D0098793

THE PLAYS OF ARNOLD WESKER

Volume 1

A JOAN KAHN BOOK

Also by Arnold Wesker:

Love Letters on Blue Paper (short stories)

THE PLAYS
of
ARNOLD WESKER

Volume 1

The Kitchen

Chicken Soup with Barley

Roots

I'm Talking about Jerusalem

Chips with Everything

Harper & Row, Publishers
New York, Hagerstown, San Francisco, London

CONTENTS

The Kitchen

INTRODUCTION
AND NOTES FOR THE PRODUCER

The lengthy explanations I am forced to make may be annoying; I am sorry, but they are necessary.

This is a play about a large kitchen in a restaurant called the Tivoli. All kitchens, especially during service, go insane. There is the rush, there are the petty quarrels, grumbles, false prides, and snobbery. Kitchen staff instinctively hate dining-room staff, and all of them hate the customer. He is the personal enemy. The world might have been a stage for Shakespeare but to me it is a kitchen, where people come and go and cannot stay long enough to understand each other, and friendships, loves and enmities are forgotten as quickly as they are made.

The quality of the food here is not so important as the speed with which it is served. Each person has his own particular job. We glance in upon him, highlighting as it were the individual. But though we may watch just one or a group of people, the rest of the kitchen staff does not. They work on.

So, because activity must continue while the main action is played out, we shall study, together with a diagram of the kitchen, who comes in and what they do.

The waitresses spend the morning working in the dining-room before they eat their lunch. But throughout the morning there are about three or four who wander in and out carrying glasses from the glassery to the dining-room and performing duties which are mentioned in the course of the play. During the service the waitresses are continually coming out of the dining-room and ordering dishes from the cooks. The dishes are served on silver and the waitresses take about six plates out of the hot plate immediately under the serving-counter. Stocks of plates are replenished all the time by the porters. These are highly efficient waitresses. They make a circuit round the kitchen calling at the stations they require. They move fast and carry large quantities of dishes in their arms.

The kitchen porters, who are a mixture of Cypriots and Maltese, are divided into various sections. Firstly there are those who do the actual washing of cutlery, tins and plates by machine; these we do not see. For our purpose we only use one porter, who continually replaces clean plates under the serving-counter so that the waitresses can take them as required. He also sweeps up at regular intervals and throws sawdust around.

The woman who serves the cheeses and desserts and coffee, we hardly and rarely see through the glass partition back of stage, but every now and then she comes to the pastry-section to replenish her supplies of tarts and pastries.

Now to the cooks. At this point it must be understood that at no time is food ever used. To cook and serve food is of course just not practical. Therefore the waitresses will carry empty dishes, and the cooks will mime their cooking. Cooks being the main characters in this play, I shall sketch them and their activity here, so that while the main action of the play is continuing they shall always have something to do.

NOTE

The section dealing with the service starting on p. 40 with 'Two veal cutlets' is the actual production worked out by John Dexter based on what was originally only an indicative framework set out by me. I wish to acknowledge his creation of this workable pattern.

The pattern of service falls into three stages of increasing speed. (1) From 'Two veal cutlets,' p. 40, to Gaston's 'Max send up steaks and mutton chops quick,' p. 43, the pace is brisk but slow. (2) From then on to Peter's cry of 'Too old, too old my sweetheart,' p. 45, the pace increases. (3) From then on to the end of the part, 'Have you all gone barking-raving-bloody-mad,' the pace is fast and hectic.

If trouble is taken to work out this pattern then the right rhythm will be found.

Any producer is at liberty to abstract this set if he can still get over the atmosphere.

CHARACTER SKETCHES IN ORDER OF STATIONS

FRANK, Second Chef: *Poultry*. A prisoner of war for four years. Now at thirty-eight he has an easygoing nature. Nothing really upsets him, but then nothing excites him either. He drinks steadily throughout the day and by nightfall is blissfully drunk though instinctively capable. Flirts with the waitresses, squeezing their breasts and pinching their bottoms.

ALFREDO: *Roast*. An old chef, about sixty-five and flat-footed. Large-muscled and strong, though of medium height. He is a typical cook in that he will help nobody and will accept no help; nor will he impart his knowledge. He is the fastest worker there and sets-to straight away, not stopping till his station is all ready. He speaks little, but he has a dry sense of humour. He is the worker and the boss is the boss, and he probably despises the boss. He hums to himself as he works.

HANS: *Fry*. A German boy, nineteen, pimply and adolescent. He is working in London through a system of exchange. He speaks very bad English and is impressed by anything flashy. Yet as a German he is sensitive.

PETER: *Boiled Fish*. Peter is the main character. Another young German, aged twenty-three, who has worked at the Tivoli for the last three years. His parents were killed in the war. He is boisterous, aggressive, too merry, and yet good-natured. After three years at the Tivoli one might say he was living on his nerves. He speaks good English but with

5

an accent, and when he is talking to people he tends to speak into their ear as though he were telling them a secret. It is a nervous moment. A strong characteristic of Peter is his laugh. It is a forced laugh, pronounced 'Hya hya hya,' instead of 'ha ha ha.' He turns this laugh into one of surprise or mockery, derision or simple merriment. There is also a song he sings – music at page 49 – which ends in exactly the same laughter. Somehow its maniacal tone is part of the whole atmosphere of the kitchen.

KEVIN: *Fried Fish.* The new young man, Irish, twenty-two. He spends most of his time being disturbed by the mad rush of the work and people around him. This is worse than anything he has ever seen.

GASTON: *Grill.* A Cypriot by birth, forty-odd, slight and dark-complexioned. Everyone-is-his-friend until he starts work, then he is inclined to go to pieces and panic and cry at everyone. When the play starts he has a loud scratch down the side of his face.

MICHAEL: *Eggs.* There is nothing particular about this boy of eighteen. He is what his dialogue will make him; but he is a cook and before long all cooks are infused with a kind of madness.

BERTHA: *Vegetable Cook.* Large woman, coarse, friendly, narrow-minded, Jewish.

MANGOLIS: *Kitchen Porter.* Young Cypriot boy, cheeky, hard-working, dashing in and out of fast-moving kitchen, replenishing plates on hot-plate.

ANNE: *Dessert and Coffee.* Irish, soft-spoken, thirty-five, easy-going. Speaks with slow, cloying lilt.

MAX: *Butcher.* A stout man of fifty. Loud-mouthed, smutty and anti anything that it is easy to be anti about. He has a cigarette continually dropping from his mouth, and like Frank drinks steadily all day till he is drunk.

NICHOLAS: *Cold Buffet.* Nicholas is a young Cypriot who has

6

lived in England three years and can therefore speak reasonable English but with an accent. Speaking the language and working in a capacity socially superior to his compatriots, who are dishwashers, he behaves with a wild heartiness, as one who is accepted. And as one who is accepted he imitates, and he chooses to imitate Frank and Max by becoming drunk by the end of the day.

RAYMOND and PAUL: *Pastrycooks.* Paul is a young Jew; Raymond is an Italian who speaks almost perfect English but with an accent. These two pastrycooks, as opposed to the madmen in the kitchen, are calm and less prone to panic. The rush of the kitchen does not affect them; they work hard and straight through without the afternoon break but have no direct contact with the waitresses. Raymond is emotional. Paul is suave, though not unpleasant.

CHEF: A large man of about fifty-nine with tiny moustache. If he could, he would work elsewhere – preferably not in the catering trade at all. The less that is brought to his attention, the happier he feels. In such a large kitchen the organization carries itself almost automatically. He rarely speaks to anyone except Frank the second chef, Max, who works near him, and Nicholas, who is immediately under him. He will not say good-morning nor communicate any of the politeness expected of a chef. Familiarity, for him, breeds the contempt it deserves.

MR MARANGO: *Proprietor.* An old man of seventy-five, stout – but not fat – with flabby jowls and a sad expression on his face. A magnificent curtain of grey hair skirts the back of his bald head and curls under itself. His sad look is really one of self-pity. The machine he has set in motion is his whole life and he suspects that everyone is conspiring to stop it.

7

THE ACTIONS

For the purpose of the action of this play, the following dishes have been allotted to the following cooks. Of course they cannot go through all the actions necessary for the cooking of these dishes. The two important things are:

1 That they have some actions to mime throughout the play in between speaking their parts and gossiping among themselves, and

2 That by the time the service is ready to begin they have an assortment of neatly arranged trays and pots of 'dishes and sauces' ready to serve to the waitresses as requested.

FRANK: Roast pheasant/chips. Roast chicken/pommes sautés. Mushrooms. Pour salt in twenty chicken carcasses, place in oven. Slice carrots and onions and boil for gravy. Salt and place pheasants in oven. (Both carcasses are cleaned elsewhere.) Chop mushrooms and fry together with sauté.

ALFREDO: Roast veal/spaghetti. Boiled ham/boiled potatoes. Roast beef for staff. Season and cook veal and beef in oven. Boil spaghetti in salt water. Chop onions and carrots and make sauce. Place ham in pot to boil.

HANS: Sausages/baked rice. Pork chops/white beans. Vegetables for the staff. Cut up ham, tomatoes, onions and mushrooms, and sauté for rice. Boil white beans. Pork chops are fried during service. Collect from cold cupboard and heat yesterday's vegetables for staff.

PETER: Mixed fish/sauce. Cod meunière/boiled potatoes. Boiled turbot/sauce hollandaise. Beat egg yellows on slow heat, add melted margarine for sauce hollandaise. This takes a long time. Slice cod and turbot into portions. Slice lemons for garniture.

KEVIN: Grilled sardines/boiled potatoes. Grilled salmon/boiled potatoes. Fried plaice/chips or boiled potatoes. Slice lemons

8

for plaice. Cut salmon into portions. Arrange four trays on bench: one for oil, one for milk, one for flour, and one with required fish. Clean grill with wire brush.

GASTON: Grilled chops/chips. Grilled steak/chips. Most of his work is done during service. Clean grill with wire brush. Collect from vegetable-room and then blanch chips. Aid Kevin.

MICHAEL: Hamburger/eggs on top/chips. Ham omelet. Onion soup. Cut ham for omelet. Cube stale bread for onion soup. Crack eggs in tin ready for omelet. We assume enough soup left over from yesterday.

MAX: Mainly carting of huge meat carcasses from cold-room to bench where he then proceeds to cut and dissect them.

NICHOLAS: Cold roast beef/potato salad. Cold ham/Russian salad. Slice meats and arrange various trays of salad. Also roll and slice in portions chipped meat for Michael's hamburgers.

CHEF: Mainly clerical and organizational work of course. He will mind his own business as much as possible.

PAUL and RAYMOND: Bands of apple and pear tart. Pastry called 'Religieuse'. First bake trays of tarts prepared day before. Spread custard sauce and then slice fruit to lay on top. Make more pastry; mix flour and fat, add water, roll out. Cut into more bands ready for tomorrow. Fill pastry with cream from cloth bag. Peel fruit.

BERTHA: Assume all her vegetables, sprouts, cabbage, spinach and sauté, were cooked day before. She merely has to heat them over. Otherwise gossips with coffee woman.

The original, shorter version was first presented by the English Stage Society at the Royal Court Theatre on September 13th, 1959. This full-length version was first presented by the English Stage Company at the Royal Court Theatre on June 27th, 1961, with the following cast:

Magi	TOMMY EYTLE
Max	MARTIN BODDEY
Bertha	JESSIE ROBINS
Molly	JANE MERROW
Winnie	IDA GOLDAPPLE
Mangolis	MARCOS MARKOU
Paul	HARRY LANDIS
Raymond	ANDRE BOLTON
Hettie	RITA TUSHINGHAM
Violet	ALISON BAYLEY
Anne	GLADYS DAWSON
Gwen	JEANNE WATTS
Daphne	SHIRLEY CAMERON
Cynthia	SANDRA CARON
Dimitri	DIMITRI ANDREAS
Betty	TARN BASSETT
Jackie	CHARLOTTE SELWYN
Hans	WOLF PARR
Monique	MARY PEACH
Alfredo	REGINALD GREEN
Michael	JAMES BOLAM
Gaston	ANDREAS MARKOS
Kevin	BRIAN PHELAN
Nicholas	ANDREAS LYSANDROU
Peter	ROBERT STEPHENS
Frank	KEN PARRY
Chef	ARNOLD YARROW
Head Waiter	CHARLES WORKMAN
Marango	ANDREAS MALENDRINOS
Tramp	PATRICK O'CONNELL

Directed by John Dexter

PART ONE

There is no curtain in this part. The kitchen is always there. It is semi-darkness. Nothing happens until the audience is quite seated (at the appointed time for commencement, that is).

The night porter, MAGI, enters. He stretches, looks at his watch, and then stands still, realizing where he is. It is seven in the morning. Then with a taper he lights the ovens. Into the first shoots a flame. There is smoke, flame, and soon the oven settles into a steady burn, and with it comes its hum. It is the hum of the kitchen, a small roar. It is a noise that will stay with us to the end. As he lights each oven, the noise grows from a small to a loud ferocious roar. There will be this continuous battle between the dialogue and the noise of the ovens. The Producer must work out his own balance.

As MAGI lights the fourth oven, MAX enters, goes straight to the lower cold cupboard and collects a bottle of beer, which he opens and starts to drink.

As MAGI lights the last oven, BERTHA enters to her station. As she passes MAX she says, 'Good morning, Max.' *He burps.*

BERTHA. Here, Magi, give us a hand with this.

MAGI. O.K., love.

BERTHA. There.

(*Enter* MANGOLIS.)

MAGI. Bertha – that ten shillings.

BERTHA. You haven't got it? So you haven't got it! You going away?

MAGI. No.

BERTHA. Then I'll wait.

MAGI. You're a good girl, Bertha.

BERTHA. Good – I am; but a girl – unfortunately not.

MAGI. Go on. *I* could fancy you.

BERTHA. Me? Boy, I'd crack you in one crush. Crrrrrunch! (*Creeps towards him like a spectre.*) First your arms – snap snap! Then your legs – snap snap! Then your eyes –

gobble! Then your ears and your nose and your throat –
gobble gobble gobble!

MAGI. And what would you do with the left-overs?

BERTHA. Kosher it with salt and prayers and hang it up to drip-
dry!

MAX. Magi, give us a hand please.

MAGI. Bertha – you worry me.

BERTHA. I worry him.

> (MAX and MAGI raise the beef on to ALFREDO's oven. As
> they do this, BETTY and WINNIE, waitresses, enter, mumbling,
> and go through to the dining-room. PAUL and RAYMOND
> enter with their tools under their arms. They go to their own
> corner. MAGI exits.)

PAUL (to anybody). Good morning, good morning. (to BERTHA)
Good morning, me old darling. (to MAX) And to you too,
Max.

MAX (his soul not yet returned). Good morning.

BERTHA. Morning.

RAYMOND. Max, it's escalope of veal on today?

MAX. How many?

RAYMOND. Three. I'll take them now and put them in my box,
before the others get there.

> (MAX goes to cold-room, and returns with three escalopes
> which he slaps down on his table and RAYMOND collects.
> MANGOLIS delivers empty dustbins to their places.)

MAX. And don't forget my puff pastry tomorrow.

RAYMOND. Usual?

MAX. Usual.

PAUL (to RAYMOND as he returns). It's Religieuse today?

RAYMOND. Yes. But you do the fruit bands, leave the pastries,
I'll do them. Motor bike working all right?

> (HETTIE and VIOLET, waitresses, pass through to the dining-
> room.)

HETTIE. This is the way to the dining-room.

VIOLET. I'm not used to working in places like this, I used to be at the old Carlton Tower.

PAUL. Bloody thing! No more second-hand gear for me.

RAYMOND. What is it?

PAUL. If I knew it wouldn't be so bad. Mechanical contraptions! It takes me all my time to find out where the alarm on a clock is.

RAYMOND. I'll look at it.

PAUL. You know about motor bikes?

RAYMOND. In the war I was a dispatch rider – I had to know.

PAUL. I left it at home though.

RAYMOND. I'll come to your home then.

PAUL. I'll make you a supper.

RAYMOND. We'll have an evening of bachelors.

PAUL. A bachelors' evening.

RAYMOND. A bachelors' evening. We'll use the veal cutlets Max promised.

PAUL. Good idea. What about your wife?

RAYMOND. Sometimes it's a good thing to miss a wife.

PAUL. Yes.

RAYMOND. I'm sorry, I forgot.

PAUL. Don't worry on my account – she was a fool. If she'd only been a bitch it wouldn't have mattered but she was a fool as well.

RAYMOND. It's not such a big hurt then?

(Enter ANNE *to her station.)*

PAUL. For me? No! But she's going to have children one day and those kids are going to have a fool for a mother – that's what hurts.

RAYMOND. You don't miss her?

PAUL. I don't miss her. Good morning, Anne. *(She doesn't hear.)* Good morning, Anne.

ANNE. Good morning, boys.

PAUL. That's better.

RAYMOND. Good morning, sweetheart.

ANNE. Hello boys, hello Max.

MAX *(his soul returned)*. Top o' the mornin' to you Anne.

ANNE *(putting coffee in metal jug to warm on oven)*. An' the rest o' the day to yersel', dear. *(stretching herself)* Ah, me bed was lovely.

RAYMOND *(lasciviously)*. I bet it was.

ANNE. Hey, Raymond, tell me, what happened to Peter in the end, you know, last night?

RAYMOND. Now he's a silly boy, eh? Don't you think so? I don't even know what it was all about anyway. You know, Paul?

PAUL. All I know is he had a fight with Gaston. Why? I don't know. Over a ladle I think, or maybe a...

MAX. He's a bloody German, a fool, that's what he is. He is always quarrelling, always. There's no one he hasn't quarrelled with, am I right? No one! That's some scheme that is, exchanging cooks! What do we want to exchange cooks for? Three years he's been here, three years! *(Exits to get more beer.)*

ANNE. Ah, the boy's in love.

RAYMOND. What love! You ever see him? When Monique does a turn as hostess by the stairs he watches her through that mirror there. *(Points to glass partition.)*

ANNE. Rubbish.

RAYMOND. And he walks round the kitchen and looks to see if she's talking or flirting with any of the customers.

ANNE. I don't believe it.

BERTHA. Never.

RAYMOND. You don't believe me?

PAUL. And they quarrel in front of everybody as well. They shout at each other. Shout! You know, sometimes she doesn't even look at him, and waits for her orders with her back turned.

14

ANNE. The poor boy. He's no parents you know. But what happened last night? I want to know.

(MAGI *re-enters.*)

MAX. Ask Magi.

MAGI. Any coffee, Anne?

ANNE. Sure dear. *(Pours.)* Help yourself.

RAYMOND. Hey Magi, what happened with Peter last night, uh?

MAGI *(unconcerned)*. They nearly killed him.

ANNE. Oh God.

RAYMOND *(gesticulating)*. But what was it all about, tell me? I don't know nothing, me.

MAGI. Well *you* should know that — I wasn't here.

PAUL. All we know is that they suddenly started shouting at each other. And you know, Peter always shouts more than the other and you can always hear Peter — well, so then it stopped, and then a few seconds later they were fighting, and I saw Gaston raise a boning knife and Peter knock it out of his hand, and then...

RAYMOND. And then he lifted him and nearly sat him on the stove and...

PAUL. And then the Chef came along and...

ANNE. Well I saw the Chef separate them and I heard Gaston say 'I haven't finished yet, it's not over yet,' but I still don't know what it was all about.

PAUL. Who cares? I say good-morning to Peter but never good-night.

MAGI. Well I came in at nine last night. The boys were changing and suddenly Peter comes and Gaston follows him. Gaston says Peter called him a lousy Cypro and the boys make circle round him and want to murder him! All of them... but Peter says 'No, everyone for me is the same — it makes no difference race, you misunderstand...' They all wanted to hit him! And he was scared! I never seen him so white.

ANNE. But what was it about to begin with?

15

MAX. A ladle, I tell you.

PAUL. Who knows? There's always fights, who knows how they begin?

MAGI *(laying down cup)*. Well, I'm going.

PAUL. Have a good kip, old son.

ANNE. And I must get started too. *(Looks round empty kitchen.)* You wouldn't think this place will become a madhouse in two hours, would you now. *(Moves off with MAGI.)*

> *(RAYMOND, PAUL and MAX continue to work in silence. Enter DAPHNE, GWEN and CYNTHIA, waitresses, to dining-room.)*

DAPHNE. So if he doesn't come home tonight I'm going to leave.

CYNTHIA. Well he does have to work in the afternoon.

GWEN. That's right.

MAX. Any luck on the pools, Ray?

RAYMOND. Huh!

MAX. Norwich and Leyton let me down. Twenty points. Twenty points!

> *(Enter HETTIE from dining-room for a coffee. Pause.)*

HETTIE. Morning, Annie love.

PAUL. Read about the man in the mental home who won thirty-five thousand pounds?

RAYMOND. And his wife turned up after eighteen years?

> *(Enter DAPHNE from dining-room for a coffee.)*

PAUL. Eighteen years!

> *(Pause. DIMITRI enters. A Cypriot kitchen porter, young, good-looking and intelligent. He is carrying in his hand a home-made portable radio. He is happy as he takes it to PAUL. He speaks with an accent.*
> *Enter MOLLY, JACKIE, waitresses, to dining-room.)*

DIMITRI. I make it Paul, I make it. There! *(Lays it on table near by.)* She does not look handsome. I'm sorry for that.

PAUL. Ah you good boy, Dimitri. Can we play it? *(He looks*

16

round to see if authority is in sight. Only DAPHNE *and* HETTIE *approach. One has a bucket in her hand and her hair is tied up with a scarf. The other one is similarly attired and carries a feather duster.)* Anyone around?

HETTIE *(pointing to portable).* What is it, Paul?

PAUL. Is Marango around yet?

DAPHNE. Not yet. Whose is it?

PAUL. It's mine. Dimitri here made it.

RAYMOND. You made it on your own? All those little wires and plugs? Tell me, what are you doing here? Why you waste your time with dishes in this place? You can't get a job in a factory?

DIMITRI. A factory? You think I find happiness in a factory? What I make there? Uh? This little wire, you see it? This I would make, or that...what you call it?

PAUL. Knob.

DIMITRI. Knob. That perhaps I could put in. All day I would screw in knobs. I tell you, in a factory a man makes a little piece till he becomes a little piece, you know what I mean?

HETTIE. It's true, he's right, you know.

DIMITRI. Sure I know, my brother, he works there. I know all right.

RAYMOND. Hey Dimitri, *you* know what happened to Peter last night?

DIMITRI. They nearly kill him. Why?

DAPHNE. Oh my Gawd.

DIMITRI. But you think it was all Peter's fault? They all wanted to fight. Listen, you put a man in the plate-room all day, he's got dishes to make clean, and stinking bins to take away, and floors to sweep, what else there is for him to do — he wants to fight. He got to show he is a man some way. So — blame him!

*(*DIMITRI *turns on the radio, which plays a loud rock 'n' roll tune.* PAUL *grabs* DAPHNE, *and starts to dance,* HETTIE *tries*

17

to dance with DIMITRI, *who won't .... * HANS *enters, grabs*
HETTIE, *they dance. At the height of the dance,* MONIQUE
enters from the dining-room.)

MONIQUE. Marango's in the dining-room.

ALL. What!

MONIQUE. Marango's in the dining-room.

(*There is a scramble to restore everything to normal, work is
resumed,* DIMITRI *vanishes into the plate-room with the
radio.* HANS *exits.*

Enter ALFREDO.)

ALFREDO. It's only me. Good morning, gentlemen.

MAX (*pointing to* ALFREDO'*s station*). The veal is there.

ALFREDO (*studying the menu on the board*). Thank you, thank
you.

PAUL (*shouting*). Is the new cook here?

ALFREDO (*shrugging his shoulders*). He didn't ask for me.

(*Enter* MONIQUE *with glasses.*)

PAUL. I thought you said Marango's coming.

MONIQUE. I said he's in the dining-room – he's still there.

RAYMOND. Monique, what happened last night, you tell us?

MONIQUE. No more Ray, there's a good man. Gaston has a
black eye.

PAUL. A right morning we're going to have this morning then.

RAYMOND. A Peter – nothing?

MONIQUE. He was lucky.

RAYMOND. You mean he was with you so they couldn't touch
him.

MONIQUE. I mean he was lucky. They waited for him outside.

RAYMOND. Outside also?

MONIQUE. 'You want to play gangsters?' he says to them,
'Go bring me Marlon Brando and I'll play gangsters.'

RAYMOND. A time like that he's funny.

MONIQUE. And then he shakes hands with them and says
'Good night, bonne nuit, gute Nacht and Kalinka' one by

one. And he leaves them all standing. *(Smiles.)* What could they do? *(Smile fades.)* The bully!

HEAD WAITER. Monique...*(As he enters from dining-room.)*

MONIQUE. Morning, Harry.

HEAD WAITER. Janey is sick.

MONIQUE. Not again. That girl's anaemic, I swear she's anaemic.

HEAD WAITER. Take over for the day, please.

MONIQUE. But I'm not dressed for hostess.

HEAD WAITER. That dress looks all right to me – just take off the apron.

MONIQUE. This one? But it's not ironed!

HEAD WAITER. You only have to show the customers to their tables, not dance with them. *(Exits.)*

MONIQUE. That's three times this week I've been hostess. Here Bertha, look after this apron for me.

BERTHA. Give it me Tchooch, I'll sit on it and keep it pressed.
    (Enter DAPHNE, GWEN and HETTIE.)

MONIQUE. Hettie, Janey's sick again, take over my station, will you love? Daphne, give her a hand will you?

DAPHNE. I'm on glasses don't forget.

MONIQUE. True...I forgot. Who's left then? Winnie's on ten. Gwen's on...Gwen, what station you on today?

GWEN. Seven.

MONIQUE. Seven...That's your hands full.

HETTIE. What about the new woman?

MONIQUE. That's marvellous, she's an old hand isn't she? She can help you, and you can keep an eye on her – come on, let's move.

PAUL. And the best of British luck.

MONIQUE. At least it means I won't have to stand in front of that bully all day.
    (The waitresses all exit.)

PAUL. Fancy that sort of relationship.

RAYMOND. Peter and Monique? They're not so bad – it's her husband I wouldn't like to be.

PAUL. No, you wouldn't.

RAYMOND. There – I've done it again. I'm sorry Paul.

PAUL. That's all right, I don't mind being cuckolded, I'm in good company.

(Enter MICHAEL.*)*

MICHAEL *(to* BERTHA*)*. Morning, fatty. How are you?

BERTHA. And you can shut up for a start, little boy. I can ring your napkins out any day. With you tucked in them, any day.

(Enter GASTON.*)*

MICHAEL *(to* GASTON*)*. Your eye's black.

GASTON. YOU TELLING ME SOMETHING.

MICHAEL. All right, all right...whew...He looked as though he wanted to kill me.

PAUL. Who'd want to kill you, Michael?

MICHAEL. Quite right...who'd want to kill me? Young man in his teens, all the world in front of him. Look at it... a lovely sight, isn't it? Isn't she beautiful? A bloody great mass of iron and we work it – praise be to God for man's endeavour – what's on the menu today? I don't know why I bother – it's always the same. Vegetable soup, minestrone, omolleteeee au jambon – ah well! One day I'll work in a place where I can create masterpieces, master bloody pieces. Beef Stroganoff, Chicken Kiev, and that king of the Greek dishes – Mousaka.

GASTON. Never. You'll never create a Mousaka. Chips you can make – chips with everything.

MICHAEL. Don't you think you Greeks have got the monopoly on good cooking, you know. There was a time when the English knew how to eat.

GASTON. There was a time.

MICHAEL. Aye – well – yes – there was a time.

(Enter HANS, *who escorts* KEVIN. *Sooner or later they all arrive to glance at the menu on the blackboard.* NICHOLAS *follows them to his station.)*

HANS *(to* KEVIN*).* I not know where you work. On fish perhaps. *(to* PAUL*)* Paul, new cook.

PAUL. Hello.

(They continue to work while KEVIN *watches them and the rest of the kitchen.)*

KEVIN. Is there much doing here?

PAUL. You'll see. Two thousand customers a day.

(While KEVIN *has been introduced and is talking to the pastrycooks,* BERTHA *goes to the cold cupboard and, after looking around inside, takes out a tray of sliced, cold potatoes. Following behind, about to start his work, is* NICHOLAS. *He has a bottle of beer in his hand, which he is drinking.)*

NICHOLAS *(to* BERTHA*).* Where you go with that?

BERTHA. I need it for sauté.

NICHOLAS *(taking tray).* Oh, no, no, no. That's for me. Me, I prepared that yesterday. That's for me for my salad.

BERTHA *(trying to hold on to tray).* You get your salad from the vegroom.

NICHOLAS. Ah no bloody hell! You get *yours* from the veg. That is for me, that is what I get ready.

BERTHA *(nastily).* You don't bloody hell me, my son. You bloody hell in your own country. *(to others)* What d'you think of him, eh? The little...

NICHOLAS. This is my country.

BERTHA. The lavatory is your country.

NICHOLAS *(taking tray eventually).* The lavatory is *your* country, and the sewers, you know that? The sewers.

BERTHA *(taking out another tray).* I'll pay you sonny. You cross me once, that's all, just once. Lousy little foreigner you!

NICHOLAS *(cheekily).* *She* calls *me* foreigner! Listen to her...

ALFREDO *(approaching cupboard for his own goods).* Excuse me

21

friends, you can carry on in a minute. *(But the quarrel has died down.)*

NICHOLAS *(approaching pastry-section).* D'you hear her? Uh? The cow! Paul, you got some tart or cake or something? I'm starving. *(PAUL hands him tart.) (to KEVIN)* You the new cook?

KEVIN. Yes.

NICHOLAS. Good luck to you! *(Laughs to the others.)* You know where your station is?

KEVIN. I don't even know what stations there are.

NICHOLAS. Here, I'll show you. Right now for a start there's the menu...That's where you find what to cook for day, our chef writes it out each night. Over here, this is where I work on the Cold Buffet. This is Max the Butcher. This is where Hans works, he does Staff and rice and cutlets and you know, and this is Alfredo on the Roast. And next here, we got the Second Chef Frank on Poultry....And here, well here you see that fat bitch down there, well she works here as the Veg Cook. And this is my Aunty Anne who is on the teas and coffees. This is Michael on Soups and Omelets. And this is my best friend Gaston, the best cook in this kitchen, he does steaks and chops. Co-Co works here but he's off today. Here are Paul and Raymondo, Pastrycooks. And here, this is where Peter works on Boiled Fish, he...

(By this time he has to take KEVIN back to left of stage and point out the other stations. As he talks on, PETER enters in a great hurry, he is late. He laughs his laugh.)

PETER. Auf geht's! Auf geht's!

HANS. Auf geht's, Pete! Was war denn los heut' Morgen?

PETER. Ach, die Weiber! Die Weiber!

NICHOLAS. Peter, the new cook, I give him to you.

PETER. So what shall I do with him? *(to KEVIN)* You know where it is you work?

KEVIN. Not yet I don't.

PETER. Where do you come from?

KEVIN. Ireland.

PETER. No, I mean what restaurant you work in before?

KEVIN. Parisito, Shaftesbury Avenue.

PETER *(rubbing his thumb and finger together)*. Good pay?

KEVIN *(shaking his head)*. That's why I came here.

PETER. Oh, you get good money here – but you work! *(raising his hands in despair)* Oh yes! Now, you help me. Can you make a sauce hollandaise? You know – eggs and…*(Makes motion of whisking.)*

KEVIN. Yes, yes.

PETER *(briskly)*. The eggs are already in a tin in the cold cupboard. There is a pot, the whisk is in the drawer and I melt margarine for you.

> *(By now almost everybody is working. Waitresses are making an appearance, they are carrying glasses back and forth; one, CYNTHIA, is handing out the printed menu for the day, another is taking round bread for lunch for the kitchen staff. As she reaches HANS, he approaches her shyly and tries to flirt with her.)*

HANS. Oh baby, wait a moment! I…I…I…Du gefällst mir, du hast mir schon vom ersten Tag an gefallen! Könnten wir nicht mal was zusammen arrangieren?

> *(FRANK, the second chef, enters and breaks up conversation.)*

MAX *(to FRANK)*. We got no lamb cutlets.

FRANK. Three carcasses came in yesterday.

MAX. So?

FRANK. So!

MAX. So you come and help me cut them up. I'm on my own today.

FRANK. What you got?

MAX. Veal cutlets.

FRANK. O.K., so veal cutlets then. *(moving to KEVIN)* New cook?

KEVIN (*sweating and still beating his sauce*). Yes, Chef.

FRANK. Right, you work on the fried fish this morning.

PETER (*approaching from cutting-table*). Thank you, thank you, but I got six dishes to prepare.

FRANK. Co-Co is off today. Someone must do the fry.

PETER. Bloody house this is. The middle of summer and we got no staff. I got six dishes.

(*The* CHEF *enters.*)

ALFREDO. Morning, Chefie.

CHEF. Morning.

MAX. Morning, Chef.

CHEF. Morning.

HANS (*cheekily*). Morning, Chefie.

(*The* CHEF *stops, turns, looks* HANS *up and down, then continues to his desk.* HANS *pulls a face, and makes a rude sign.*)

FRANK. Morning, Leo. (*to* KEVIN) Here, you, get that fish out of that cupboard and come here, I want to show you something.

HANS (*to* PETER). Du, gestern Abend hat's dich aber beinah erwischt!

PETER. Sie sind nur mutig, wenn sie zusammen sind!

HANS. Haben sie draussen auf dich gewartet?

PETER. Ja, da warin auch welche. Leider war ich mit Monika zusammen und jetzt spricht sie nicht mehr mit mir.

HANS. Sie wird auch wieder mit dir reden!

PETER. Ach egal! Auf geht's! (*Sings his song, in which* HANS *joins him, ending in laughter.*) Hi lee, hi lo, hi la!

GASTON (*passing at that moment*). Madmen, lunatics!

PETER. Hey Gaston, I'm sorry – your black eye, I'm sorry about it.

GASTON. DON'T TALK TO ME.

PETER. I say I'm sorry, that's all.

GASTON. You sorry because half a dozen Cypriot boys make you feel sorry – but we not finished yet!

PAUL. Gaston! What's the matter with you? A man is saying sorry – so accept!

GASTON. Accept? He gives me this *(pointing to black eye)* and I must accept? *(to* PETER*)* We not finished yet, I'm telling you.

PETER. What you not finished with? Tell me! What you want to do now? You want to give me a black eye? That make you feel happier? All right! Here, give me one and then we'll be finished, eh? *(Adopts quixotic stance.)*

GASTON. Don't laugh, Peter, I'm telling you, it gets worse, don't laugh.

*(*PETER *adopts another quixotic stance.)*

PAUL *(to* PETER*).* So what are you tantalizing him for? Lunatic! *(to* RAYMOND*)* Nobody knows when to stop. A quarrel starts and it goes on for months. When *one* of them is prepared to apologize so the other doesn't know how to accept – and when someone knows how to accept so the other...ach! Lunatics! *(Throws a hand of disgust, while* PETER *sings loudly.)*

*(*MONIQUE *approaches* GASTON *and lays a friendly arm on his shoulder as they both watch* PETER's *antics.)*

MONIQUE. He makes a lot of noise but he's not really dangerous.

GASTON. Listen to him – your boy-friend!

MONIQUE. Show me the eye. Beautiful! First prize!

GASTON. Now Monique, don't protect him.

MONIQUE. But you know he wouldn't hurt anyone – not intentionally.

GASTON. This eye –

MONIQUE. It was an accident, you know it was, just between us you know it was, don't you? Why don't you just let me try and handle him?

GASTON. You? You're like a bit of paper – the wind blows you about.

MONIQUE. I manage.

GASTON. Manage? What sort of a life is manage? Manage! He needs a big scare, a big fright.

MONIQUE. Fright? Nothing frightens that boy.

GASTON. Boy! A baby! You just threaten to leave him and you'll see how frightened he'll get. Listen to him — baby!

(The HEAD WAITER *enters to* CHEF'S *desk.)*

HEAD WAITER *(handing* CHEF *a letter)*. Read it.

CHEF. What's this one about?

HEAD WAITER. Read it. Read it.

CHEF. Sour soup, what sour soup?

HEAD WAITER. Yesterday's.

CHEF. I was off yesterday, see Frank.

HEAD WAITER. He was off yesterday...A kitchen he runs. *(Goes to* FRANK.)

FRANK. What do you want? Nicholas! Twelve chickens.

NICHOLAS. There are only six.

FRANK. Well order some more! What's this sour soup...?

HANS. Auf geht's, Nicholas! Come on, Nicholas! Twelve chickens, please! Bonjour Raymond, comment ça va?

RAYMOND. Ça va, toujours au boulot, etcetera.

HANS. Vive le frigue!

MAX *(suddenly and violently to* HANS). You're in England now, speak bloody English. *(*HANS *is nonplussed for the day.)* Everybody speaking in a different language, French, Italian, German. *(to* HANS) You come here to learn English didn't you? Well speak it then!

PETER. What's the matter Max? You frightened of something? Have another beer.

MAX. I'm not frightened of you, I tell you that straight. So *you* can keep quiet.

PETER *(approaching close to* MAX *and talking in his ear)*. You know your trouble Max? You been here too long.

MAX *(moving away from him)*. Yes, yes, yes Peter, all right.

PETER *(following him)*. How long have you been here? Twenty-one years? You need a change.

MAX *(moving away again)*. Yes, yes.

PETER *(following him)*. Why don't you go work a season in Germany?

MAX. Sure to.

PETER. Visit other kitchens! Learn more!

MAX. Yes, yes. Get on with your work.

PETER. Don't you worry about my work!

HANS. Genug, Pete.

PETER. You can't bear a change? A new face upsets you?

MAX. Let's drop it? Erwigt yes?

HANS. Stop it, Pete!

CHEF. All right, Peter — let's have some work!

(MR MARANGO appears.)

HANS. Marango!!

(PETER returns to his work and winks at RAYMOND in passing. MARANGO walking slowly round the kitchen inspecting everything, placing his hand on the hot-plate to see if it is still working. It is a mechanical movement — sometimes he puts a hand on the cold pastry slab to see if it is still hot — it is a mechanical tour. Meanwhile —)

KEVIN *(to PETER)*. Is it like this every day? *(wiping sweat from forehead)* Look at me, I never sweated so much since me glorious honeymoon.

PETER. It is nothing this. This is only how it begins. Wait till we start serving, then. *(Raises his hands.)* You in place?

KEVIN. More or less. I got me salmon to cut.

PETER. Good, we eat soon.

MARANGO *(gently to KEVIN)*. You're the new cook?

KEVIN *(wiping his brow again)*. Yes sir.

MARANGO. It's hot eh, son?

KEVIN. Sure, an' a bit more.

MARANGO. Never mind, I pay you well. Just work, that's all, just work well. *(Continues tour.)*

KEVIN *(to* PETER*)*. He seems a kind old man.

PETER. You think he is kind? He is a bastard! He talks like that because it is summer now. Not enough staff to serve all his customers, that is why he is kind. You going to stay till winter? Wait till then. You'll see. The fish is burnt! Too much mise-en-place! The soup is sour! He is a man, he is a restaurant. I tell you. He goes to market at five thirty in the morning; returns here, reads the mail, goes up to the office and then comes down here to watch the service. Here he stands, sometimes he walks round touching the hot-plate, closing the hot-plate doors, then looking inside this thing and that thing. Till the last customer he stays. Then he has a sleep upstairs in his office. Half an hour after we come back, he is here again – till nine thirty, maybe ten at night. Every day, morning to night. What kind of a life is that, in a kitchen! Is that a life I ask you? Me, I don't care, soon I'm going to get married and then whisht – *(Makes movement with his arm to signify 'I'm off.')*

HANS *(approaches with large tray in his hand which he later puts in cold cupboard)*. Auf geht's, Irishman! I must not speak German to you. I'm in England and have to speak *bloody* English. Hi lee, hi lo, hi la!

(At this point, MONIQUE *passes by where* PETER *is working. She is carrying glasses.)*

MONIQUE *(to* PETER*)*. Bully!

PETER *(to Monique)*. Go to hell! *(to* KEVIN *proudly)* That's my wife, or she will be soon. Look *(takes out card from wallet)* – this card she sent me when she was on holiday. *(reading aloud)* 'I am not happy till you come. I love you very much.' And look, her lipstick marks. She is very lovely, yes?

KEVIN. She looks like a girl I knew, all bosom and bouncing you know?

PETER *(not really understanding what* KEVIN *said).* We eat soon, eh? *(*KEVIN *goes off to pursue his printed menu.) (to* HANS*)* Hans, hilf mir. *(They take a large heavy pot off from the oven, and pass the contents through a strainer into a small pot which* PETER *has prepared on the ground.)*

KEVIN *(showing menu to* PETER*).* Look here, it says on the printed menu fried plaice and on the board it says fried sole.

PETER. See the Chef.

KEVIN *(approaching* CHEF*).* Good morning, Chef. Look, it says here fried plaice and on the board it's got fried sole.

CHEF. I don't know anything about it. It was my day off yesterday, see the Second Chef.

KEVIN. Have we got any plaice?

CHEF *(sarcastically looking inside his apron).* It's not here.

KEVIN *(moves away to* RAYMOND*).* Now that's a helpful person for you. Doesn't he care about anything?

RAYMOND. He don't want to know nothing, only when it's gone wrong.

*(*MONIQUE *again passes in front of* PETER *to glassery.* PETER *is angry. Tries to make his quarrel secret but of course this is impossible.)*

PETER. Why do you still call me bully, all day you call me bully.

MONIQUE *(moves away across front of stage).* Bully!

PETER *(following her and talking, as is his habit, in her ear).* You think to make me angry? What is it you wanted me to do? Let him fight me?

MONIQUE *(turning to him at last).* He's got a black eye now you see?

PETER. I see, I see. But he raised a knife to me.

MONIQUE. Bully. *(She turns away.)*

PETER *(following her like the pathetic, jealous lover).* And remember you're hostess today, I can see you in the glass. No flirting, do you hear? *(Grips her arm.)* No flirting.

MONIQUE. I shall talk to who I like. *(Moves off.)*

PETER *(hoping no one can hear him).* Cow! Disgusting cow! All the restaurant can see you.

(At this point, HANS draws out the table from the pastry-section more to the centre of the stage, and begins to lay it with cutlery and glasses and bread, ready for lunch. MAX, ALFREDO, NICHOLAS and FRANK prepare to eat at MAX's table. KEVIN, MICHAEL, PETER and HANS will eat at the table HANS is now laying. GASTON will not eat because he will not sit with PETER. These two continue to ignore each other throughout the day.)

MICHAEL *(shouting).* Who has the strainer? Gaston? Peter?

PETER. I got it here, you'll have to clean it. *(to a kitchen porter who is near by)* Hey, Mangolis, you clean this for Michael please?

(MANGOLIS makes a rude sign with his hand and moves off. PETER shrugs his shoulder, and MICHAEL heaves up strainer himself, and carts it off. HETTIE stops in her work to speak to PETER.)

HETTIE *(as though to confide in her only).* Hey, Peter, what happened last night, they didn't...?

PETER *(briskly, as she only wants to gossip).* No, no. Cowards, all of them. It was nothing.

PAUL *(to same waitress as she passes his section).* Hettie, did you go last night?

HETTIE *(ecstatically).* Mmm.

PAUL. He's a good actor?

HETTIE *(even more ecstatically and hugging herself).* What a man. Oh one night, just one night with him, and then I wash dishes all my life. *(Moves off.)*

RAYMOND *(to PAUL).* So what chance do we stand? You wonder my wife doesn't make love like she used to?

PAUL. And that's why I'm not going to get married. I buy picture books and I'm happy.

GWEN. All right boys, staff meal, coming up.

(*While* PAUL *and* RAYMOND *are talking, a long procession of straggling, gossiping and giggling waitresses have come down stage on the left and are moving around to* HANS *and* ALFREDO, *who have laid trays of food on the serving-counters. Beside food are piles of plates. The waitresses help themselves.*)

GWEN. What've you got for us this morning?

ALFREDO. Curried cats and dogs.

GWEN. Is this cabbage from yesterday?

HANS. It's all right, it's all right, eat it, eat.

VIOLET. What are these?

HANS. Very good, very good. Cauliflower and white sauce.

VIOLET. White sauce? It smells.

MOLLY. Got anything good, Hans?

HANS. If you don't like – go to Chef.

MOLLY. Got any boiled potatoes?

HANS. Not cooked yet, not ready, ach...

(HANS *moves away in disgust leaving them to serve themselves. He watches* PETER *working a second, and then goes into steam-room. As the waitresses are serving themselves and grumbling and eventually moving off to the dining-room, we discover that* NICHOLAS *has been arguing with* DAPHNE. *He is making his quarrel much too public for her liking. He is probably a little drunk already.*)

NICHOLAS. Me? Me? Me a liar?

DAPHNE. Yes, you.

NICHOLAS. Oh! So I lied when I say I pass the catering exams, eh? I lie when I say I got a rise, eh? I lie when I say I got us a flat, eh? I always *do* and you always say I don't. That's a good marriage is it?

DAPHNE. You're not satisfied? Move!

NICHOLAS. Well listen to that twist! Listen-to-that-woman's-twisting! Come and ask him then, come on. You don't believe *me*, believe *him* then.

DAPHNE. No, Nicky, no...now stop.

NICHOLAS. Well, why don't you believe me then? If I tell you I got to stay the afternoon, why don't you believe me? *(shouting)* Frank! Frank! Where is he now. *(Wanders off in search of Frank while waitress waits wondering what he is going to do.)*

RAYMOND *(shouting to waitress)*. Hit him! Go on, you're big enough. *(Nudges PAUL, they laugh.)*

FRANK *(as he is dragged into the scene by NICHOLAS)*. What do you want me for? What is it now, eh?

DAPHNE. Oh Nicky, don't be a fool. *(to RAYMOND and PAUL despairingly.)* Oh for Christ's sake, what do you think of him now!

NICHOLAS. No, ask him, go on. You don't believe me.

FRANK. Ask him what, for hell's sake?

NICHOLAS. Have I got to work in the afternoon or haven't I?

FRANK *(moving away, incredulous that he has been called away for this)*. You called me for *that*? You mad or something? Do me a favour and leave me out of this, will you. *(grinning to the others)* Asks me to solve his marriage problems. *(to NICHOLAS)* I'll tell you how to do it as well, ha, ha, ha!

(Crashing in on laughter is a loud scream from the steam-room. HANS comes running out with his hands covering his face. A number of people run and crowd him.)

HANS. My face! My face! I burnt my face.

FRANK. What is it Hans?

HANS. Who bloody fool put a pot of hot water on steamer?

PETER. It fell on you?

HANS *(moving away from crowd)*. Bastard house! I never worked before so bad. Never, never...(PETER *takes him away for some first aid.)*

FRANK. He'll live. *(to the crowd)* All right, it's all over, come on. *(Crowd disperses. FRANK moves over to CHEF.)*

MOLLY *(calling after them)*. Put some of that yellow stuff on him.

FRANK. No matter how many times you tell them they still rush around.

CHEF *(he is not interested, shrugs shoulders)*. Is the new chap all right?

FRANK. He seems to be. Look out. *(MARANGO approaches.)*

MARANGO. What happened to the boy?

CHEF *(as though concerned)*. I don't know. I wasn't there. Frank, what happened?

FRANK *(wearily)*. Someone left a pot of boiling water on one of the steamers and he tipped it over his face.

MARANGO. He's burnt his face. It's not serious, *(to CHEF)* but it might have been. *(He shakes his head sadly and moves away.)*

CHEF. What can I do, Mr Marango? They rush about like mad, I tell them but they don't listen.

(MARANGO moves off shaking his head still.)

CHEF *(to FRANK)*. Much he cares. It interrupts the kitchen so he worries. Three more years, Frank, three, that's all and then the whisht! Retire, finish! Then you can take over.

FRANK. Oh no! Not this boy. I'm in charge one day a week — enough! They can find another madman.

CHEF. Do you think I'm mad?

FRANK. Do you enjoy your work?

CHEF. Who does?

FRANK. So on top of not enjoying your work you take on responsibility — that isn't mad?

CHEF. I've got a standard of living to keep up — idiot!

FRANK *(moving off)*. So go mad!

CHEF. Idiot! Michael!

MICHAEL. Chef?

CHEF. The soup was sour yesterday.

MICHAEL. Sour?

CHEF. Sour!

MICHAEL. But it was only a day old.

33

CHEF. I've had letters from customers.

MICHAEL. Customers!

CHEF. And Michael – don't take chickens home with you.

MICHAEL. Chickens?

CHEF. Take cutlets, take cold meats but not chickens. Chickens are bulky. Wait till you're my age before trying chickens.

MICHAEL. Oh, I must graduate to it like.

CHEF. That's right, you must graduate to it like. You can have your lunch now.

(PETER and HANS return.)

KEVIN. You all right?

(HANS makes a movement of his hands to say 'Ach, I'm fed-up, forget it.')

PAUL. You look beautiful.

KEVIN. A Red Indian.

PETER. Come on, let's eat.

(They all move to their places to eat; PAUL returns to his work; there is less activity in the kitchen now – the calm before the storm. A few waitresses wander around, a porter sweeps the floor.)

KEVIN *(to PETER)*. How long have you been here?

PETER. Three years.

(MICHAEL laughs.)

KEVIN. How did you stick it?

MICHAEL. Sick all ready?

KEVIN. I don't think I'll last the day.

PETER. People are always coming and going.

HANS *(he is not eating much)*. I think me I'll go soon.

MICHAEL *(to KEVIN)*. The worse is to come. *(to others)* Am I right? You wait till the service, ah!...But you'll get used to it after a while.

PETER. We all said we wouldn't last the day, but tell me what is there a man can't get used to? Nothing! You just forget where you are and you say it's a job.

MICHAEL. He should work on the eggs. Five dishes I've got, five! Hey Paul, any cakes?

PAUL. They're all gone – I got some tart from yesterday. *(raising his shoulders)* Sorry!

MICHAEL *(not too loudly)*. Liar!

KEVIN. I thought you could eat what you liked here.

MICHAEL. You can, but you have to swipe it. Even the food for cooking. If I want to make an onion soup that's any good, I go to the cold-room and I take some chickens' wings to make my stock. No questions, just in and out – whisht!

PAUL *(to* RAYMOND*)*. Why do we say there isn't any cake when there is?

RAYMOND. Don't you worry – they eat plenty.

PAUL. So do we. Have you ever caught yourself saying something you don't mean to say? Why did I refuse Michael a cake? Doesn't hurt me to give him a cake, most times we do but there's always that one time when we don't. First thing in the morning I joke with him and half way through the day I lie to him, defending the governor's property as though it was me own. I don't know what to be bloody loyal to half the time.

PETER. Hey, where's Gaston? Why is he not with us, eating here? I black his eye not his arse.

PAUL. Leave off, Peter – the row's over now, patch it up.

MICHAEL. When husbands and wives can't patch up their rows, who are we to succeed?

PAUL. My wife was a mean-minded woman, Michael. She came from a well-run and comfortable-off home but she was mean-minded. I did right by her so don't you be concerned about that. *(*FRANK, ALFREDO *and* MAX *laugh amongst themselves.)* Every time someone asked us how we were she used to say 'Busybody.' Oh yes you can laugh, cocker, but I used to have to spend hours listening to her being bitchy about other women. I tried everything. Hours I spent – I even tried to – aaah what the hell do I bother to explain to you for, here – take your bloody bit of cake. *(Embarrassed silence.)*

HANS. I think I go to America.

KEVIN. America?

HANS *(grins sheepishly, he is about to surprise* KEVIN*).* I been to New York already.

KEVIN. You have?

HANS. I already been twice. *(Nods head to say 'What do you think of that!')* Worked on a ship. *(Pause.)* On a ship you waste more than you eat. *(Lets this sink in.)* You throw everything into the sea before you come on land. *(Sinks in further.)* Whole chickens! The gulls, you know, they eat it.

KEVIN. What about New York?

HANS *(kissing his fingers).* New York? New York, das ist die schönste Stadt der Welt! Wenn du ankommst – When you arrive: The skyline! The Empire State Buildings! Coney Island! And Broadway, Broadway – you heard of Broadway? *(*KEVIN *nods with his mouth full.)* Ah...beautiful city.

KEVIN. I heard it, yes.

HANS *(in his stride now. Grimace, meaning – 'No question of it!').* And Kevin! Women! Three in the morning! And bars and night-clubs! Rush here and rush there! *(More grimace. Secretly, the others jeer good-naturedly.)* A beautiful city! I think this house not very good...here.

KEVIN. It's not, eh?

PETER *(moving to get glass of water).* You got to turn out food hot and quickly. Quality – pooh! No time!

KEVIN. Even in the small restaurants they're not after caring much.

 HAEL *(lighting cigarette).* Why should they! It's this *(rubs thumb and finger together)* that counts, you know that.

KEVIN. Oh I don't know. You'd've thought it was possible to

36

run a small restaurant that could take pride in its food and made money too.

PETER. Of course it's possible, my friend – but you pay to eat in it. It's money. It's all money. The world chase money so you chase money too. *(snapping his fingers in a lunatic way)* Money! Money! Money!

(PETER *is now near* FRANK. *On an impulse he places glass in the cup of* FRANK'S *tall white hat, and creeps back laughing his laugh to himself.*)

PETER. Frank!

(FRANK *of course moves and the water spills over him. More laughter from* PETER.)

FRANK *(shouting across to* PETER*)*. One day you'll lay an egg too many and it'll crack under you. Yes – you laugh.

PETER. Frank is also unhappy. *(*GWEN *approaches table.)* Yes?

GWEN *(lays hand on* MICHAEL'S *shoulder; he lays his on her buttocks)*. Who's on fish today?

MICHAEL. Do you love me?

GWEN. I think you're irresistible. Who's on fish?

KEVIN. Me.

GWEN. Right, I order four plaice. *(Moves off.)*

PETER *(easing* KEVIN *back to seat because he has just risen to serve that order)*. You got time. You not finished your lunch yet. The customer can wait. *(to* KEVIN*)* Be like Mr Alfredo. Nothing disturbs Mr Alfredo. Mr Alfredo is a worker and he hates his boss. He knows his job but he does no more no less and at the right time. Mr Alfredo is an Englishman – look at that!

(*At this point* MR ALFREDO *comes to the front of the stage and looks around to see that no one is watching. No one is. He tucks something first into the right of his apron. Then, straightening himself out, he returns to pick his teeth.* MOLLY *approaches* FRANK.)

MOLLY. Mr Marango wants a leg of chicken and some sauté.

FRANK. Mr Marango can go to hell, I'm eating.

MOLLY *(moves off)*. I'll call for it in five minutes.

FRANK. They don't give you a chance to eat here.

MAX. Hey, you heard they nearly killed Peter last night?

FRANK. Don't talk to me about that boy. He's mad. I've had too much of him already...three years.

NICHOLAS. They should kill 'em off! Kill 'em off! The lot! Boche! I hate them, you know? I don't hate no one like I hate them. And they want to abolish hanging now. You read about it?

MAX *(to* FRANK*)*. Do you think that Bill'll go through?

FRANK. How should I know! I suppose it's worth a try.

MAX. They'll be sorry, I'm telling you.

NICHOLAS *(self-righteously)*. What I say is if a man he kills another then he should be killed too.

MAX *(approvingly)*. An eye for an eye.

NICHOLAS. And we should use the electric chair. It's no good the hanging.

MAX *(enjoying what he is about to say)*. Remember those two they put on the chair in America not long ago, for spying? The bloody thing misfired – ha – they had to do it again. I bet the duty electrician on that job got a rollicking.

FRANK. What do you want them to use – gas ovens?

(MONIQUE *walks past* PETER *to front of stage and waits for him by his station. She has a cup of tea in her hand.* PETER *jumps up and goes to her. They do this every meal-break.)*

PETER. You forgive me?

MONIQUE. I can't keep up a row, I laugh after a while.

PETER. I'm a good boy, really. When's your day off?

MONIQUE. Tomorrow.

PETER. Then I won't see you.

MONIQUE. No.

PETER. What are you going to do?

MONIQUE. In the morning I'm going shopping. In the afternoon I'm going to have my hair done, and in the evening I'm going dancing at the Astra.

PETER. Why do you have to go there? All the prostitutes go there.

MONIQUE. I'm going with Monty.

PETER. Listen Monique. Tell Monty tonight. Ask for a divorce, eh? We can't go on like thieves, we do damage to ourselves, you know that?

MONIQUE. Peter, not here, please. I can't tell him yet.

PETER. Here — inside here *(knocks at his head with his hand)* we do damage. We insult ourselves. I'm not going to wait much longer, you'll see. You think I like this Tivoli?

MONIQUE. Now stop it. Why do you always choose a public place to talk about it? You go on and on, and I keep telling you to give me time. I've promised I will, and I will, so be patient.

PETER. Patient...me, patient?...You don't believe me I won't wait, do you?

MONIQUE. Please yourself.

PETER *(despairingly)*. What do you want me to do? Do you want to make me something to laugh at? Three years I'm here now, three...

MONIQUE. Oh, ye gods!

(MONIQUE leaves him. PETER is about to become furious but controls himself.)

PETER *(shouting)*. Auf geht's, Irishman. Finish now. Auf geht's. *(KEVIN takes no notice so PETER repeats louder.)*

PETER. Auf geht's, Irishman, auf geht's.

KEVIN. All right all right.

(PETER sings his song, lifting HANS to his feet. HANS, KEVIN and PETER return to their stations.)

CHEF. O.K., Frank.

FRANK. All right, let's get some work done.

CHEF. All right, Michael. Mangolis clear.

MANGOLIS. Sir.

(All return to their stations. CHEF approaches KEVIN.)

CHEF. You all right?

KEVIN. Yes, Chef.

CHEF. In place and everything?

KEVIN. Yes, Chef.

CHEF. Let me see. *(Watches KEVIN start to work.)* All right, but quicker, quicker, quicker.

PETER. Quicker, quicker, quicker, Irishman.

HANS. Quicker, quicker.

PETER. Watch him now the Irishman, soon he won't know what's happening....Hya...Hya, hya. *(He and HANS start to sing their song.)*

KEVIN. Does your mother know you're out?

(The waitresses begin to enter, shouting their orders at the required station. They take plates from hot-plate, cradle them in their arms and order. They appear in greater numbers as the service swings into motion. Queues form in front of first one cook, then another.)

MOLLY *(to HANS).* Two veal cutlets.

HANS. Two veal cutlets.

GWEN *(to PETER).* Four cod...do we order cod?

PETER. Yes, back in five minutes.

WINNIE *(to PETER).* Three turbot.

PETER. Three turbot.

CYNTHIA *(to HANS).* Four veal cutlets.

HANS. Four veal cutlets! Oh baby wait a moment! I...I...I... Hast du dir's überlegt? Gehen wir zusammen aus? Ich lade dich ein! Wir gehen ins Kino und nachher tanzen. Willst du?

CYNTHIA. No, I – have – to – go – and – get – my – plaice.

(said as to someone who doesn't understand a word of English)

HANS. Oh Gott! My cutlets!

DAPHNE *(to FRANK).* Three legs of chicken.

40

FRANK. Three legs of chick.

HETTIE *(to* NICHOLAS*)*. Two chicken salad.

NICHOLAS. Two chicken salad.

HANS *(who has been watching* CYNTHIA*)*. Oh my cutlets.

CYNTHIA *(to* KEVIN*)*. Party of eight plaice to begin with.

KEVIN. Eight plaice. She's a worker.

JACKIE *(to* GASTON*)*. Five grilled chops.

GASTON. Five grilled chops.

DAPHNE *(to* NICHOLAS*)*. Three french salad.

HETTIE. I was first.

DAPHNE. Special.

NICHOLAS. Three french salad.

MOLLY *(to* GASTON*)*. Six steaks.

GASTON. Six steaks.

MOLLY *(to* MICHAEL*)*. Four minestrone.

MICHAEL. Four minestrone.

GWEN *(to* FRANK*)*. Two roast chicken and sauté.

FRANK. Two roast chicken and sauté.

CYNTHIA *(to* HANS*)*. These my veal cutlets?

HANS. These are your cutlets! Four Kalbskotletts only for you
   baby!

CYNTHIA. Oh really!

HANS *(to* PETER*)*. Wunderbar! Peter look! Wie die geht! Wie
   die aussieht, die ist genau meine Kragenweite!

PETER *(singing)*. 'Falling in love again.'

KEVIN. Hey Peter, any more plaice?

PETER. In the cold cupboard.

   (In exiting, KEVIN *knocks into* DAPHNE.*)*

DAPHNE. Watch it, Irishman.

PETER *(continuing to tease* HANS*)*. 'Falling in love again.'

HANS. Oh Pete, stop it! Ich weiss nicht, was ich anstellen soll!
   I speak quite good English already

VIOLET. Four cod.

   (They obviously don't hear her.)

41

HANS. But with her I forget every word.

VIOLET. I said four cod!

HANS (*to* VIOLET). Shut up, baby! (*to* PETER) She is smashing!!
(VIOLET *goes off.*)

MONIQUE (*to* CHEF). Chef, complaint, minestrone.

PETER (*to* MONIQUE). Now remember, don't forget to remember.

MONIQUE. Remember what?

PETER. What are you doing...you don't know what you are
doing.

CHEF. Michael, the soup is sour.

MONIQUE (*to* PETER). Your work...your work.
(*While she isn't looking,* MICHAEL *tips the soup straight from
one bowl into another, and hands the plate to her.*)

BETTY (*to* ALFREDO). Two roast beef.

ALFREDO. Hold it, hold it.

BETTY. Oh, is it ready?

ALFREDO. Of course it's ready.

PETER. Mangolis, plates!

MANGOLIS. Plates coming up.

GWEN (*to* PETER). Is my four cod ready?

DAPHNE (*to* NICHOLAS). One salad.

WINNIE (*to* FRANK). Two roast pheasant, darling.

FRANK. Oh charming. I love you.

HETTIE (*to* HANS). Two sausages.

JACKIE (*to* ALFREDO). One roast pork.

ALFREDO. One roast pork.

DAPHNE (*to* KEVIN). Two plaice. Oh, where the hell is he?
(*Waits for* KEVIN.)

HETTIE (*to* KEVIN). Three grilled turbot.

JACKIE (*to* PETER). Two cod.

PETER. Two cod.

DAPHNE (*to* KEVIN). Two plaice. Come on, come on Irishman.

KEVIN *(re-entering)* Oh Jesus, Mother of God, and the Holy Virgin.

GASTON *(who is passing at the same time)*. Exo.

DAPHNE *(to KEVIN)*. Two plaice.

MOLLY *(to HANS)*. My veal cutlets ready?

HANS. What do you think?

HETTIE *(to KEVIN)*. Three grilled turbot.

KEVIN. Three grilled turbot.

MOLLY *(to NICHOLAS)*. One lobster, one ham salad.

NICHOLAS. One lobster, one ham.

CYNTHIA *(to MICHAEL)*. Three omelets au jambon.

MICHAEL. Three jambons.

BETTY *(to GASTON)*. Three entrecote steaks.

GASTON. Three entrecote steaks.

ANNE *(to PAUL)*. My fruit flans ready?

PAUL. I'll bring them up, me old darling.

GWEN *(to NICHOLAS)*. Two ham salads.

NICHOLAS. Two ham salads.

GWEN. I want two coffees, Annie love.

ANNE. All right dear.

WINNIE *(to HANS)*. Two veal cutlets.

HANS. Two veal cutlets...Oh God. Max, veal cutlets and sausages.

MAX. Yes...all right. *(Takes tray which HANS throws to him.)*

GASTON. Max send up steaks and mutton chops quick. *(Almost hysterical.)*

MAX *(angrily)*. Wait a bloody minute will you!

GASTON *(in panic)*. I got six steaks ordered already.

MAX. So what am I supposed to do?

GASTON *(to nobody in particular)*. Everybody the same in this bloody house. I've always got a big queue before I start. *(Returns mumbling.)*

WINNIE *(to KEVIN)*. One plaice please.

KEVIN. One plaice? Right.

BETTY *(to* FRANK*)*. One roast chicken.

FRANK. One roast chicken.

HANS. Come on, Max.

HETTIE *(to* KEVIN*)*. Two grilled salmon, do we order it?

KEVIN. Yes, five minutes. Go on, hop it!

JACKIE *(to* KEVIN*)*. One grilled trout please.

KEVIN *(rushing around)*. Right away!

MOLLY *(to* KEVIN*)*. Two plaice please.

KEVIN. All right, all right.

PETER *(shouting while he serves)*. Ha-ha! He-he! Ho-ho! They're here! They come!

HETTIE *(to* NICHOLAS*)*. One chicken, one ham salad.

CYNTHIA *(to* PETER*)*. One cod.

PETER. One cod.

WINNIE *(to* MICHAEL*)*. One hamburger.

MICHAEL. One hamburger.

VIOLET. Are my four cod ready?

GWEN *(to* HANS*)*. One veal cutlet.

PETER *(to* VIOLET*)*. When did you order them?

HANS. One veal cutlet.

VIOLET. Five minutes ago. I come past and you were talking to Hans – remember?

PETER. I remember nothing. Come back in five minutes. Next?

VIOLET. You weren't listening, that's what it was.

PETER. You ordered nothing, I say.

MOLLY *(to* MICHAEL*)*. Two minestrone.

PETER. Now come back five minutes' time...next.

VIOLET. Well really.

GWEN *(to* PETER*)*. One steamed turbot.

PETER. One steamed turbot.

BETTY *(to* HANS*)*. Three veal cutlets please.

HANS *(mimicking)*. Three veal cutlets please.

HEAD WAITER. Violet.

JACKIE *(to* NICHOLAS*)*. Two ham, one lobster salad.

44

DAPHNE *(to* ANNE*).* Three fruit flan.

HANS *(to* BETTY, *who has waited).* What's the matter with you...
you can't see the cutlets cook.

BETTY. Well, last time I waited.

HANS. Well, last time I waited.

BETTY. Oh get lost...excuse me Harry. *(to* HEAD WAITER, *who
is passing)*

WINNIE *(to* GASTON*).* Three steaks.

HEAD WAITER *(to* CHEF*).* Ten minutes ago, Violet ordered
four cod. They're not ready yet.

*(*KEVIN, GASTON *and* MICHAEL *call for plates.)*

CHEF. Peter...the cod not ready yet?

PETER. She's a liar that one, she ordered nothing.

CHEF. Come on, come on.

PETER. One cod, two cod.

DAPHNE *(to* ANNE*).* Two coffees.

PETER. Three cod, four cod.

(As VIOLET *turns with the plates,* MANGOLIS, *who is passing,
knocks her, and the plates fall to the ground.)*

JACKIE *(to* ANNE*).* Three coffees.

VIOLET. Oh God, God, God, I can't, I can't.

GWEN. Don't upset yourself, love.

VIOLET. Look at it all, I can't work like this. I'm not used to
this way of working.

BETTY *(to* MICHAEL*).* One minestrone.

VIOLET. I've never worked like this before, never, never.

(During this the CHEF *calls* FRANK, *who calls* MANGOLIS, *to
clear the broken china.)*

PETER. Too old, too old my sweetheart. Go home old woman –
for the young this work – go home.

HANS *(to* PETER*).* Oh stop it, shut up.

*(*PETER *makes a face after* CHEF, *and when it is safe he
begins to sing his song while working. Half way through, he
breaks off, and rushes to oven. There is something vast and*

Shakespearian in the way PETER *moves — he is always wanting to play the fool.)*

GWEN *(to* HANS*).* One veal cutlet.

PETER *(to* KEVIN*).* Oh God! She burns! The cod! Hya, hya, hya. She burns, Irishman. No good, no good. *(Rushes the frying-pan with the burnt fish to the dustbin nearby, and covers it with paper.)* Ssh, ssssh. Hya, hya, hya.

HANS *(to* PETER, *loudly in the midst of his own work).* That is not too good work, Peter, not good work mein Lieber. Pig's work. *(Laughs and points to* KEVIN, *who has large queue at his station.)* We have busy time, Irishman, yes?

KEVIN. Bloody comedian.

HETTIE *(to* KEVIN*).* My salmon ready?

KEVIN. Your what?

HETTIE. Me grilled salmon.

KEVIN. How many do you want?

HETTIE. Two.

CYNTHIA *(to* MICHAEL*).* My three omelets.

MICHAEL. Your three omelets.

DAPHNE *(to* KEVIN*).* Two salmon.

JACKIE *(to* KEVIN*).* Three sardines.

KEVIN. Peter, for God's sake will you give me a hand?

HETTIE *(to* MICHAEL*).* Two veg soups.

PETER *(helping* KEVIN*).* Let's go Irishman, let's go. The next.

DAPHNE. Two salmon.

PETER. Right.

BETTY *(to* HANS*).* My veal cutlets.

HANS. Your veal cutlets.

PETER. And the next?

JACKIE *(to* PETER*).* Three sardines.

BETTY *(to* HANS*).* Oh come on, lobster-face.

HANS. What does it mean, lobster-face?

PETER. And the next?

WINNIE *(to* PETER*).* Three plaice.

HANS *(to* BETTY*)*. Ein, zwei, drei.

PETER *(to* WINNIE*)*. One, two, three.

BETTY *(to* PETER*)*. Two plaice.

> *(While* PETER *has been helping* KEVIN, *the following three orders pile up on his unattended station.)*

MOLLY. One turbot.

GWEN. One steamed halibut.

CYNTHIA. Two cod.

MOLLY. Oh come on, Peter.

> *(*PETER *rushes to his station, laughing like a merry fool going into battle.)*

PETER. Look at this – hya, hya – good morning ladies – and the next...

MOLLY *(to* PETER*)*. One turbot. *(*PETER *serves her, and cries out* 'Next, next,' *and so on.)*

GWEN *(to* PETER*)*. One steamed halibut.

JACKIE *(to* FRANK*)*. Three legs of chicken.

FRANK. Three chicken.

KEVIN *(to* PETER*)*. I've run out of lemons!

PETER *(with rude indifference)*. Well cut some more then. The next?

KEVIN. Let me borrow your cutting-board then, please. *(He moves to take it from* PETER'*s bench.)*

PETER *(stops his work, and jumping on* KEVIN, *grabs board: in the kitchen it is every man for himself now)*. Oh no, no, no, no my friend. The plate-room, the plate-room, in the plate-room, you'll find them. This is mine, I have need of it.

KEVIN. But I'll give it back in a few seconds.

PETER *(pointing)*. The plate-room. *(Slams his hand down on the board for emphasis; to a waitress –)* What do you want?

KEVIN *(going to plate-room)*. Well, speak a little human like, will yer please?

PETER. No time, no time. Next.

CYNTHIA *(to* PETER*).* Two cod.

JACKIE *(to* NICHOLAS*).* One cheese salad.

VIOLET *(to* NICHOLAS*).* One ham salad. *(tearfully)*

BETTY *(to* GASTON*).* My steaks ready yet?

VIOLET *(to* ANNE*).* A fruit flan and two coffees.

GASTON *(to* BETTY*).* About time.

BETTY. I'm sorry.

DAPHNE *(to* FRANK*).* Two roast chicken.

FRANK. Two roast chicken.

WINNIE *(to* ALFREDO*).* Two roast veal and spaghetti.

JACKIE *(to* MICHAEL*).* One prawn omelet.

MICHAEL. One prawn.

GWEN *(to* ALFREDO*).* Two roast beef.

ALFREDO. Two roast beef.

MOLLY *(to* Kevin*).* Two sole.

CYNTHIA *(to* Kevin*).* Three plaice.

DAPHNE *(to* GASTON*).* Two lamb chops.

HETTIE *(to* MICHAEL*).* Two minestrones.

MONIQUE *(to* PETER*).* Four cod.

PETER. What?

MONIQUE. Violet's four cod.

MOLLY *(about* Kevin*).* He's never here, this one.

PETER *(to* MONIQUE*).* You wait for me afterwards.

MONIQUE. I'll wait for you.

CYNTHIA *(to* Kevin*).* Come on Irishman, my plaice.

BETTY *(to* MICHAEL*).* One minestrone.

PETER *(to* MONIQUE*).* We go for a stroll?

MONIQUE. Yes, we go for a stroll.

MOLLY *(to* CYNTHIA*).* We'll lose all those tips.

GWEN *(to* HANS*).* Four veal cutlets.

HANS. Four veal cutlets.

MOLLY *(to* KEVIN*).* Me sole, luvvy, where's me sole?

KEVIN *(re-entering).* Wait a bloody minute, can't you.

MOLLY *(to* KEVIN*).* Two.

GWEN *(to* PETER*)*. Two halibut.

BETTY *(to* MICHAEL*)*. Three hamburgers.

CYNTHIA *(to* KEVIN*)*. Three plaice. There's no time for breathing here, you know.

KEVIN. Jesus is this a bloody madhouse.

MICHAEL. Three hamburgers.

NICHOLAS. Plates.

MANGOLIS. Plates.

KEVIN. Have you all gone barking-raving-bloody-mad.

(At this point all the waitresses have got into a continuous circle of orders round and round the kitchen, as the volume of the ovens increases and the lights slowly fade to blackout. The calls of orders and for plates and more meat, etc., continue through the blackness until the stage is clear and ready for the interlude. The author would prefer there to be no interval at this point but recognizes the wish of theatre bars to make some money.)

PETER'S SONG

Hi lee hi lo hi la   Hi lee hi lo hi la   hi lee

hi lo   hi la ha ha ha ha ha   *continue down the scale in laughter*

hya hya hya hya.

INTERLUDE

Lights fade up on the sound of a guitar.

It is afternoon break. The sounds of the oven are at half. PAUL *and* RAYMOND *are working in their corner. These are the only two who stay through the afternoon.* KEVIN *is flat out on his back on a wooden bench, exhausted.* DIMITRI *is slowly sweeping up.* PETER *is sitting by a table waiting for* MONIQUE. HANS *is in a corner with a guitar, singing 'Ah sinner-man' in German.*

KEVIN. Finished! I'm done! I'm boiled! You can serve me up for supper!

PAUL *(as if ordering a meal)*. Two portions of boiled Irishman please! With garnish!

RAYMOND *(also calling)*. Two fried tomatoes on his ears, potatoes round his head, and stuff his mouth with an extra helping of peas.

KEVIN. I'll produce me own gravy! But did you see it? Did-you-see-that? Fifteen hundred customers, an' half of them eating fish. *I* had to start work on a Friday!

RAYMOND. It's every day the same, my friend.

KEVIN *(raising himself up)*. Look at me. I'm soaking. Look at this jacket. I can wring it out. That's not sweat, no man carries that much water. *(flopping back again)* Kevin, you'll drop dead if you stay. I'm warning you Kevin, take a tip from a friend, hop it! Get out! You've got your youth Kevin, keep it! This is no place for a human being -- you'll drop dead, I'm telling yous.

DIMITRI. Hey Irishman, what you grumbling about this place for? Is different anywhere else? People come and people go, big excitement, big noise. *(Makes noise and gesticulates.)* What for? In the end who do you know? You make a friend, you going to be all you life his friend but when you go from here -- pshtt! You forget! Why you grumble about this one kitchen?

PETER. You're a very intelligent boy, Dimitri.

DIMITRI. And you're a bloody fool. I'm not sure I want to talk with you.

KEVIN. Oh not the Gaston row again. All the morning I hear how Peter give Gaston a black eye. It's the break, no rows please, it's peace. Can you hear it? It's lovely, it's silence. It's nothing – ahhh! (*Moves.*) Oooh – I'm drowning, in my own sweat. Christ! What a way to die.

DIMITRI (*to* PETER). A bloody fool you!

(PETER *picks up a cardboard box, and puts it over* DIMITRI's *head.* DIMITRI *flings it off angrily and is about to throw it back, but he sees* PETER *with his head in his hands. Instead, he takes out a cigarette box, and begins rolling* PETER *a cigarette. He gives the paper to* PETER *to lick, then continues folding it, and hands it to him.*)

PETER. Hey Irishman, I thought you didn't like this place. Why don't you go home and sleep.

KEVIN. Me home is a room and a bed and a painting of the Holy Virgin. It'll always be there.

PETER. Like this place, this house – this too, it'll always be here. That's a thought for you Irishman. This – this madhouse it's always here. When you go, when I go, when Dimitri go – this kitchen stays. It'll go on when we die, think about that. We work here – eight hours a day, and yet – it's nothing. We take nothing. Here – the kitchen, here – you. You and the kitchen. And the kitchen don't mean nothing to you and you don't mean to the kitchen nothing. Dimitri is right you know – why do you grumble about this kitchen? What about the offices and the factories? There Irishman – what do you say to that?

KEVIN. You want to come in one morning and find it gone?

PETER. Just one morning. Imagine it, eh? Gone. All this gone.

KEVIN. So you'd be out of work!

PETER. So I'd die?

KEVIN. It doesn't worry you I suppose.

HANS. Du träumst schon wieder.

KEVIN. What's he say?

PETER. He say – I'm dreaming.

(PETER *stands up, and begins idly strolling round the kitchen. Picks up dustbin-lid, a long ladle – shield and sword – lunges at* RAYMOND. RAYMOND *picks up a whisk. A few seconds' duel.* PETER *raises his arms in surrender.*)

PETER. Yah! War! Did you used to play like this, at war, with dustbin-lids and things? I did. Yah! Not very good, eh Irishman? War? Kids playing at war grow up peaceful they say, I think not so simple, eh? Me I never liked war games. I had my own group – boys, we'd build things. Castles, huts, camps.

(*During this,* PETER *has taken two dustbins, puts one on the corner of the stove and one on the opposite corner of his hot-plate. He then puts a tall container on top of each and sauce-pans on top of these. Next he puts* DIMITRI'*s broom across the top, and hangs dish-cloths on the handles. He then notices a vase of flowers on the Chef's table, and, selecting the largest, he gives the remainder to* PAUL; *he puts his flower through one of the saucepan handles. With his back to the audience, he faces his creation.*)

PAUL. Beautiful, what is it?

PETER. It's my arch, and I was...And I was...(*grabbing a long ladle to use as a saluting sword*) I was ein grosser Deutscher Ritter!

HANS. Hey Peter – weisst du noch?

(*At this point* HANS *starts to play the Horst Wessel song on the guitar.* PETER *does the goose-step through his arch while* PAUL *throws flowers over him and* HANS.)

KEVIN (*sings*). And the Irish Republican Army made muck of the whole bloody lot. Now isn't that something mad, now.

52

PETER. You think this is madness?

KEVIN. Well, isn't it? Isn't it kids playing and all that carry-on?

PETER. This one says games and that one says dreams. You think it's a waste of time? You know what a game is? A dream? It's the time when you forget what you are and you make what you could be. When a man dreams – he grows, big, better. You find that silly?

HANS. Du bist zu alt, Peter!

PETER. I'm *not* too old, never, never too old, don't tell me that. Too old! When you're dead you're too old.

HANS. Aha, und du glaubst wir haben hier Zeit zum träumen.

PETER. There is! There is time to dream. I want to dream. Everyone should dream, once in a life everyone should dream. Hey Irishman, you dream, how do you dream, tell us?

KEVIN. You play your own games, Peter, leave me out of it, I'm past it.

PETER. You know when a man is not a man? When he's ashamed of being a child. That's you Irishman. You're ashamed of being a child. Why you ashamed? We all friends here, why you ashamed to dream, I give you the chance.

KEVIN. I'm obliged!

PETER. Hey Paul, Raymondo, Dimitri, stop work a minute. You got time. Here, come here. We are all given a chance to dream. No one is going to laugh, we love each other, we protect each other – someone tell us a dream, just to us, no one else, the ovens are low, the customers gone, Marango is gone, it's all quiet. God has given us a chance now, we never have the opportunity again, so dream – someone – who? Dimitri – you, you dream first.

DIMITRI. In this place? With iron around me? And dustbins? And black walls?

PETER. Pretend! There's no dustbins, that's a big beautiful arch there. Pretend! The walls are skies, yes? The iron, it's rock on a coast; the tables, *(thinks)* they're rose bushes; and the ovens are the noise of the winds. Look at the lights – stars, Dimitri.

HANS. Peter, du verschwendest deine Zeit!

PETER. So what! So what if I waste time? It's good to be able to waste time. I got another sixty years to live, I can afford it. Dimitri – dream – a little dream, what you see?

DIMITRI. A little, a little er – what you call it – a small house, sort of –

PAUL. A hut?

DIMITRI. No –

KEVIN. A shed?

DIMITRI. That's right, a shed. With instruments, and tools, and I make lots of radios and television sets maybe, and...

PETER. Ach no, silly boy. That's a hobby, that's not what you really want. You want more, more, Dimitri –

DIMITRI. I – I – I can't, Peter, I can't see more, I try but I can't see more.

PETER. Poor Dimitri – hey Irishman, you – you dream.

KEVIN. if you think because I'm Irish I'm going to start prattling on about goblins and leprechauns you've got another think coming –

PETER. No, no, not fairies, a real dream, about men –

KEVIN. But I don't dream of men –

PETER. What then?

KEVIN. Sleep! Sleep me. Most people sleep and dream; me – I dream of sleep!

PETER. What is it with you all? Hans – you, what are your dreams?

(HANS *sings on, as though not answering the question. Then –)*

HANS. Money! Geld, Peter, Geld! With money I'm a good

man! I'm generous! I love all the world! Money, Pete!
Money! Money! Money! *(Continues singing.)*

PETER. How can you talk of money, Hans, when you're singing?

HANS. Dreaming, mein Lieber, dreaming, dreaming.

PETER. Raymondo?

RAYMOND. Me? Women!

PETER. Which women? Large, small? Happy? Black? Yellow?
What kind?

RAYMOND. There *is* more than one kind?

PETER. Raymond – you make me very sad. Paul – you.

PAUL. Do me a favour.

PETER. Please!

PAUL. No. *(Relents)* Listen, Peter...I'll tell you something. I'm
going to be honest with you. You don't mind if I'm
honest? Right! I'm going to be honest with you. I don't
like you. Now wait a minute, let me finish. I don't like you!
I think you're a pig! You bully, you're jealous, you go mad
with your work, you always quarrel. All right! But now
it's quiet, the ovens are low, the work has stopped for a
little and now I'm getting to know you. I still think you're
a pig – only now, not so much of a pig. So that's what I
dream. I dream of a friend. You give me a rest, you give
me silence, you take away this mad kitchen so I make
friends, so I think – maybe all the people I thought were
pigs are not so much pigs.

PETER. You think people are pigs, eh?

PAUL. Listen, I'll tell you something. I agree with Dimitri also;
when the world is filled with kitchens you get pigs – I'll
tell you. Next door to me, next door where I live is a bus
driver. Comes from Hoxton, he's my age, married and got
two kids. He says good-morning to me, I ask him how he
is, I give his children sweets. That's our relationship. Somehow he seems frightened to say too much, you know?

God forbid I might ask him for something. So we make no demands on each other. Then one day the busmen go on strike. He's out for five weeks. Every morning I say to him 'Keep going mate, you'll win.' Every morning I give him words of encouragement; I say I understand his cause. I've got to get up earlier to get to work but I don't mind. We're neighbours. We're workers together, he's pleased. Then, one Sunday, there's a peace march. I don't believe they do much good but I go, because in this world a man's got to show he can have his say. The next morning he comes up to me and he says, now listen to this, he says 'Did you go on that peace march yesterday?' So I says Yes, I did go on that peace march yesterday. So then he turns round to me and he says, 'You know what? A bomb should have been dropped on the lot of them! It's a pity,' he says, 'that they had children with them cos a bomb should've been dropped on the lot!' And you know what was upsetting him? The march was holding up the traffic, the buses couldn't move so fast! Now I don't want him to say I'm right, I don't want him to agree with what I did, but what terrifies me is that he didn't stop to think that this man helped me in my cause so maybe, only *maybe*, there's something in his cause. I'll talk about it. No! The buses were held up so drop a bomb he says, on the lot! And you should've seen the hate in his eyes, as if I'd murdered his child. Like an animal he looked. And the horror is this – that there's a wall, a big wall between me and millions of people like him. And I think – where will it end? What do you do about it? And I look around me, at the kitchen, at the factories, at the enormous bloody buildings going up with all those offices and all those people in them, and I think, Christ! I think, Christ, Christ, Christ! I agree with you Peter – maybe one morning we should wake up and find them all gone. But then I think: I should stop making pastries? The factory

worker should stop making trains and cars? The miner should leave the coals where it is? *(Pause.)* You give *me* an answer. You give me your dream.

KEVIN. Hush pâtissier! Hush! It's quiet now. Gently now.

(HANS throws one of the red flowers to PAUL. There is a long silence. HANS, who had stopped playing, now continues. The ovens hum. PAUL sticks the flower in his lapel.)

PETER. I ask for dreams — you give me nightmares.

PAUL. So I've dreamt! Is it my fault if it's a nightmare?

KEVIN. We're waiting for your dream now, Peter boy.

DIMITRI *(jumping up suddenly).* This is the United Nations, eh? A big conference. Is Russia here, and America and France and England — and Germany too. Is all here. And they got on a competition. Is finished the wars, is finished the rows. Everybody gone home. We got time on our hands. A prize of one million dollars for the best dream. Raymondo he want a new woman every night. I want a workshop. Paul he wants a friend. Irishman he wants a bed and Hans he just want the million dollars. Big opportunity! Come on Peter, a big dream.

PETER *(looking around).* All this gone?

DIMITRI. You said so. One morning you come here, to this street here, and the kitchen is gone. And you look around for more kitchens and is none anywhere. What you want to do? The United Nations wants to know.

PAUL. Come on, come on!

PETER. Shush, shush!

(PETER suddenly confronted with his own idea becomes embarrassed and shy. He laughs.)

PETER. I can't. I can't.

(MONIQUE arrives and PETER forgets everything and becomes the all-consumed lover, the excited child.)

MONIQUE. Ready?

PETER. Finished? I come I come. Hey Irishman, you'll soon be coming back. Go home. Change. You catch pneumonia. *(excitedly)* Auf geht's, auf geht's!

(The mad PETER *rushes out with his* MONIQUE. *The rest are left. The guitar and the hum of the ovens.)*

DIMITRI *(shouting at the absent Peter)*. Fool! Bloody fool! We wait for a dream.

PAUL. I don't know what you see in him.

DIMITRI. I don't know what I see in him either. Bloody fool!

KEVIN. Bloody volcano if you ask me. I'm away. *(Rises.)*

PAUL *(returning to his work)*. He hasn't got a dream.

KEVIN. It's all mad talk if you ask me. I don't see no point in it. I don't see no point in that Peter bloke either. He talks about peace and dreams and when I ask him if I could use his cutting-board to cut me lemons on this morning he told me – get your own. Dreams? See yous!

*(*KEVIN *exits.* HANS *is still playing.* DIMITRI *returns to his sweeping.)*

PAUL *(to* DIMITRI*)*. So *you* tell me the point of all that. I don't even know what I was saying myself.

DIMITRI. Why should I know? Sometimes things happen and no one sees the point – and then suddenly, something else happen and you see the point. Peter not a fool! You not a fool! People's brain moves all the time. *All* the time. I'm telling you.

*(*DIMITRI *sweeps on.* HANS *finishes his song, rises, bows, slings his guitar and exits.*

This next scene happens very, very slowly to denote the passing of the afternoon.)

PAUL. Best part of the day.

RAYMOND. When they're gone I slow down.

PAUL *(throwing a cigarette end to* DIMITRI*)*. Here's another bit of debris for you. Longest part of the day though, isn't it?

RAYMOND *(offering to* PAUL *from Nicholas's table)*. Tomato?

Carrot? Cucumber? (PAUL *declines all.*) Yes, the longest part.

(Enter MANGOLIS. DIMITRI *strikes the bench and table and part of the arch. The afternoon is over.* MANGOLIS *is singing a Greek air;* GASTON *enters followed by* NICHOLAS, *and the four of them gradually start a Greek dance....)*

PART TWO

...At the end of the Greek dance, DIMITRI *starts to kick a cardboard box, as in football;* MICHAEL, *entering, intercepts it.*

MICHAEL. And that great little inside left, Michael Dawson, has the ball again. Will he miss this golden opportunity? Can he hold his own against the great Arsenal backs? He *does!* Yes! Past Wills, past MacCullough, past Young and he's going to shoot, he *shoots!* – and it's a goal, a goal, yes, his fifth goal, making the score Leyton Orient eighteen, Arsenal nil. What a game! What a boy! Look at this place, like a battlefield, grrr – it smells of the dead.

*(*MONIQUE *enters, slamming the door, and exits into the dining-room, in a furious temper.)*

PAUL. Well, they started the afternoon happy. Did you have a good afternoon, Michael?

MICHAEL. Too bloody good... St James Park. Lying in the sun. Dozing. The girls – aaaah! Hey, I saw Nick and Daphne in the park.

PAUL. There's nice for you.

MICHAEL. Rowing on the lake.

RAYMOND. How touching. Aaaaaah!

MICHAEL. He wasn't doing the row though! You boys are lucky, not having to break in the afternoon, come back to work.

PAUL. I thought you liked the place.

MICHAEL. I don't mind the coming in, it's the coming back. Not old Alfred though. Look at him – in, out, cook, serve – he doesn't mind.

*(*ALFREDO *has entered and gone straight to his work. Following him is* PETER, *who hangs back.)*

ALFREDO. Well come on Peter boy, work, it won't hurt you. Come on then, stock up, replenish, boy.

PETER. My arch — where is it? Who took it down, who took my arch away? Let it stay — let Marango see it.
(GASTON is emptying waste into one dustbin.)
PETER *(to GASTON)*. You leave it! You leave it!
(ALFREDO approaches him. During this conversation the others enter.)
ALFREDO. You are not ill, are you?
PETER. Who knows.
ALFREDO. No pain nor nothing?
PETER. No. Alfredo, look —
ALFREDO. Good! You have all your teeth?
PETER. Yes.
ALFREDO. Good! You have good lodgings?
PETER. Yes.
ALFREDO. So tell me what you're unhappy for.
PETER. Alfredo, you are a good cook, uh? You come in the morning, you go straight to work, you ask nobody anything, you tell nobody anything. You are ready to start work before we are, you never panic. Tell me, is this a good house?
ALFREDO *(drily)*. Depends. It's not bad for Mr Marango, you know.
MICHAEL *(approaching PETER)*. Peter, give me a cigarette please!
(PETER does so. MICHAEL stays on to listen.)
ALFREDO. I'm an old man. It's finished for me. Mind you I've worked in places where I could do good cooking. But it doesn't matter now. Now I work only for the money.
MICHAEL. Quite right! A match Peter please.
PETER *(to MICHAEL, looking for matches)*. You like it here, don't you?
MICHAEL. The ovens —
PETER. No, I got no matches.
MICHAEL. I love the sound of the ovens. Nick, got a light?
(NICHOLAS throws him matches.)

PETER. Idiot! He loves the sound of the ovens! You stand before them all day! They're red hot! You fry first a bit of
ham and an egg in a tin; then someone orders an onion
soup and you put soup and bread and cheese in another tin,
and you grill that; then someone orders an omelet and you
rush to do that; then someone throws you a hamburger
and you fry that. You go up you go down you jump here
you jump there, you sweat till steam comes off your back.

MICHAEL *(moving across to* NICHOLAS *for a light).* I love it.

PETER *(returning head to arms).* Good luck to you.

ALFREDO *(to* MONIQUE*).* Here, you talk to him – he's your
generation. *(Moves off.)*

PAUL *(to* RAYMOND*).* Come on Lightning, let's get some work
done.

MONIQUE *(to* PETER*).* Are you still sulking? It was your fault
we rowed, not mine, you're just like a little boy.

(The CHEF *and* FRANK *enter. The* CHEF *breaks between*
PETER *and* MONIQUE.*)*

PETER. Would you like me old and fat, like your husband?
Then you'd have to find a new lover! I sympathize with
Monty sometimes.

MONIQUE. You feel sorry for him?

PETER. Would you like me to hate him? I can't! I try but I
can't, it would be easier but I can't. A good man, kind and
no vices – who can hate such persons?

MONIQUE. I'm sorry I left you standing in the street.

PETER. You're always sorry afterwards, like a dog she leaves me.

MONIQUE. Where did you go?

PETER. Never mind – I went. Go on, go. Go wipe your glasses,
it's nearly time. Go, leave me.

MONIQUE. Look at you. Look at you...is it any wonder I don't
know where the hell I am...you behave like this. I come
to apologize, I say I'm sorry, I speak reasonably and now
you...you...*(Exits.)*

MAX *(to* NICHOLAS*).* What did you marry her for then?

NICHOLAS. Because I love her, that's why. Ha – *(digs* FRANK*)* did you hear that? Why did I marry her, because I love her. And you?

MAX *(also digging* FRANK*).* Because she told me I was big for my age. Hey, did you read about the man who took a young girl into his house, his wife was there, and they all sat undressed watching television. His wife was there! With him! All undressed! Watching television!

FRANK *(drily).* So what happened? They caught cold? *(to* KEVIN*)* Hey, this isn't a rest room, get on with your work.

(Enter DAPHNE *and* HETTIE, *giving out new menus.)*

KEVIN. I'll be taking *my* leave tonight by Christ.

GASTON. You'll get used to it. It's good money.

(Enter VIOLET *chatting with* ANNE, *followed by* HEAD WAITER, *who goes to* CHEF'*s table.)*

KEVIN. To hell with the money an' all. I like me pay but not for this. It's too big here, man, it's high pressure all the time. An' the food! Look at the food! I never cooked so bad since I was in the army. An' no one is after caring much either!

VIOLET. And what about the waitresses, we're the animals, everybody pushing everybody else out of the way.

HEAD WAITER. Never mind, Violet. You got over your first morning all right. This evening won't be so bad, nobody will push you. It'll just be hot – hot and close – for everyone.

VIOLET. I can remember working in places where you had to move like a ballet dancer, weave in and out of tables with grace. There was room, it was civilized.

KEVIN. Starch and clean finger-nails – I heard about it.

*(*HETTIE *goes off sniggering at* VIOLET.*)*

VIOLET *(to* HETTIE*).* And we didn't mind either – we had to queue up and be inspected, all of us, chefs too – it was

63

civilized. I once served the Prince of Wales. Look at me, bruises.

KEVIN. Look at her! Look at me, three stone lighter!

HANS (*to* KEVIN). Marango will try to make you stay.

KEVIN. Now there's a man. Have you watched him? One of the girls dropped some cups by there this morning and he cried, 'me wages' he cried. 'All me wages down there!' And do take notice of the way he strolls among us all? I thought he'd a kind face, but when he's done talking with you his kindness evaporates. In thin air it goes, sudden, and his face gets worried as though today were the last day and he had to be closing for good and he were taking a last sad glance at everything going on. This mornin' he watched me a while, and then walked away shaking his head as though I were dying and there was not a drop of hope for me left an' all.

HANS (*to* PETER). What he has said?

PETER. Marango spielt den lieben Gott!

(DAPHNE *wanders away but not before she takes a piece of cake from* PAUL.)

PAUL (*to* DAPHNE). Bon appetit.

GASTON. Paul you got some cake?

PAUL (*to* RAYMOND). Give the boy some cake. (*to* HANS) You got over this morning yet?

HANS (*taking a cake* RAYMOND *is offering round*). This morning, ach! He's a big fool, that Max. He's like a dustbin.

RAYMOND. So why you take notice? Look at them.

(MAX *and* NICHOLAS *are pointing at each other in some sort of argument, waving fingers, pulling faces and swaying.*)

NICHOLAS. No! No! No! I'm never going to listen to you again, never.

MAX. Good, very good. I'm fed up with you hanging around me anyway. 'Max should I do this, Max should I do that?' Well, Max isn't your father.

64

NICHOLAS. You're damn right he's not my father. My father was a man with kindness, my father never betray what I tell him.

MAX. Well *I* didn't betray what you told me either, I keep telling you –

NICHOLAS. My father brought up nine children and all of them good people –

MAX. I didn't tell anyone, I keep telling you –

NICHOLAS. My father –

MAX. Your father nothing! He's been dead since you was three years old so give that one a miss also.

RAYMOND. The first thing in the morning they come in and drink a bottle of beer. Then they're happy. All day they drink.

PAUL *(to* HANS*).* What did Max say then exactly?

HANS. He dosn't like I talk in German. *(tragically)* You know Paul you – you are a Jew and me – I'm German; we suffer together.

*(*PAUL *stiffens, relaxes, laughs ironically, hands* HANS *the red flower from his lapel.* HANS *returns to his station.)*

KEVIN *(to* HANS*).* Is that a Jew then?

HANS *(sentimentally).* A very good boy.

KEVIN. Well who'd have thought that, now.

(At this point a TRAMP *wanders into the kitchen. He is looking for the* CHEF*. Everyone stares at him and grins.)*

MAX *(shouting across to* BERTHA*).* Bertha, ha, ha, is this your old man come after you? *(General laughter.)*

BERTHA. I'll come after you in a minute, pack it in.

(The TRAMP *comes over to the group of young men and talks to* KEVIN*.)*

TRAMP. 'Scuse me. The Chef please, which'n is he?

KEVIN. Napoleon there.

TRAMP. 'Scuse me, Chef *(touching his knee),* war disabled, I don't usually ask for food but I lost me pensions book see? I don't like to ask but...

CHEF. Michael, clean a tin and give him some soup.

TRAMP *(to* KEVIN*).* Don't usually do this. Can't do anything till they trace me book. *(to* HANS*)* Got it in the desert, 'gainst Rommel.

HANS. Rommel! Aha!

TRAMP. Got papers to prove it too. Here, look, papers! Always carry these around with me, everyone got to have his papers and I always carry mine. Be daft for the like o' me to leave them anywhere, wouldn't it? Who'd believe me otherwise, see? Papers! Whatcha making? Spaghetti bolonaizeeee? That's good that Italian food. Do you put bay leaves in? Good with bay leaves, not the same without. Bay leaves, red peppers, all that stuff. What's this? *(Sees half-made arch.)* A castle? *(Sees dish-cloth, picks it up, and idly balances it on the tip of one of the handles, laughs and looks to see whether others are amused.* MICHAEL *hands him a tin of soup.)*

MICHAEL. Here you are.

TRAMP. Got a cigarette?

MICHAEL. Yes, and I'm smoking it.

MAX. Go on, 'op it, be quick, we got work.

PETER *(goes up to* TRAMP, *and looks in the tin; takes tin from* TRAMP *and offers it to* MAX*).* You drink it?

MAX. Ah get out of it, you and your high and bloody mighty gestures. *I* work for my living. Fool!

*(*PETER *ignores him and tosses the tin into the dustbin. Then he moves to* HANS's *station, and brings back two meat cutlets which he gives to the* TRAMP.*)*

PETER. Take these cutlets. *(gently pushing him)* Now go, quick, whist!

(But he is not quick enough. The CHEF *approaches, and stands looking on.)*

CHEF *(quietly).* What's that?

PETER. I gave him some cutlets.

CHEF. Mr Marango told you to give him?

PETER. No, but...

66

CHEF. You heard me say, perhaps?

PETER. No, I...

CHEF. You have authority suddenly?

PETER *(impatiently)*. So what's a couple of cutlets, we going bankrupt or something?

CHEF. It's four and six that's what, and it's me who's Chef that's what and...(PETER *moves away muttering* 'ach.' *The* CHEF *follows him, annoyed now.)* Don't think we're too busy I can't sack you. Three years is nothing you know, you don't buy the place in three years, you hear me? You got that? Don't go thinking I won't sack you.

(By this time MR MARANGO *appears on his round, hands in pocket.)*

MARANGO. Yes?

CHEF. The tramp – Peter gave him a cutlet, it was his own supper.

*(*CHEF *returns to his work, dispersing the crowd on the way.* MR MARANGO *simply nods his head at* PETER. *It is a sad nodding, as though* PETER *had just insulted him. He walks from right of stage to the left in a half circle round* PETER, *nodding his head all the time.)*

MARANGO *(softly)*. Sabotage. *(Pause.)* It's sabotage you do to me. *(sadly taking his right hand out of his pocket, and waving it round the kitchen)* It's my fortune here and you give it away. *(He moves off muttering* 'sabotage.'*)*

PETER. But it...

MARANGO *(not even bothering to look round)*. Yes, yes, I'm always wrong – of course – yes, yes. *(Moves off into dining-room.)*

(Everyone settles back into place. PETER *goes to get a cup of coffee and makes faces at Marango's back, then he returns beside* ALFREDO. HANS *joins them.)*

HANS. Ou, pass auf, der ist wirklich hinter dir her!

PETER. Ach, er erwartet, dass die ganze Welt auf seine Küche aufpasst!

67

KEVIN. I seem to remember being told not to grumble by someone.

PETER. A bastard man. A bastard house.

KEVIN. And he also said you could get used to anything.

PETER. But this house is like – is like –

PAUL. Yeah? What is it like?

PETER. God in heaven, I don't know what it's like. If only it –
if only it –

KEVIN. Yes, yes, we know all that – if only it would all go.

PETER. Just one morning – to find it gone.

PAUL. Fat lot of good you'd be if it went – you couldn't even
cough up a dream when it was necessary.

PETER. A dream?

HANS. Ja, Pete, wo bleibt der Traum, den du uns versprochen
hast?

PETER. I can't, I can't. *(sadly)* I can't dream in a kitchen!
(Violently kicks down other half of arch.)

HANS. Aha! Und jetzt spielst du wieder den wilden Mann!
*(Enter BERTHA with a colander and MONIQUE. Both watch
this.)*

BERTHA *(to MONIQUE)*. Why don't you hop it, out of here, girl
like you –

MONIQUE. Girl like me *what?*

BERTHA. Pack it in, Monique. Peter I mean – dissolve it.

MONIQUE. Just like that?

BERTHA. Just like that.

MONIQUE. Just – like – that, huh! Twice he's given me a baby,
twice I've disappointed him. He wanted them both. Dissolve that.

BERTHA. Aaaaah why don't we all hop it?

MONIQUE. Good question, Aunty Bertha.

PETER *(moving to MONIQUE)*. I'm sorry.

MONIQUE. Not an attractive future, is it? Apologizing backwards and forwards. First you, then me...

PETER. Did you see that tramp?

MONIQUE. What tramp?

PETER. You didn't hear?

MONIQUE. Hear what?

PETER *(boasting and laughing, trying to pacify her)*. I had a row about him, Mr Marango and the Chef there, they wanted to give him a dirty tin full of soup so I threw it away and gave him some cutlets.

MONIQUE. And Marango caught you?

PETER *(imitating)*. 'Sabotage,' the old man said. 'Sabotage, all my fortune you take away.'

MONIQUE. Oh Peter!

PETER *(tenderly)*. Listen, do you want to know where I went this afternoon? To buy your birthday present.

MONIQUE. A present?

WINNIE *(to* HANS*)*. One veal cutlet.

WINNIE *(to* KEVIN*)*. Two plaice.

(PETER *takes out a necklace, and places it round her neck. She relents, turns to him, and pulls him to her, bites his neck.)*

CYNTHIA *(to* HANS*)*. One veal cutlet.

HANS. One veal cutlet. *(long sad glance at her)*

CYNTHIA *(to* MICHAEL*)*. One minestrone.

MICHAEL. One minestrone.

GWEN *(to* MICHAEL*)*. Minestrone.

PETER. Ah, you want to eat me. How do you want me? Grilled? Fried? Underdone? Well done?

(While PETER *and* MONIQUE *continue to talk affectionately, a sudden cry comes up from the back of the kitchen.* WINNIE *has doubled up in pain, and passed out. A crowd rushes to her — it all happens very quickly, hardly noticed. The boys at the table simply glance round and watch but do not move.* PETER *and* MONIQUE *do not even hear it. We can only hear a few confused voices.)*

ALFREDO. All right, now don't crowd round, take her into the dining-room. Don't crowd round. *(Crowd disperses as* WINNIE *is taken into dining-room.)*

PAUL. Who was it? What's happened, then?

MOLLY. It's Winnie, she's passed out.

KEVIN. Well what was all that now?

GASTON. The heat. Always affecting someone. Terrible.
(Meanwhile...)

PETER *(to* MONIQUE*)*. Did you – er – you still going to do it. I mean I...

MONIQUE. Don't worry Peter, I shall see to it now. It's not the first time is it?

PETER. You don't think we should go through with it? I don't mind being responsible. After all it is my baby.

MONIQUE. Enough, I'm not going to talk about it any more.

PETER. You told Monty about us then?

MONIQUE. You really must stop rowing with Marango, darling.

PETER. Did you speak to Monty as we said?

MONIQUE. They won't stand it all the time, you know. I'm always telling you about this, Peter.

PETER. Listen Monique, I love you. Please listen to me that I love you. You said you love me but you don't say to your husband this thing.

HETTIE *(to* FRANK*)*. Two chicken.

MONIQUE. Now not this again.

PETER. You are not going to leave him are you? You don't really intend to?

MONIQUE. Oh Peter, please.

PETER. What do you want I should do then?

MONIQUE. Did the Chef say much?

PETER. We could leave any day. We could go for a long holiday first. Ski-ing in Switzerland perhaps.

MONIQUE. I am going to the hairdresser tomorrow as well.

PETER. Monique, we row this morning, we row in the after-

noon too, this evening we are almost in love again…
Answer me.

MONIQUE. Did I tell you Monty's going to buy me a house?

PETER *(screaming)*. Monique!

*(*MONIQUE *looks round in embarrassment and, muttering* 'You fool,' *stalks off.* VIOLET *approaches* PETER*.)*

VIOLET *(subdued — to* PETER*)*. You serving yet, Peter? I want three turbot. Special for Marango.

PETER. It's half past six yet?

VIOLET. It's nearly…

PETER. Half past six is service.

VIOLET. But it's special…

PETER. Half past six!

DAPHNE *(to* HANS*)*. Two sausages.

(Service is just beginning. Evening service is not so hectic and takes a longer time to start up. Waitresses appear, most people are at their stations.)

BETTY *(to* KEVIN*)*. Two plaice.

KEVIN. Me, I'd have a Jaguar. It's got a luxury I could live with.

GASTON. Have you seen the new French Citroën? Just like a mechanical frog it looks.

HANS. And the Volkswagen? It's not a good car?

KEVIN. Now there's a good little car for little money.

HANS. No country makes like the Volkswagen.

KEVIN. You've gotta hand it to the Germans.

(More waitresses are coming in, but the service is easy and orders ring out in comfort. CYNTHIA, *however, breaks her journey round the kitchen, and, with a glass of wine, goes up to the* CHEF *to gossip.* MAX *and* NICHOLAS *stand by listening.)*

CYNTHIA. Heard what happened to Winnie? She's been rushed to hospital.

MAX. What did she do wrong then?

CYNTHIA. She was pregnant.

MAX. She didn't look it.

CYNTHIA. I know. She didn't give herself a chance.

CHEF. Misfired?

CYNTHIA. I'll say, and it weren't no accident neither.

MAX *(shaking his head)*. Silly woman, silly woman.

CHEF. She's got seven children already, though.

CYNTHIA. That's right. Marango's hopping mad. It started happening on the spot, in there, in the dining-room. May and Sophie had to take her away.

MAX. What did she do, then?

CYNTHIA. She took pills, that's what. And I'll tell you something else, there are four other girls here took the same pills. There! Four of them!

BETTY *(to HANS)*. Two veal cutlets.

CYNTHIA. And you know who one of the four is? *(She inclines her head in Peter's direction.)*

MAX. Monique?

CYNTHIA *(nodding her head triumphantly)*. Now don't you tell anyone I told you, mind. But you ask Hettie, ask her, she bought the stuff. *(Continues on the round to KEVIN.)* Two plaice, please.

GWEN *(to HANS)*. Two hamburgers.

MAX. Knew this would happen.

HETTIE. Two halibut. *(This is said to PETER, who sits on stool centre, back to audience.)*

MAX. Knew it. Can't be done, though. What makes them think that by taking a tablet through the mouth it will affect the womb.

HETTIE. Oh come on Peter, two halibut.

(PETER slowly rises to serve her.)

MAX. There's only one way, the way it went in... What happens with a tablet? Nothing... Nothing can.

(PETER serves only one halibut.)

HETTIE *(to PETER)*. I said two.

MAX. The stomach is irritated, that's all, squeezed see? Forces
the womb. Presses it.

NICHOLAS. Now what do you know about this? A doctor now!

MAX. Oh I know about this all right. Only one drug is effective
through the mouth. *(secretively)* And you know what that
is? Ergot? Heard of it? Only thing to do it. And that's rare.
Oh yes, I studied this in the forces when I had nothing else
to do. Very interesting, this psychology. Complicated. I
knew Winnie was in pod as soon as she came here.

*(All the time, the pastrycooks have been clearing away their
station and are now ready to go. They are saying goodbye
to everyone. MAX shouts to them as they go.)*

MAX. Some people have it easy!

*(The pastrycooks begin to leave, and, as they do so, an argu-
ment flares up suddenly at PETER's station.)*

MOLLY *(to HANS)*. Two sausages.

GWEN *(to PETER)*. One turbot.

DAPHNE *(to PETER)*. Three cod.

PETER. It's not ready yet.

DAPHNE. Oh come on Peter, three cod.

PETER. It's not ready yet, come back five minutes' time.

(All the other chefs sing 'Hi lee, hi lo, hi la' at him.)

MOLLY *(to HANS)*. Four veal cutlets.

GWEN *(to PETER)*. Six turbot.

JACKIE *(to PETER)*. Two halibut.

VIOLET *(to PETER)*. Two turbot. *(As there is a queue she tries to
help herself.)*

PETER *(to VIOLET)*. You wait for me yes? *I* serve you. You
ask *me*.

VIOLET. But you were busy.

PETER. I don't care. This is my place and there *(points to the side
of bar)*, there is for you.

VIOLET. Now you wait a bloody minute will you? Who the
hell do you think you are, you?

PETER. You don't worry who I am. I'm the cook yes? And you're the waitress, and in the kitchen I do what I like yes? And in the dining-room you do what you like.

VIOLET *(taking another plate from off the oven).* I won't take orders from you, you know, I...

PETER *(shouting and smashing the plate from her hand for a second time).* Leave it! Leave it there! I'll serve you. Me! Me! Is *my* kingdom here. This is the side where *I* live. This.

VIOLET *(very quietly).* You Boche you. You bloody German bastard!

(She downs plates on the bar and walks off. PETER follows her. There is a general uproar and protest from the other waitresses who are waiting to be served.)

PETER. What you call me? What was it? Say it again. *(He screams at her.)* SAY IT AGAIN! *(She halts, petrified.)*

(The scream calls the attention of most people to him. They all stare at him as at a frightened animal. Suddenly he wheels round and in a frenzy searches for something violent to do. He rushes up to VIOLET. *Seems about to attack her, but she is not the enemy. He knocks plates off one of the counters. Other chefs rush to hold him. He breaks away and reaches for a large chopper. Everyone backs away. Then with a cry of* 'auf geht's,' *he dashes to a part under a serving-counter and smashes something underneath. There is a slow hiss and all the fires of the ovens die down. There is a second of complete silence before anybody realizes what has happened, and then* FRANK *and two others are upon him, trying to hold him down. The* CHEF, *at last moved to do something, rushes to the scene, but* PETER *breaks away again and flees to the dining-room.* FRANK *and others follow. All this has happened too quickly for anyone to do a great deal about it, but in the scuffle the following cries were heard —)*

MICHAEL. He's broken the gas lead! Someone turn off the main!

(MANGOLIS *exits to do so.*)

FRANK. Hold him, grab hold of him!

KEVIN. Jesus Christ he'll murder her.

HANS. Sei nicht dumm! Beherrsch dich! Lass sie laufen!

(When PETER *has rushed into the dining-room, there is another silence as everybody waits to hear what will happen next. Some are not even sure what has already happened. Suddenly there is a tremendous crash of crockery and glass to the ground. There are screams, some waitresses come back into kitchen from dining-room.)*

KEVIN. Holy mother o' Mary, he's gone berserk.

GASTON. The lunatic! He's swept all the plates off the table in there.

MICHAEL. He's ripped his hands.

KEVIN. I knew something like this would happen, now I just knew it.

(The crowd by the entrance to the dining-room makes way as ALFREDO *and* HANS *bring* PETER *back.* PETER's *hands are covered in blood. Some smears have reached his face. He looks terribly exhausted. They bring him down stage.* MICHAEL *hurriedly finds a stool.)*

CHEF *(to* MICHAEL*).* Phone an ambulance.

WAITRESS. Monique is doing that now.

*(*MONIQUE *pushes through the crowd. She is sobbing but she carries the medical box and a table-cloth.* ALFREDO *snatches the cloth from her and rips it up. She tries to dab some liquid on* PETER's *hands, he jumps and pushes her away. This is too much for her; she leaves it all and rushes away.* ALFREDO, *however, simply takes* PETER's *hands and ties them up.)*

PETER. It hurts, Christ it hurts.

ALFREDO. Shut up!

CHEF *(bending close to* PETER*).* Fool! *(He straightens up, and, finding nothing else to say for the moment, bends down to repeat again.)*

75

Fool! *(Pause.)* So? What? The whole kitchen is stopped.
Fool!

PETER *(to* ALFREDO*).* Now he cares.

CHEF *(incredulous and furious).* What do you mean, 'Now he
cares'?

ALFREDO *(gently moving* CHEF *out of the way so that he might tie
up* PETER's *hands).* Leave him Chef, leave him now.

CHEF *(reaching* PETER *another way).* What do you mean, 'Now
he cares'? *You* have to make me care? Forty years and
suddenly you have to make me care? You? You? Who
are you, tell me? In all this big world who are you for
Christ's sake?

(At this point the crowd breaks away to let MARANGO *in.
He surveys the damage.)*

MARANGO *(with terrible calm).* You have stopped my whole
world. *(Pause.)* Did you get permission from God? Did
you? There – is – no – one – else! You know that? No
ONE!

FRANK. All right, take it easy Marango. The boy is going, he's
going. He's ill, don't upset yourself.

MARANGO *(turning to* FRANK *and making a gentle appeal).* Why
does everybody sabotage me, Frank? I give work, I pay
well, yes? They eat what they want, don't they? I don't
know what more to give a man. He works, he eats, I give
him money. This is life, isn't it? I haven't made a mistake,
have I? I live in the right world, don't I? *(to* PETER*)* And
you've stopped this world. A shnip! A boy! You've stopped it. Well why? Maybe you can tell me something I
don't know – just tell me. *(No answer.)* I want to learn
something. *(to the kitchen)* Is there something I don't know?
*(*PETER *rises and in pain moves off. When he reaches a point
back centre stage* MARANGO *cries at him.)* BLOODY FOOL!
(Rushes round to him.) What more do you want? What is
there more, tell me? *(He shakes* PETER, *but gets no reply.*

76

PETER *again tries to leave. Again* MARANGO *cries out.)* What is there more? (PETER *stops, turns in pain and sadness, shakes his head as if to say — 'if you don't know, I cannot explain.' And so he moves right off stage.* MARANGO *is left facing his staff, who stand around, almost accusingly, looking at him. And he asks again —)* What is there more? What is there more? What is there more?

Chicken Soup with Barley

For
Leah and Joe

CHARACTERS OF THE PLAY

SARAH KAHN
HARRY KAHN, *her husband*
MONTY BLATT
DAVE SIMMONDS
PRINCE SILVER
HYMIE KOSSOF, *Sarah's brother*
CISSIE KAHN, *Harry's sister, a trade-union organizer*
ADA KAHN, *daughter of Sarah and Harry*
RONNIE, *son of Sarah and Harry*
BESSIE BLATT, *wife of Monty*

★

ACT I
Scene 1: October 4th 1936
Scene 2: The same evening

ACT II
Scene 1: June 1946
Scene 2: Autumn 1947

ACT III
Scene 1: November 1955
Scene 2: December 1956

★

First presented at the Belgrade Theatre, Coventry,
on 7th July 1958

81

THE SOLO GAME

	Clubs	Hearts	Diamonds	Spades
CISSIE:	K,4,3,2	3	K,2˙	A,K,J,6,4,2
SARAH:	A,Q,6	10,5,4	A,6,5,4	9,8,3
PRINCE:	J,10,8	K,7,J	J,10,9,8,7	Q,5
HYMIE:	9,7,5	A,Q,9,8,6,2	Q,3	10,7

1st *Hand:* CISSIE: 3 Hearts – 10 – K – A
            HYMIE: 3 Diamonds – 2 – 4 – J
            PRINCE: Q Spades – 10 – J – 9
            PRINCE: 5 Spades – 7 – 6 – 8
            SARAH: 5 Hearts – 7 – 6 – K Diamonds
            PRINCE: 7 Diamonds – Q – K Clubs – A
            SARAH: 3 Spades – J Clubs – 9 Clubs – 2 Spades
            [CISSIE *shows Hand*]

NOTE TO ACTORS AND PRODUCERS

My people are not caricatures. They are real (though fiction), and if they are portrayed as caricatures the point of all these plays will be lost. The picture I have drawn is a harsh one, yet my tone is not one of disgust — nor should it be in the presentation of the plays. I am at one with these people: it is only that I am annoyed, with them and myself.

ACT ONE

Scene 1

October 4th, 1936.

The basement of the Kahns' house in the East End of London. The room is warm and lived in. A fire is burning. One door, at the back and left of the room, leads to a bedroom. A window, left, looks up to the street. To the right is another door which leads to a kitchen, which is seen. At rear of stage are the stairs leading up into the street.

SARAH KAHN is in the kitchen washing up, humming to herself. She is a small, fiery woman, aged 37, Jewish and of European origin. Her movements indicate great energy and vitality. She is a very warm person. HARRY KAHN, her husband, comes down the stairs, walks past her and into the front room. He is 35 and also a European Jew. He is dark, slight, rather pleasant looking, and the antithesis of Sarah. He is amiable but weak. From outside we hear a band playing a revolutionary song.

SARAH (*from the kitchen*). You took the children to Lottie's?

HARRY (*taking up book to read*). I took them.

SARAH. They didn't mind?

HARRY. No, they didn't mind.

SARAH. Is Hymie coming?

HARRY. I don't know.

SARAH (*to herself*). Nothing he knows! You didn't ask him? He didn't say? He knows about the demonstration, doesn't he?

HARRY. I don't know whether he knows or he doesn't know. I didn't discuss it with him — I took the kids, that's all. Hey, Sarah — you should read Upton Sinclair's book about the meat-canning industry — it's an eye-opener ...

SARAH. Books! Nothing else interests him, only books. Did you see anything outside? What's happening?

HARRY. The streets are packed with people, I never seen so

83

many people. They've got barricades at Gardiner's Corner.

SARAH. There'll be such trouble.

HARRY. Sure there'll be trouble. You ever known a demonstration where there wasn't trouble?

SARAH. And the police?

HARRY. There'll be more police than blackshirts.

SARAH. What time they marching?

HARRY. I don't know.

SARAH. Harry, you know where your cigarettes are, don't you? (*This is her well-meaning but maddening attempt to point out to a weak man his weakness.*)

HARRY. I know where they are.

SARAH. And you know what's on at the cinema?

HARRY. So?

SARAH. And also you know what time it opens? (*He grins.*) So why don't you know what time they plan to march? (*Touché!*)

HARRY. Leave me alone, Sarah, will you? Two o'clock they plan to march — nah!

SARAH. So you do know. Why didn't you tell me straight away? Shouldn't you tell me something when I ask you?

HARRY. I didn't know what time they marched, so what do you want of me?

SARAH. But you did know when I nagged you.

HARRY. So I suddenly remembered. Is there anything terrible in that?

(*She shakes a disbelieving fist at him and goes out to see where the loudspeaker cries are coming from. The slogan 'Madrid today — London tomorrow' is being repeated. As she is out HARRY looks for her handbag, and on finding it proceeds to take some money from it.*)

SARAH (*she is hot*). Air! I must have air — this basement will kill me. God knows what I'll do without air when I'm dead. Who else was at Lottie's?

84

HARRY (*still preoccupied*). All of them.

SARAH. Who's all of them?

HARRY. All of them! You know. Lottie and Hymie and the boys, Solly and Martin.

(*He finds a ten-shilling note, pockets it and resumes his seat by the fire, taking up a book to read. SARAH returns to front room with some cups and saucers.*)

SARAH. Here, lay these out, the boys will be coming soon.

HARRY. Good woman! I could just do with a cup of tea.

SARAH. What's the matter, you didn't have any tea by Lottie's?

HARRY. No.

SARAH. Liar!

HARRY. I didn't have any tea by Lottie's, I tell you. (*Injured tone*) Good God, woman, why don't you believe me when I tell you things?

SARAH. *You* tell *me* why. Why don't I believe him when he tells me things! As if he's such an angel and never tells lies. What's the matter, you never told lies before I don't think?

HARRY. All right, so I had tea at Lottie's. There, you satisfied now?

SARAH (*preparing things as she talks*). Well, of course you had tea at Lottie's. Don't I know you had tea at Lottie's? You think I'm going to think that Lottie wouldn't make you a cup of tea?

HARRY. Oh, leave off, Sarah.

SARAH. No! This time I won't leave off. (*Her logic again.*) I want to know why you told me you didn't have tea at Lottie's when you know perfectly well you did. I want to know.

(HARRY *raises his hands in despair.*)

I know you had tea there and *you* know you had tea there — so what harm is it if you tell me? You think I care whether you had a cup of tea there or not? You can drink tea there till it comes out of your eyes and I wouldn't care only as long as you tell me.

85

HARRY. Sarah, will you please stop nagging me, will you?
What difference if I had tea there or I didn't have tea there?

SARAH. That's just what I'm saying. All I want to know is
whether you're all of a liar or half a liar!

HARRY (*together with her*). ... all of a liar or half a liar!

(*A young man,* MONTY BLATT, *comes down the stairs. He is
about* 19, *Jewish, working-class, and cockney. His voice is
heard before he is seen, shouting:* 'Mrs Kahn! Sarah! Mrs
Kahn!' *He has interrupted the row as he dashes into the room
without knocking.*)

MONTY. Ah, good! You're here! (*Moves to window and, looking
out, shouts up.*) It's O.K. They're here. Here! (*Offering
parcel*) Mother sent you over some of her strudel. C'mon
down. (*To* HARRY) Hello, Harry boy, how you going? All
fighting fit for the demo?

HARRY. I'm fit, like a Trojan I'm fit!

SARAH. You won't see him at any demo. In the pictures you'll
find him. (*Goes to landing to make tea.*)

MONTY. The pictures? Don't be bloody mad. You won't hear
a thing! You seen the streets today? Sarah, you seen the
streets yet? Mobbed! Mo-obbed! The lads have been there
since seven this morning.

(*Two other young men in their early twenties come down the
stairs,* DAVE SIMMONDS *and* PRINCE SILVER. *They are
heatedly discussing something.*)

PRINCE. But Dave, there's so much work here to do. Hello,
Sarah!

DAVE. I know all about the work here, but there are plenty of
party members to do it. Hello, Sarah. Spain is the battle-
front. Spain is a real issue at last.

SARAH. Spain? Spain, Dave?

HARRY. Spain?

PRINCE. Dave is joining the International Brigade. He's leaving
for Spain tomorrow morning. (*To* DAVE) But Spain is only

one issue brought to a head. You're too young to ...

HARRY. Dave, don't go mad all of a sudden. It's not all glory, you know.

DAVE. Harry, you look as though you didn't sleep last night.

MONTY. He didn't — the old cossack. (*To the tune of 'All the nice girls love a sailor'*) For you know what cossacks are ...
Am I right, Harry?

PRINCE. I saw your sister Cissie at Aldgate, Harry. She was waving your mother's walking-stick in the air.

HARRY. She's mad.

MONTY (*loudly calling*). Where's this cup of tea, Sarah?

SARAH (*bringing in tea*). Do your fly-buttons up, Monty, you tramp you. Now then, Dave, tell me what's happening and what the plans are.

(*Everyone draws up a chair by the table.*)

DAVE. It's like this. The Party loudspeaker vans have been out all morning — you heard them? The Fascists are gathering at Royal Mint Street near the bridge. They plan to march up to Aldgate, down Commercial Road to Salmon Lane in Limehouse — you know Salmon Lane? — where they think they're going to hold a meeting. Then they plan to go on to Victoria Park and hold another meeting.

SARAH. *Two* meetings? What do they want to hold two meetings for?

HARRY. Why shouldn't they hold two meetings?

SARAH. What, *you* think they should hold two meetings?

HARRY. It's not what I think — she's such a funny woman — it's not what I think, but they want to hold two meetings — so what's so strange about that?

SARAH. But it costs so much money.

HARRY. Perhaps you want we should have a collection for them?

DAVE. Now. They could go along the Highway by the docks and then up Cable Street, but Mosley won't take the High-

87

way because that's the back way, though the police will suggest he does.

SARAH. I bet the police cause trouble.

PRINCE. They've had to call in forces from outside London.

SARAH. You won't make it a real fight, boys, will you? I mean you won't get hurt.

MONTY. Sarah, you remember they threw a seven-year-old girl through a glass window? So don't fight the bastards?

PRINCE. Now Monty, there's to be discipline, remember. There's to be no attack or bottle-throwing. It's a test, you know that, don't you, it's a test for us. We're to stop them passing, that's all.

MONTY. Sure we'll stop them passing. If I see a blackshirt come by I'll tap his shoulder and I'll say: 'Excuse me, but you can't come this way today, we're digging up the road.' And he'll look at my hammer and sickle and he'll doff his cap and he'll say: 'I beg your pardon, comrade, I'll take the Underground.'

DAVE. Comrades! You want to know what the plans are or you don't want to know? Again. As we don't know what's going to happen we've done this: some of the workers are rallying at Royal Mint Street — so if the Fascists want to go through the Highway they'll have to fight for it. But we guess they'll want to stick to the main route so as not to lose face — you follow? We've therefore called the main rally at Gardiner's Corner. If, on the other hand, they do attempt to pass up Cable Street —

SARAH. Everything happens in Cable Street.

HARRY. What else happened in Cable Street?

SARAH. Peter the Painter had a fight with Churchill there, didn't he?

MONTY. You're thinking of Sidney Street, sweetheart.

HARRY. You know, she gets everything mixed up.

SARAH. You're very wonderful I suppose, yes? You're the clever one!

HARRY. I don't get my facts mixed up, anyway.

SARAH. Per, per, per, per, per! Listen to him! My politician!

MONTY. Sarah, do me a favour, leave the fists till later.

DAVE. If, on the other hand, they do try to come up Cable Street then they'll meet some dockers and more barricades. And if any get through that lot then they still can't hold their meetings either in Salmon Lane or Victoria Park Square.

SARAH. Why not?

PRINCE. Because since seven this morning there's been some of our comrades standing there with our platforms.

MONTY. Bloody wonderful, isn't it? Makes you feel proud, eh Sarah? Every section of this working-class area that we've approached has responded. The dockers at Limehouse have come out to the man. The lot!

PRINCE. The unions, the Co-ops, Labour Party members and the Jewish People's Council —

SARAH. The Board of Deputies?

HARRY. There she goes again. Not the Jewish Board of Deputies — *they* asked the Jewish population to keep away. No, the Jewish People's Council — the one that organized that mass demo against Hitler some years back.

(SARAH *pulls face at him.*)

MONTY. There's been nothing like it since the General Strike.

HARRY. Christ! The General Strike! That was a time, Sarah, eh?

SARAH. What you asking me for? You want I should remember that you were missing for six days when Ada was ill?

HARRY. Yes, I was missing, I'm sure.

SARAH. Well, sure you were missing.

HARRY. Where was I missing?

SARAH. How should I know where you were missing. If I'd

have known where you were missing you wouldn't have been missing.

(*There is heard from outside a sound of running feet and voices shouting. Everyone except* HARRY *moves to the window.*)

FIRST VOICE. They're assembling! They're assembling! Out to the barricades — the Fascists are assembling!

SECOND VOICE. Hey, Stan! Where's the best place?

FIRST VOICE. Take your boys to Cable Street. The Fascists are assembling! Come out of your houses! Come out of your houses!

MONTY. What about us, Dave?

SARAH. You haven't suggested to Harry and me where to go yet.

DAVE. There's plenty of time. They won't try to march till two, and it's only twelve thirty.

SARAH. You eaten? You boys had lunch?

PRINCE. We all had lunch at my place, Sarah; sit down, stop moving a few seconds.

DAVE. Take your pick, Sarah. If you fancy yourself as a nurse then go to Aldgate, we've got a first-aid post there, near Whitechapel Library.

SARAH. Such organization! And you lot?

DAVE. Monty is taking some of the lads to the left flank of Cable Street, Prince is organizing a team of cyclist messengers between the main points and headquarters, I'm going round the streets at the last minute to call everyone out and — and that's the lot.

MONTY (*rubbing his hands*). All we have to do is wait.

DAVE. Where is Ada?

SARAH. Ada and Ronnie are at Hymie's place. I thought it best they get right out of the way.

DAVE (*guiltily*). You think she'll stay away? Your precocious daughter is a born fighter, Sarah.

MONTY. 'Course she is! She'll be round the streets organizing the pioneers — you see.

SARAH. Never! I told her to stay there and she'll stay there.

HARRY. I'm sure!

SARAH. God forbid she should be like you and run wild.

HARRY. All right, so she should be like you then!

SARAH. I'm jolly sure she should be like me! Ronnie isn't enough for him yet. A boy of five running about at nights and swearing at his aunts. (*Smiles at thought.*) Bless him! (*To the others*) He didn't half upset them: they wouldn't let him mess around with the radio so he started effing and blinding and threw their books on the floor. (*Turning again to* HARRY) Like you he throws things.

HARRY. Have you ever come across a woman like her before?

MONTY. I'd love another cup of tea.

HARRY (*jumps up and goes to kitchen*). I'll make it. I'll make it.

SARAH. He's so sweet when anybody else is around. I'll make some sandwiches.

PRINCE. But we've eaten, Sarah.

SARAH. Eat. Always eat. You don't know what time you'll be back.

> (SARAH *goes to cupboard and cuts up bread ready for cheese sandwiches. A very distant sound of people chanting is heard:* 'They shall not pass, they shall not pass, they shall not pass.')

MONTY. The boys! Listen. Hear them? You know, Sarah, that's the same cry the people of Madrid were shouting.

PRINCE. And they didn't get past either. Imagine it! All those women and children coming out into the streets and making barricades with their beds and their chairs.

DAVE (*sadly*). It was a slaughter.

PRINCE. And then came the first International Brigade.

DAVE. The Edgar André from Germany, Commune de Paris from France, and the Dombrovsky from Poland.

MONTY. Wait till our Dave gets over there. You'll give 'em brass balls for breakfast, Dave, eh?

SARAH. You really going, Dave? Does Ada know?

DAVE. Don't tell her, Sarah. You know how dramatic calf-love is.

PRINCE. Calf-love? If you get back alive from Spain she'll marry you at the landing stage — mark me.

SARAH. How are you going?

DAVE. They tell me it's a week-end trip to Paris and then a midnight ramble over the Pyrenees. The back way!

SARAH. It's terrible out there, they say. They say we've lost a lot of good comrades already.

PRINCE. We've lost too many good comrades out there — you hear me, Dave?

MONTY. Sammy Avner and Lorimer Birch at Boadilla, Felicia Brown and Ernst Julius at Aragon.

SARAH. Julius? The tailor who used to work with us at Cantor's? But he was only a young boy.

PRINCE. And Felicia an artist and Lorimer an Oxford undergraduate.

MONTY. And Cornford was killed at Cordova.

PRINCE. And Ronnie Symes at Madrid.

MONTY. And Stevie Yates at Casa del Campo.

SARAH. Casa del Campo! Madrid! Such beautiful names and all that killing.

(*Pause.*)

MONTY. Hey! You know who organized the first British group? Nat Cohen! I used to go to school with him. Him and Sam Masters were on a cycling holiday in France. As soon as they heard of the revolt they cycled over to Barcelona and started the Tom Mann Centuria.

HARRY (*coming to the door*). He's a real madman, Nat Cohen. He chalks slogans right outside the police station. I used to work with him.

SARAH. God knows if they'll come back alive.

DAVE. When three Fascist deserters were asked how they

reached our lines they said they came through the hills of
the widows, orphans and sweethearts; they'd lost so many
men attacking those hills.

MONTY. And may they lose many more!

DAVE (*angrily*). The war in Spain is not a game of cards,
Monty. You don't pay in pennies when you lose. May
they lose many more! What kind of talk is that? Sometimes, Monty, I think you only enjoy the battle, and that
one day you'll forget the ideal. You hate too much. You
can't have brotherhood when you hate. There's only one
difference between them and us — we know what we're
fighting for. It's almost an unfair battle.

(HARRY *now returns to kitchen to pour out tea.*)

MONTY. Unfair, he says! When Germany and Italy are
supplying them with guns and tanks and aeroplanes and
our boys have only got rifles and mortars — is that unfair?
You call that unfair, I don't think?

DAVE. When you fight men who are blind it's always unfair.
You think I'm going to enjoy shooting a man because he
calls himself a Fascist? I feel so sick at the thought of
firing a rifle that I think I'll board that boat with a blind-
fold over my eyes. Sometimes I think that's the only way
to do things. I'm not even sure that I want to go, only I
know if I don't then — then — well, what sense can a man
make of his life?

SARAH. You're really a pacifist, aren't you, Dave?

DAVE. I'm a terribly sad pacifist, Sarah.

HARRY. I understand you, Dave — I know what you mean,
boy. What do you want we should say? You go — we're
proud of you. You stay behind — we love you. Sometimes you live in a way you don't know why — you just
do a thing. So you don't have to shout — you're shouting
at yourself! But a pacifist, Dave? There's going to be a big
war soon, a Fascist war: you think it's time for pacifism?

SARAH. He's right, Dave.

DAVE. I know it's not time yet. I know that. I know there is still some fighting to be done. But it'll come. It will come, you know — when there'll be a sort of long pause, and people will just be frightened of each other and still think they *have* to fight. That'll be the time — But now — well, I feel like an old gardener who knows he won't live through to the spring to plant his seeds.

(HARRY *comes in with the teas and at the same time a voice from the streets is heard frantically shouting:* 'Man your posts! Men and women of the East End, come out of your houses! The blackshirts are marching! Come out! Come out!' *There is a hurried movement from the people in the room.* DAVE *and* MONTY *rush to the window.* PRINCE *rushes upstairs, knocking a cup of tea out of* HARRY's *hand.*)

MONTY. Christ! They've started before time.

DAVE. It might be a false alarm.

PRINCE (*from the stairs*). We can't take the risk. Let's get going.

(MONTY *moves off quickly, taking a poker from the fireplace on his way out and concealing it in his clothes.*)

MONTY. I'll clean it and bring it back later.

HARRY. But I've made your tea.

DAVE. Stick it back in the pot. We'll drink it later. Now you two, you know where the posts are — Cable Street, Royal Mint Street and Gardiner's Corner.

HARRY (*at the window*). The street is mobbed. Jesus! Look at them, everybody is coming out, everybody.

SARAH (*putting on her coat in general rush*). Where's the first-aid post?

DAVE (*having helped* SARAH *with coat, moves off*). Whitechapel Library. Harry, you coming?

HARRY (*still at window*). I'm coming, I'm coming. You go on. Good God, there's Alf Bosky and his wife. She's got the baby with her. (*Shouts up.*) Hey Alf — good luck, com-

94

rade — we're coming. Sarah, there's Alf Bosky and his wife.

SARAH (*looking for something in kitchen*). I heard, I heard! (*She finds a rolling pin and, waving it in the air, dashes into the front room.*) Are you coming now, Harry? I'm going to Gardiner's Corner — come on, we'll be late.

HARRY (*backing away from rolling pin*). Don't hit anybody with that thing, Sarah, it hurts.

SARAH. Fool!

(SARAH *dashes to the stairs but stops and, remembering something, returns to front room. From a corner of the room she finds a red flag with a hammer and sickle on it and thrusts it in* HARRY'S *hand.*)

SARAH. Here, wave this! Do something useful!

(*Exits upstairs.*)

HARRY (*grabbing his coat*). Hey, Sarah, wait for me — Sarah! Hey, wait for me!

(*He follows her, banner streaming. The voices outside grow to a crescendo:* 'They shall not pass, they shall not pass, they shall not pass!')

CURTAIN

Scene 2

Same room, later that evening. There is commotion and some singing from the streets outside. MONTY *and* PRINCE *are coming down the stairs leading* HYMIE KOSSOF. *He has blood all over his face. He is a short, rotund man with a homely appearance.*

MONTY (*leaving* PRINCE *and* HYMIE *to go into the room*). I'll get some water on the stove. Sit him in a chair. (*Shouts upstairs.*) Cissie! Don't come down yet, go and get some first-aid kit from somewhere. (*Fills kettle.*)

95

PRINCE. Now don't talk too much and don't move, Hymie. Jesus! What a state you're in. Sarah'll go mad.

HYMIE. Well, clean me up quickly then.

MONTY (*rushing from kitchen to window*). Cissie! *Cissie!* Try that sweet shop near Toynbee Hall. I saw a first-aid group there. They might still be there. (*Comes away, but, remembering something else, sticks his head out again.*) *Aspros!* Try and get hold of some Aspros.

SARAH (*from the top of the stairs — off*). Monty! Is Hymie down there?

HYMIE. Oh, my goodness, she's here. If there is one thing Sarah loves it's someone who's ill to fuss over. Why didn't I go home?

MONTY. Because you know Lottie would say serves you right!
(SARAH *appears;* MONTY *rushes to her.*)
Now don't panic, Sarah, he's all right, he's all right.

SARAH (*entering*). Hymie!

HYMIE. Sarah Nightingale!

MONTY. Now don't frighten him, I tell you.

SARAH (*taking over towel and wiping him*). Fool you! They told me you were hurt — I nearly died.

HYMIE. So did I!

SARAH. Fool! *You* had to go straight into it.

HYMIE. I was only hit by a truncheon. Now do me a favour, Sarah, and just make some tea, there's a good girl.

SARAH. Nobody else got hurt. Only him. The brave one!

MONTY (*significantly handling the poker*). Plenty got hurt! Oh, he's all right. Aren't you all right, Hymie?

HYMIE. I'm here, aren't I?

SARAH (*taking off her coat*). Well, why hasn't anybody done something?

PRINCE. Cissie has gone to get some first aid.

SARAH. Cissie? Harry's sister?

PRINCE. Yes. Where is Harry, by the way? Anybody seen him?

SARAH (*ominously*). Wait till I see him. I'll give him. You expected him to stay there?

MONTY. I saw him at Cable Street; he was waving the old red flag, but he didn't stay long. He took one look at the artillery and guns and said he was going to find us some sandwiches.

SARAH. They had guns at Cable Street? Did they use them?

MONTY. Nah! it was only brought out to frighten us. *Frighten* us, mark. If they'd have dropped a bomb today we wouldn't have been frightened. Christ! What a day!

HYMIE. I mean, did you ever see anything like it? We threw stones and bottles at them, Sarah. They were on horseback with batons and they kept charging us, so we threw stones. And you should have seen Monty when one policeman surrendered. Surrendered! A policeman! It's never happened before. He didn't know what to do, Monty didn't. None of us knew. I mean, who's ever heard of policemen surrendering? And after the first came others — half a dozen of them. My goodness, we made such a fuss of them. Gave them cigarettes and mugs of tea and called them comrade policemen.

PRINCE. There's no turning back now — nothing can stop the workers now.

MONTY. I bet we have a revolution soon. Hitler won't stop at Spain, you know. You watch him go and you watch the British Government lick his arse until he spits in their eye. Then *we'll* move in.

HYMIE. I'm not so sure, Monty. We won today but the same taste doesn't stay long. Mosley was turned back at Aldgate pump and everyone shouted hurrah. But I wonder how many of the people at Gardiner's Corner were just sightseers. You know, in every political movement there are just sightseers.

MONTY. Ten thousand bloody sightseers? Do me a favour, it wasn't a bank holiday.

(SARAH *goes to kitchen to pour the water into the bowl.* CISSIE *appears.*)

HYMIE. Any big excitement can be a bank holiday for a worker, believe me.

(*Enter* CISSIE. *Woman of about* 33. *She is a trade-union organizer — precise in her manner, dry sense of humour.*)

CISSIE. Ointment, lint, bandage and plaster. Let's have a look at him.

SARAH (*entering with bowl of water*). I'm coming, it's all right, I can manage.

(CISSIE *makes way and* SARAH *begins to sponge her brother's face and then puts bandage round his head.*)

PRINCE. Where were *you*, Cis?

CISSIE. Gardiner's Corner holding a banner. The union banner. And you?

MONTY. Digging up the paving stones in Cable Street.

CISSIE. Paving stones? (*She hoists the back of her skirt to warm her behind in front of the fire.*)

MONTY. We pulled out the railings from a near-by church and the stones from the gutter. I'll get some more coal for the fire. (*Goes to kitchen, pinching* CISSIE's *behind on the way.*) We turned over a lorry.

SARAH. A lorry?

HYMIE. But it was the wrong one. The lorry we'd laid on was in a near-by yard and when the call went up to bring the lorry the boys, if you don't mind, grabbed one at the top of the street. I ask you!

SARAH. Keep still. There, you look more respectable now.

(MONTY *re-enters with coal and on his way to fire takes a feather from a hat near by and plants it among* HYMIE's *bandages.*)

HYMIE. Anyone get hurt your way, Cissie?

98

CISSIE. Some of the boys from my union got arrested.

SARAH. I'll go and make some tea now.

CISSIE. Mick and Sammy and Dave Goldman — and that bloody fool, if you'll excuse the expression, Sonny Becks. Everybody is standing behind the barricades waiting for the blackshirts to appear. The place is swarming with policemen waiting, just waiting, for an opportunity to lay their hands on some of us. So look what he does: not content with just standing there — and Sonny knew perfectly well that the orders were for the strictest discipline — not content with just standing he chose that moment to get up on Mrs O'Laoghaire's vegetable barrow and make a political speech. 'Let us now remember the lessons of the Russian revolution,' he starts like he was quoting Genesis, the nitwit. And then he finds that the barrow isn't safe so he steps over to an iron bedstead and put his foot through the springs just as he was quoting Lenin's letter to the toiling masses!

MONTY. You can never stop Sonny making a speech.

CISSIE. But not in bed! Anyway, you know Sonny — a mouth like a cesspool and no shame — so he lets out a torrent of abuse at the capitalist bed-makers and the police just make a dive at him. Mick and Sammy tried to argue with the police so they were hauled off and then Dave Goldman tried to explain — that was when he was hauled off, poor bastard, if you'll excuse the expression!

HYMIE. What'll happen?

CISSIE. The union'll have to find the lawyers and probably pay their fine — what else? Which reminds me — Monty and Prince. Get all the boys and girls you can find and bring them to that social next Saturday, the one for Sally Oaks.

HYMIE. Wasn't it her husband caught his bicycle in a tram line and was killed?

CISSIE. That's right. She's a Catholic. The local priest is trying

99

to raise some money to keep her going for a bit and we promised we'd support it. Well, I'm going.

SARAH (*entering with tea*). Cissie, have you seen Harry?

CISSIE. Harry? No!

SARAH. He's not at your place, I suppose?

CISSIE. How should I know? I haven't been there all day.

SARAH. He always is at your place.

CISSIE. Sarah, I'm not responsible for my brother's actions. None of us have ever been able to control him, the eldest brother! We warned you what you were taking on — you wanted to change him! She wanted to change him.

SARAH. It's your mother who spoils him, you know that?

CISSIE. Spoils him! Do me a favour — the woman's been bed-ridden for the last ten years. Spoils him!

SARAH. He knows he can go to her — she'll feed him.

CISSIE. He's her son, for God's sake.

SARAH. Don't I know it. He's her son all right — and he wants to be looked after like everyone looks after her. Only it's such a pity — he can walk!

CISSIE. Yes, yes — so I know all this already. Good night, everyone.

(CISSIE *exits amid varied goodbyes and* 'I'll be seeing you'.)

SARAH. I hate her!

HYMIE. Don't be a silly girl. Cissie is a good trade-union organizer.

SARAH. She's a cow! Not a bit of warmth, not a bit! What's the good of being a socialist if you're not warm.

HYMIE. But Cissie has *never* liked Harry.

SARAH. Not a bit of warmth. Everything cold and calculated. People like that can't teach love and brotherhood.

PRINCE. Love comes later, Sarah.

SARAH. Love comes now. You have to start with love. How can you talk about socialism otherwise?

MONTY. Hear, hear, Comrade Kahn. Come on now, what is

this? We've just won one of the biggest fights in working-class history and all we do is quarrel.

(MONTY *settles down and all is quiet. Suddenly, softly, he starts to sing.*)

England arise, the long long night is over.

(*Others join in.*)

Faint in the East behold the dawn appears.
Out of your evil sleep of toil and sorrow,
England arise, the long long day is here.

England arise ...

SARAH (*suddenly*). Hymie! The children! God in heaven, I've forgotten the children.

HYMIE. They're at my place. What's the matter with you?

SARAH (*putting on her coat*). But I can't leave them there. How could I forget them like that; what am I thinking of? Won't be long.

(*Exits.*)

HYMIE (*calling up to her*). But Ronnie'll be asleep. Don't tell Lottie I got hit. Tell her I'm coming home soon. (*Returning to front room*) Impetuous woman!

(*They all settle themselves comfortably round the fire. SARAH is heard calling from the street.*)

SARAH (*off*). Make yourself some food! And there's tea in the pot.

HYMIE (*coming away from window*). Make yourself some food! With her it's food all the time. Food and tea. No sooner you finished one cup than you got another.

MONTY. She's a sweetheart.

HYMIE. God forbid you should ever say you're not hungry. She starts singing that song: As man is only human he must eat before he can think.

MONTY (*picking up the song and singing it*).

As man is only human

He must eat before he can think,
Fine words are only empty air
But not his meat or his drink.
(*Others join in chorus.*)
    Then left right left, then left right left,
    There's a place, comrade, for you.
    March with us in the ranks of the working class
    For you are a worker too.
(HARRY *enters. As they finish the song he stands in the door-way and, waving the banner, cries*)

HARRY. We won! Boys, we won the day!

MONTY. Harry! Welcome home the hero! Where are those bloody sandwiches?

HYMIE. Your wife's looking for you.

HARRY. What, she's gone *out* for me? (*Places banner in corner and looks concerned.*)

MONTY. Yes! Just this minute.

HARRY. Did she have a rolling pin in her hand?

HYMIE. No, no. She's gone to my place to collect the children.

HARRY. Blimey, Hymie! What happened to you? You all right, Hymie?

HYMIE. Now don't you fuss, Harry; drink your tea.

MONTY. That's it, Harry, swill up, mate.

HARRY. Sure, sure. (*Goes to kitchen.*) The children, you say? But I saw Ada in the streets.

PRINCE (*looking to* MONTY). She was helping me, Harry, but don't tell Sarah. She was taking messages from Cable Street to headquarters. I knew she wouldn't stay in on such a day. Marched with us on the victory march, then went to look for Dave.

MONTY. She'll break her little heart when she hears he's going to Spain.
(ADA *comes tearing down the stairs at this point — she is the Kahns' daughter, aged* 14.)

ADA. Mother! Mother! Hello everyone — Dad, where's Mother? (*She snatches a slice of bread and butter from table.*)

HARRY. Hello, Ada — you haven't seen her yet? You'll cop it. She's gone to look for Ronnie.

ADA. (*going off again*). Be back in quarter of an hour — excuse me.

HARRY. Where you going now?

ADA Must check up on the last few posts, see that all the other pioneers are safe. (*She calls back through the window.*) Christ, what a day, comrades! (*Exits.*)

HARRY. Comrades! And *we* didn't force her to be in the pioneers. Wasn't necessary. I tell you, show a young person what socialism means and he recognizes life! A future! But it won't be pure in our lifetime, you know that, don't you, boys? Not even in hers, maybe — but in her children's lifetime — *then* they'll begin to feel it, all the benefits, despite our mistakes — you'll see, despite our mistakes. Now boys, tell me everything that happened.

PRINCE. Don't you know? Sir Philip Game, the police commissioner, got the wind up and banned the march. He told Mosley to fight it out with the Home Secretary. He wasn't going to have any trouble. And what happened to you?

HARRY (*proudly*). I was nearly arrested.

MONTY. You?

HARRY. I was running through the streets waving a red banner Sarah gave me and a policeman told me to drop it.

PRINCE. So?

HARRY. I dropped it! And then I turned into Flower and Dean Street and raised it again. He must have guessed what I was going to do. Christ! I never saw so many policemen appear so quickly. They seemed to pour out of all the windows when they heard that penny-farthing whistle. I only just had time to hop into my mother's place.

MONTY. And you stayed there?

HARRY. I had a cup of tea and at about four o'clock I came out. I got to Gardiner's Corner and police were charging the barricades. I didn't see no Fascists. Any get there?

PRINCE. They stayed in the back streets. The police did all the attacking. So?

HARRY. So I saw the police were picking our boys off like flies and then I saw my policeman — his hat was missing by this time. Oooh! There was a vicious look came into his eye when he saw me. I didn't stop to ask him where he'd lost it. I just ran back to my mother's and read a book.

HYMIE (*ominously*). So you *were* at your mother's. (*To the others*) I think we'd better go before Sarah comes back. Harry, we're going.

HARRY. You're not staying for something to eat?

HYMIE. Lottie's waiting for me, Harry. Come on, you two.

HARRY. Hey, Hymie. You won't tell her I was at my mother's all the time, will you? No?

(*The boys assure him with pats and shakes of the head. HARRY pours himself out a cup of tea and, taking it into the front room, he settles down to a book by the fire. After some seconds SARAH comes down the stairs with RONNIE, a boy of about five. He is asleep in her arms. She takes him straight into the bedroom. HARRY tries to appear very absorbed. SARAH comes out of the room, takes off her coat and hangs it up. She is eyeing HARRY most of the time with a gaze to kill while he does his best to avoid it. She clears a few things from the table, then goes out to get herself a cup of tea. As she watches HARRY she seats herself at the table and slowly stirs her drink. He shrinks under her gaze as her head begins to nod. It is an 'I-know-you-don't-I' nod.*)

SARAH. You think I'm a fool, don't you?

(*HARRY shifts uncomfortably, doesn't answer. SARAH watches him.*)

Think I can't see, that I don't know what's going on.

(*Pause.*) Look at him! The man of the house! Nothing matters to him! (*Pause.*) Well, Harry, why don't you look at me? Why don't you talk to me? I'm your wife, aren't I? A man is supposed to discuss things with his wife.

HARRY (*at last*). What do you want me to say?

SARAH. Must I tell you what to say? Don't you know? Don't you *just* know! (*Pause.*) Artful! Oh, you're so artful!

HARRY. Yes, yes. I'm artful.

SARAH. Aren't you artful, then? You think because you sit there pretending to read that I won't say anything? That's what you'd like — that I should just come in and carry on and not say anything. You'd like that, wouldn't you? That you should carry on your life just the same as always and no one should say anything.

HARRY. Oh, leave me alone, Sarah.

SARAH. Oh, leave me alone, Sarah! I'll leave you alone all right. There'll be blue murder, Harry, you hear me? There'll be blue murder if it carries on like this. All our life is it going to be like this? I can't leave a handbag in the room. You remember what happened last time? You left me! Remember?

(HARRY *tries to turn away out of it all and* SARAH *shakes him back again.*)

Remember? And you wanted to come back? And you came back — full of promises. What's happened to them now?

HARRY. Nothing's happened! Now stop nagging! Good God, you don't let a man live in peace.

SARAH. You can still pretend? After you took ten shillings from my bag and you know that I know you took it and you can still be righteous? Say you don't know anything about it, go on. Say you don't know what I'm talking about.

HARRY: No. I *don't* know what you're talking about.

105

SARAH (*finally unable to control herself, cursing him*). Fire on your head! May you live so sure if you don't know what I'm talking about. The money fell out of my purse, I suppose. I dropped it in the street. (*Screaming at him*) Fire on your head!

HARRY (*rising and facing her in a rage*). I'll throw this book at you — so help me I'll throw this book at you.

(*At this point* ADA *rushes in.*)

ADA. Harry, stop it. (*She cries.*) Oh, stop it!

HARRY (*shouting*). Tell your mother to stop it, she's the cause, it's her row. Don't you know your mother by now? (*He has moved away to the door.*)

SARAH. I'm the cause? Me? You hear him, Ada, you hear him? I'm the cause! (*Throws a saucer at him.*) Swine, you!

HARRY (*in speechless rage, throws his book to the ground*). She's mad, your mother, she's stark raving mad!

(HARRY *rushes out of the room up the stairs.* SARAH *follows him to bottom of stairs and, picking up a basin in her hands, brandishes it.* ADA *goes to look out of the window.*)

SARAH. That's it, run away. Go to your mother! She'll give you peace! She'll do everything for you! Weakling, you! *Weakling!*

ADA (*crying*). Everybody's outside, Mummy. Everybody is looking down at us.

SARAH (*turning to comfort her*). There, there, Boobola. There, there, meine kindt. Shuh! Shuh! I'm sorry. (*Bends over her and strokes her.*) Shuh! Shuh! It's finished, I'm sorry, it's over.

HARRY (*from the street*). She's mad, she's gone mad, she has.

SARAH. Shuh! shuh! Ada, don't listen. It'll pass. Shuh — shuh! (*Cooing*) loolinka, Ada, Ada, Ada.

(*As she comforts* ADA, RONNIE *comes out and stands watching them — listening and bewildered ...*)

CURTAIN

106

ACT TWO

Scene 1

June 1946 — the war has come and gone.
The scene is now changed. The Kahns have moved to an L.C.C.
block of flats in Hackney — the 1930 kind, with railings. The
working class is a little more respectable now, they have not long
since voted in a Labour Government. The part of the flat we can see
is: the front room, from which lead off three rooms; the passage to
the front door — and a door leading from the passage to the kitchen
(off); and part of the balcony with its iron railings.
It is late on a Friday afternoon. HARRY *is lying down on the*
sofa. SARAH *walks along the balcony, puts her hand through the letter*
box, withdraws the key, and enters the front room — energetic as
ever.

SARAH. What! you here already? (*Accepting the fact*) You
haven't been working!

HARRY. The place closed down.

SARAH (*takes off coat and unpacks shopping bag*). The place closed
down! But you only started there on Monday.

HARRY. Well! So the place closed down! Is it my fault?

SARAH. It always happens where *he* works. You can't bring
luck anywhere, can you! When it's a slump you always
manage to be the first one sacked and when the season
starts again you're the last one to find work. Ah, Harry,
you couldn't even make money during the war. The war!
When *everybody* made money.

HARRY (*laying pay packet on table*). Nah!

SARAH (*reading it*). What's this? Seven pounds thirteen? Why
only seven pounds thirteen?

HARRY. Four days' work.

SARAH. You haven't worked *all* day today? So what you been
doing?

107

HARRY. I felt tired.

SARAH. Sleep! That's all he can do. You didn't peel potatoes or anything? (*No answer.*) Oh, what am I standing here talking to you for? Don't I know you by now?

HARRY. I got a headache.

SARAH (*going to kitchen and talking from there*). Yes, yes — headache! Ronnie not home yet?

HARRY. He's distributing leaflets.

SARAH. What leaflets?

HARRY. I don't know what leaflets. What leaflets! Leaflets!

SARAH. Come and make some tea. Ada will be here soon.

HARRY. Leave me alone, Sarah.

SARAH (*from the kitchen*). Make some tea when I ask you!

> (HARRY *rises, and* ADA *is seen coming along the balcony. She enters through the front door in the same manner as Sarah. She is 25 years of age, well-spoken, a beautiful Jewess and weary of spirit.*)

HARRY (*kissing her*). Hello, Ada.

SARAH. Ada? Ada? You here? Go inside, Daddy'll make some tea. Supper will soon be ready. (*Appears cheerfully from kitchen with all the signs of a cook about her. Kisses* ADA.) Got a nice supper.

ADA. What nice supper?

SARAH. Barley soup. I left it on a small light all day while I was at work. (*Returns to kitchen.*)

ADA. Do you know if Ronnie has gone to my place to see if there is mail from Dave?

SARAH. Suppose so. He usually does when he knows you're coming here straight from work.

> (RONNIE *appears on the balcony and lets himself in. Aged 15, enthusiastic, lively, well-spoken like his sister.*)
>
> (*Hearing the noise at the door*) Ronnie?

RONNIE. I'm here.

SARAH. He's here.

RONNIE (*to* ADA *as he enters*). Two hundred and fifty leaflets in an hour and a half!

ADA. Very good. What for?

RONNIE. The May Day demo. Are you coming?

ADA. I doubt it.

RONNIE (*mocking her*). I doubt it! Don't you find the march exciting any longer?

ADA. I do *not* find the march exciting any longer.

RONNIE. Can't understand it. You and Dave were such pioneers in the early days. I get all my ideas from you two — and now —

ADA. And now the letters, please.

RONNIE. Letters? Letters? What letters?

ADA. Oh, come on, Ronnie — Dave's letters.

RONNIE (*innocently*). But I've been distributing leaflets!

ADA. You didn't go to my home to find ... ?

RONNIE. Miles away — other direction.

ADA (*sourly*). Thank you.

(*While* ADA *sits down to read a newspaper* RONNIE *withdraws three letters from his pocket and reads some initials on the back.*)

RONNIE. I.L.T. Now what could that mean — I love thee?

ADA. Give me those letters, please.

RONNIE (*teasing*). Oh, I love thee, sister.

ADA. You've been reading them.

RONNIE (*reading front of envelope*). Letter number 218 — Christ! he's prolific. And here's number 215 — lousy service, isn't it? And number 219. This one says I.L.T.T., I love thee terribly, I suppose. And if I loved you I'd also love you terribly. (*Bends over and kisses her.*)

ADA. Idiot! (*Reads.*)

RONNIE. Isn't it time that husband of yours was demobbed? The war's been over a year already. Imagine! I was only nine when he left. I've still kept all his letters, Ada, all of them. (*Ambles round the room to wall and tears off a little piece of wallpaper which he hurriedly crumples and stuffs into his pocket, making sure no one has seen him.*) We've been living here for five years—he hasn't even seen this place, God help him! (*Shouting to kitchen*) Harry! Harry! Where's Harry?

(HARRY *comes in with some tea and* RONNIE *goes to take a cup.*)

Good old Pops. Dad, I saw Monty Blatt. He says you must attend the meeting tonight.

HARRY. Ach! Do me a favour!

RONNIE. Listen to him! Party member! Won't attend branch meetings! How can you know what's going *on* in the world? That's where Ada gets her apathy from. She's you! And you're a lazy old sod — whoopee!

(RONNIE *hoists* HARRY *over his shoulder, fireman fashion, and dances round the room.*)

RONNIE. Are you going to the meeting?

HARRY. Let me down, you fool! Let me down!

RONNIE. The meeting?

HARRY. Stop it, you idiot — I've got a headache.

ADA. Do be quiet, you two.

RONNIE (*lowering his father*). I'll fight you. Come on, fists up, show your mettle; I just feel in the mood. (*Assumes quixotic boxing stance.*)

HARRY (*grinning*). Bloody fool! Leave off!

RONNIE. Windy! (*Playfully jabs* HARRY.)

HARRY (*raising his fists*). I'll knock your block off.

(*They follow each other round — fists raised. First* RONNIE *moves forward, then he backs away and* HARRY *moves forward. Thus they move — to and fro, without touching each other, until* SARAH *comes in with some soup in plates.*)

SARAH. The table! the table! Lay the table someone.

RONNIE. The table, the table — oh, oh, the table!

(*Everyone moves to lay the table;* RONNIE *in haste,* ADA

while reading, and HARRY *clumsily. Then they all sit down.*)

ADA. Lovely soup, Mummy.

RONNIE. Magnificent!

SARAH. You like it?

HARRY. They just said they did.

SARAH. I wasn't talking to you.

RONNIE. She wasn't talking to you.

HARRY. Your mother never talks *to* me.

RONNIE. You're so ugly, that's why. I wouldn't talk to you either only you wouldn't give me any spending money.

SARAH. He won't give you any spending money this week anyway.

RONNIE. Don't tell me. He's out of work.

HARRY (*pathetically*). The shop closed down.

ADA. Oh, Daddy, why does it always happen to you?

HARRY. It doesn't always happen to me.

ADA. Always! All my life that's all I can remember, just one succession of jobs which have fallen through.

HARRY. Is it my fault if the garment industry is so unstable?

ADA. It's not the industry — it's you.

HARRY. Yes, me.

ADA. Well, isn't it you?

HARRY. Oh, Ada, leave off. I have enough with your mother. I've got a headache.

ADA. I don't wonder you have a headache, you spend most of your time sleeping.

HARRY. Yes, sleeping.

ADA. What are you going to do now?

HARRY. I'll look for another job on Monday.

ADA. What's wrong with Sunday — on the Whitechapel Road? There's always governors looking for machinists.

HARRY. Those people aren't there for work. They go to gossip. Gossip, that's all! Monday I'll find a job and start straight away. It's busy now, you know.

111

SARAH (*collecting the soup dishes and taking them out*). Morgen morgen nor nischt heite, sagen alle faule leite.

ADA. Daddy — you are the world's biggest procrastinator.

RONNIE. Give the boy a break, Addy, that's a big word.

ADA. He ought to be ashamed of himself. The industry's booming with work and he's out of a job. You probably got the sack, didn't you?

HARRY (*offended*). I did not get the sack.

ADA. All her life Mummy's had to put up with this. I shall be glad to get away.

> (SARAH, *entering with the next course, hears this remark and glares bitterly at* HARRY.)

RONNIE. Get away where?

ADA. Anywhere. When Dave comes back we shall leave London and live in the country. That'll be our socialism. Remember this, Ronnie: the family should be a unit, and your work and your life should be part of one existence, not something hacked about by a bus queue and office hours. A man should see, know, and love his job. Don't you want to feel your life? Savour it gently? In the country we shall be somewhere where the air doesn't smell of bricks and the kids can grow up without seeing grandparents who are continually shouting at each other.

SARAH. Ada, Ada.

RONNIE. And no more political activity?

ADA. No more political activity.

RONNIE. I bet Dave won't agree to that. Dave fought in Spain. He won't desert humanity like that.

ADA. Humanity! Ach!

RONNIE. Listen to her! With a Labour majority in the House? And two of our own Party members? It's only just beginning.

ADA. It's always only just beginning for the Party. Every defeat is victory and every victory is the beginning.

RONNIE. But it is, it is the beginning. Plans for town and country planning. New cities and schools and hospitals. (*Jumping up on chair to* HARRY'*s facetious applause.*) Nationalization! National health! Think of it, the whole country is going to be organized to co-operate instead of tear at each other's throat. That's what I said to them in a public speech at school and all the boys cheered and whistled and stamped their feet — and blew raspberries.

ADA. I do not believe in the right to organize people. And anyway I'm not so sure that I love them enough to *want* to organize them.

SARAH (*sadly*). This — from *you*, Ada? You used to be such an organizer.

ADA. I'm tired, Mother. I spent eighteen months waiting for Dave to return from Spain and now I've waited six years for him to come home from a war against Fascism and I'm tired. Six years in and out of offices, auditing books and working with young girls who are morons — lipsticked, giggling morons. And Dave's experience is the same — fighting with men who he says did not know what the war was about. Away from their wives they behaved like animals. In fact they wanted to get away from their wives in order to behave like animals. Give them another war and they'd run back again. Oh yes! the service killed any illusions Dave may have once had about the splendid and heroic working class.

HARRY (*pedantically*). This is the talk of an intellectual, Ada.

ADA. God in heaven save me from the claptrap of a three-penny pamphlet. How many friends has the Party lost because of lousy, meaningless titles they gave to people. *He* was a bourgeois intellectual, *he* was a Trotskyist, *he* was a reactionary Social Democrat. Whisht! Gone!

HARRY. But wasn't it true? Didn't these people help to bolster a rotten society?

113

ADA. The only rotten society is an industrial society. It makes a man stand on his head and then convinces him he is good-looking. I'll tell you something. It wasn't the Trotskyist or the Social Democrat who did the damage. It was progress! There! Progress! And nobody dared fight progress.

SARAH. But that's no reason to run away. Life still carries on. A man gets married, doesn't he? He still has children, he laughs, he finds things to make him laugh. A man can always laugh, can't he?

ADA. As if that meant he lived? Even a flower can grow in the jungle, can't it? Because there is always some earth and water and sun. But there's still the jungle, struggling for its own existence, and the sick screeching of animals terrified of each other. As if laughter were proof!

HARRY. And we and the Party don't want to do away with the jungle, I suppose?

ADA. No, you do not want to do away with the jungle, I suppose. You have *never* cried against the jungle of an industrial society. You've never wanted to destroy its *values* — simply to own them yourselves. It only seemed a crime to you that a man spent all his working hours in front of a machine because he did not own that machine. Heavens! the glory of owning a machine!

SARAH. So what, we shouldn't care any more? We must all run away?

ADA. Care! Care! What right have we to care? How can we care for a world outside ourselves when the world inside is in disorder? Care! Haven't you ever stopped, Mother — I mean stopped — and seen yourself standing with your arms open, and suddenly paused? Come to my bosom. Everyone come to my bosom. How can you possibly imagine that your arms are long enough, for God's sake? What audacity tells you you can harbour a billion people in a theory? What great, big, stupendous, egotistical audacity, tell me?

RONNIE. Whoa, whoa!

HARRY. But it *is* an industrial age, you silly girl. Let's face facts —

ADA (*mocking*). Don't let us kid ourselves.

HARRY (*with her*). Don't let us kid ourselves — it's a challenge of our time.

ADA. Balls!

HARRY. You can't run away from it.

ADA. Stop me!

HARRY. Then you're a coward — that's all I can say — you're a coward.

SARAH (*sadly*). She had a fine example from her father, didn't she?

HARRY (*to this stab in the back*). What do you mean — a fine example from her father?

SARAH. You don't understand what I'm saying, I suppose?

HARRY (*he is hurt and throws a hand at her in disgust*). Ach! you make me sick.

SARAH (*mocking*). Ach, you make me sick. *I* make *him* sick. Him, my fine man! You're the reason why she thinks like this, you know that?

HARRY. Yes, me.

SARAH. Well, of course you. Who else?

RONNIE (*collecting dishes and escaping to the kitchen*). I'll wash up.

HARRY. I didn't bring her up — she's all your work.

SARAH. That's just it! You didn't bring her up. You weren't concerned, were you? You left it all to me while you went to your mother's or to the pictures or out with your friends.

HARRY. Yes. I went out with my friends. Sure!

SARAH. Well, didn't you? May I have so many pennies for the times you went up West to pictures.

115

HARRY. Oh, leave off, Sarah.

SARAH. Leave off! That's all he can say — leave off, leave me alone. That was it. I did leave you alone. That's why I had all the trouble.

ADA. I'm going home, Mummy.

SARAH (*caressingly and apologetically*). Oh no, Ada, stay, it's early yet. Stay. We'll play solo.

ADA. I'm feeling tired and I must write to Dave.

SARAH. Well, stay here and write to Dave. We'll all be quiet. Ronnie's going out. Daddy'll go to bed and I've got some washing to do. Stay, Ada, stay. What do you want to rush home for? A cold, miserable, two-roomed flat, all on your own. Stay. We're a family, aren't we?

ADA (*putting on her coat*). I've also got washing to do, I must go—

SARAH. I'll do it for you. What's a mother for? Straight from work I'll go to your place and bring it back with me. Stay. You've got company here — perhaps Uncle Hymie and Auntie Lottie'll come up. What do you want to be on your own for, tell me?

ADA. I'm not *afraid* of being on my own — I must go.

SARAH (*wearily*). Go then! Will we see you tomorrow?

ADA. Yes, I'll come for supper tomorrow night. Good night. (*Calling*) Good night, Ronnie.

RONNIE (*appearing from kitchen*). 'Night, Addy.

SARAH. You washing up, Ronnie?

RONNIE. I'm washing up.

SARAH. You I don't have to worry about — but your sister runs away. At the first sight of a little bother she runs away. Why does she run away, Ronnie? Before she used to sit and discuss things, now she runs to her home — such a home to run to — two rooms and a shadow!

RONNIE. But, Ma, she's a married woman herself. You think she hasn't her own worries wondering what it'll be like to see Dave after all these years?

SARAH. But you never run away from a discussion. At least I've got you around to help me solve problems.

RONNIE. Mother, my one virtue — if I got any at all — is that I always imagine you can solve things by talking about them — ask my form master! (*Returns to kitchen.*)

SARAH (*wearily to* HARRY). You see what you do? That's your daughter. Not a word from her father to ask her to stay. The family doesn't matter to you. All your life you've let the family fall around you, but it doesn't matter to you.

HARRY. I didn't drive her away.

SARAH (*bitterly*). No — you didn't drive her away. How could you? You were the good, considerate father.

(HARRY *turns away and hunches himself up miserably.*)

Look at you! Did you shave this morning? Look at the cigarette ash on the floor. Your shirt! When did you last change your shirt? He sits. Nothing moves him, nothing worries him. He sits! A father! A husband!

HARRY (*taking out a cigarette to light*). Leave me alone, please leave me alone, Sarah. You started the row, not me, you!

SARAH (*taking cigarette from his hand*). Why must you always smoke? — talk with me. Talk, talk, Harry.

HARRY. Sarah! (*He stops, chokes, and then stares wildly around him.*) Mamma. Mamma. (*He is having his first stroke.*)

SARAH (*frightened but not hysterical*). Harry! Harry! What is it?

HARRY (*in Yiddish, gently*). Vie iss sie — der mamma?

SARAH. Stop it, Harry.

HARRY. Sie iss dorten — der mamma?

SARAH. Ronnie! Ronnie!

(RONNIE *comes in from the kitchen.*)

Doctor Woolfson — quick, quick, get him.

RONNIE. What's happening?

SARAH. I don't know.

(RONNIE *runs out.*)

117

Harry, it was only a quarrel, you silly man. None of your
tricks now, Harry — Harry, you hear me?
HARRY. Vie iss sie? Mamma, mamma.

CURTAIN

Scene 2

October 1947. We are in the same room. RONNIE *is making a fire
in the grate. When this is done he puts on the radio and goes into the
kitchen. The 'Egmont' overture comes over the radio.* RONNIE
*comes out of the kitchen with a cup of tea. On hearing the music he
lays down the cup and picks up a pencil and proceeds to conduct an
imaginary orchestra, until* CISSIE *is seen moving along the balcony.
She lets herself in and surprises* RONNIE. *She is carrying a brief-case.*

RONNIE. Aunt!
CISSIE. Hello, Junior. I've come to see your father.
RONNIE. Not back from work yet. Just in time for a cuppa.
    (*Goes off to make one.*)
CISSIE. He still has that job, then?
RONNIE (*from kitchen*). Can't hear you.
CISSIE. Turn this bloody wireless down. (*Does so.*)
RONNIE. Aunty! Please! Beethoven!
CISSIE. I know, I know. Some other time. I'm not feeling so
    good. (*Takes cigarette from handbag.*)
RONNIE (*entering with tea*). What price partition in Palestine,
    Aunt?
CISSIE. Russia's backing the plan.
RONNIE. Yes — and haven't the Arabs got upset over that.
    They're taking it to the high courts. They expected Russia
    to attack the United Nations plan if only to upset the
    West. Power politics!
CISSIE. Has your father still got that job?

RONNIE. No, he's a store-keeper in a sweet factory now. Look. (*Shows her a biscuit tin full of sweets.*) Jelly babies. Can't help himself. Doesn't do it on a large scale, mind, just a handful each night. Everyone does it.

CISSIE. How long has he been there?

RONNIE. Three weeks. You know he can't stay long at a job — and now he has got what he has always wanted — a legitimate excuse.

CISSIE. He can *walk*, can't he?

RONNIE. He walks — slowly and stooped — with his head sunk into his shoulders, hands in his pockets. (*Imitates his father.*) His step isn't sure — frightened to exert himself in case he should suddenly drop dead. You ought to see him in a strong wind — (*moves drunkenly round the room*) like an autumn leaf. He seems to have given up the fight, as though *thank God* he was no longer responsible for himself. You know, Aunt, I don't suppose there is anything more terrifying to a man than his own sense of failure, and your brother Harry is really a very sensitive man. No one knows more than he does how he's failed. Now that's tragedy for you: having the ability to see what is happening to yourself and yet not being able to do anything about it. Like a long nightmare. God! fancy being born just to live a long nightmare. He gets around. But who knows how sick he is? Now we can't tell his lethargy from his illness.

CISSIE. It sounds just like Mother. Mother was bed-ridden for years. He seems to be moving that way —

RONNIE. Almost deliberately. Here! (*Goes to a drawer and takes out a notebook.*) Did you know he once started to write his autobiography? Listen. (*Reads.*) 'Of me, the dummy and my family.' How's that for a poetic title! 'Sitting at my work in the shop one day my attention was drawn to the dummy that we all try the work on. The rhythm of the machines and my constant looking at the dummy

119

rocked me off in a kind of sleepy daze. And to my surprise the dummy began to take the shape of a human, it began to speak. Softly at first, so softly I could hardly hear it. And then louder and still louder, and it seemed to raise its eyebrows and with a challenge asked: Your life, what of your life? My life? I had never thought, and I began to take my mind back, way back to the time when I was a little boy.' There, a whole notebook full, and then one day he stopped! Just like that! God knows why a man stops doing the one thing that can keep him together.

CISSIE. How's Ada and Dave?

RONNIE. Struggling in a tied cottage in the country. Ada suckles a beautiful baby, Dave lays concrete floors in the day-time and makes furniture by hand in the evening.

CISSIE. Lunatics!

RONNIE. They're happy. Two Jews in the Fens. They had to get a Rabbi from King's Lynn to circumcise the baby. A Rabbi from King's Lynn! Who'd ever think there were Rabbis in King's Lynn?

CISSIE. And you?

RONNIE. A bookshop.

CISSIE. Same one?

RONNIE. Same one.

CISSIE. You're also crazy and mixed up, I suppose?

RONNIE (*highly indignant*). Don't call me that! God in heaven, don't call me that! I'm a poet.

CISSIE. Another one!

RONNIE. A socialist poet.

CISSIE. A socialist poet!

RONNIE. I have all the world at my fingertips. Nothing is mixed up. I have so much life that I don't know who to give it to first. I see beyond the coloured curtains of *my* eyes to a world — say, how do you like that line? Beyond the coloured curtains of *my* eyes, waiting for time and timing nothing but the slow hours, lay the thoughts in the mind. Past the pool of *my* smile ...

CISSIE. What does that mean?

RONNIE. What, the pool of my smile? It's a metaphor — the pool of my smile — a very lovely metaphor. How's trade-union activity?

CISSIE. We've got a strike on. Dillingers are probably going to lock out its workers.

RONNIE. Ah, Dillingers! 'Dillinger styles gets all the men's smiles, this is the wear for everywhere!' No wonder the workers don't like poetry.

CISSIE. The old boy wants to reduce their wages because they're doing sale work.

RONNIE. What's that?

CISSIE. You know — sale work — specially made-up clothes for the big West End sales.

RONNIE. You mean a sale is not what is left over from the season before?

CISSIE. Oh, grow up, Ronnie. You should know that by now. It's cheaper stuff, inferior quality.

RONNIE. And the union doesn't protest? (*Jumping on a chair and waving his arms in the air*) Capitalist exploiters! The bastards — if you'll excuse the expression. I'll write a book about them! I'll expose them in their true light. What a novel, Aunt — set in a clothing factory, the sweat shops, the —

CISSIE. Look, you want to hear about this strike or you don't want to hear about this strike?

(RONNIE *sits down.*)

So because it's sale work Dillinger wants to cut the women's wages by ten per cent and the men's by twelve and a half per cent. So what does he plan to do? I'll tell you what he plans to do — he plans to pay all thirty of them for one full week, sack them, and then re-employ them, which would mean they were new employees and only entitled to Board of Trade rate, which is considerably less.

RONNIE. But can he do that?

CISSIE. He did it! He did it! The girls told me. But this year the shop stewards got together and asked me to go down and negotiate. They didn't all want it, mind you. One wagged his finger at me and cried: 'We're not taking your advice, we're not taking your advice!' I gave them — you know me. First I read the Riot Act to them and then I lashed out. You ought to be ashamed of yourselves, I told them, after the union struggled hard, tooth and nail, for every penny you get and at the first sign of intimidation you want to give in. For shame! I yelled at them — for shame! I tell you, Ronnie — a boss you can always handle because he always wants to bribe you, and that gives you the upper hand — but the worker ...

(HARRY *has by this time entered through the front door, and he shuffles down the passage into the front room. He is slightly paralysed down one side but is still very able to move around. The first stroke has just made him age prematurely.*)

HARRY. Hello, Cissie, what are you doing here?

CISSIE. I've come to see you. Well, how are you?

HARRY. I'm all right, Cissie, I'm fine.

CISSIE. Can you work all right?

HARRY. I can't move my left hand very well. Lost its grip or something. (*Clutches and unclutches fist to prove the point.*)

RONNIE (*gripping* HARRY'S *hand in a shake*). Strong as an ox. You're a sham, Harry boy. Want some tea?

HARRY. Yes please, son.

CISSIE. What do the doctors say is wrong with you?

HARRY. I had a stroke — that's all they know. They don't tell you anything in the hospitals these days. Sarah's gone to the doctor's now to find out if I can go back again for observation.

CISSIE. More observation?

HARRY. Ach! Don't talk to me about them, they make me sick.

CISSIE. All those blood tests they took and they still don't know — after a year. I'm surprised you had that much blood. Well, I'm going. Here, smoke yourself to death. (*Hands him forty cigarettes.*)

RONNIE (*bringing in the tea*). Going?

CISSIE. I've got a strike meeting.

RONNIE. In the evening?

CISSIE. Any time. So long, Junior.

> (*She kisses* HARRY *and* RONNIE *and goes out. On the landing she meets* SARAH.)
>
> Hello, Sarah. I just come to see Harry. Sorry I must go. How are you?

SARAH. I'm all right. Why don't you stay for supper?

CISSIE (*out of sight by now*). I've got a strike meeting. I'll be seeing you.

HARRY (*to* SARAH *as she comes in*). Did you go to the doctor's?

SARAH (*wearily*). I've been, I've been. Oh, those stairs will kill me.

HARRY. What does he say?

SARAH (*taking out a letter from her bag and placing it on the mantelpiece*). He gave me a letter: you should take it to the hospital.

HARRY. What does it say; show me.

SARAH. It's sealed; you mustn't open it.

HARRY. Show me it.

SARAH. What can you see? It's sealed.

HARRY (*irritably*). Oh, I want to see who it's addressed to.

> (*Too tired to cope with him she hands him the letter and then goes to the kitchen.*)

SARAH (*from the kitchen*). Did anybody make supper?

RONNIE. We've not long come in. (*To* HARRY, *taking away the*

123

envleope he is trying to open) Uh-uh. Mustn't open. It's for the hospital.

SARAH (*entering with a cup of tea and sitting down*). I've got a branch meeting tonight. Ronnie, you can take your own supper. It's fried fish from yesterday. You want to come with me, Harry?

HARRY. I don't feel like going to any branch meeting.

SARAH. You want to get well, don't you? You don't want to become an invalid, do you? So come to a meeting tonight. Mix with people. They're your comrades, aren't they?

HARRY. Yes, my comrades.

SARAH. Nothing is sacred for him. Ach! Why should I worry whether you come or not. What are you doing, Ronnie?

RONNIE. An evening in. I want to write a novel tonight.

SARAH. What, all in one night? Ronnie, do you think you'll ever publish anything? I mean, don't you have to be famous or be able to write or something? There must be such a lot of people writing novels.

RONNIE. Not socialist novels. Faith, Mother, faith! I am one of the sons of the working class, one of its own artists.

HARRY. You mean a political writer like Winston Churchill?

SARAH. What, does he write novels as well? I thought he was only a politician.

RONNIE. Well, he's both — *and* he paints pictures.

SARAH. A painter? He paints pictures? Landscapes and things?

RONNIE. Of course! And in his spare time he —

SARAH. What, he has spare time also?

RONNIE. In his spare time he builds walls at the bottom of his garden.

SARAH (*in admiration*). A bricklayer! Ronnie, I told you you should take up a trade! Why don't you? Go to evening classes. Why should you waste your time in a bookshop? If I were young, oh, what wouldn't I study! All the world I would study. How properly to talk and to write and

124

make sentences. You'll be sorry — don't be like your father, don't be unsettled. Learn a good trade and then you have something to fall back on. You can always write — and when you work then you'll have something to write about.

RONNIE. Give me a chance, Ma. I only left school a year ago.

SARAH. That's what he kept on saying. Give me a chance! Everybody had to give him a chance: now look at him. Harry — you're not working in the sweet factory any more, are you?

HARRY. Who said I'm not?

RONNIE. Well, isn't he?

SARAH. Well, ask him, he knows.

(RONNIE *inclines his head inquiringly.*)

HARRY. Of course I'm still working there.

SARAH (*wearily, for the time has gone for violent rows*). Harry, answer me. What do you gain by telling me this lie? Tell me, I want to know. All my life I've wanted to know what you've gained by a lie. *I* know you're not working because I saw the foreman. You're not even a good liar. I've always known when you've lied. For twenty-five years it's been the same and all the time I've not known what it's about. But *you* know — no one else knows, but you do. I'm asking you, Harry — let me be your doctor, let me try and help you. What is it that makes you what you are? Tell me — only tell me. Don't sit there and say nothing. I'm entitled to know — after all this time, I'm entitled to know. Well, aren't I, Ronnie?

(*Nobody answers her.* HARRY *avoids her gaze,* RONNIE *waits till it's all over.*)

So look at him. He sits and he sits and he sits and all his life goes away from him. (*To* RONNIE) You won't be like that, will you?

RONNIE. I shall never take up a trade I hate as he did — if that's what you mean; and I shall never marry — at least not until I'm real and healthy. (*Cheerfully*) But what's there to grumble about, little Sarah? You have two splendid children, a fine son-in-law and a grandson.

SARAH. I haven't seen my grandson yet. My daughter lives two hundred miles away from me and my husband is a sick man. That's my family. Well, it's a family, I suppose. (*She rises to go.*)

RONNIE. What about me? (*He regards himself in a mirror.*) Young, good-looking, hopeful, talented ... hopeful, anyway.

SARAH (*sadly*). You? I'll wait and see what happens to you. Please God you don't make a mess of your life, please God. Did you ask for that rise?

RONNIE. I did ask for that rise. 'Mr Randolph,' I said — he's the manager of that branch — 'Mr Randolph, I know that the less wages you pay us bookshop assistants the more you get in your salary. But don't you think I've sold enough books for long enough time to warrant you forgoing some of your commission?'

SARAH. So what did he say, you liar?

RONNIE. 'You're our best salesman,' he said, 'but I've got to keep head office happy.'

SARAH. So what did you say, you liar?

RONNIE. So I said, 'It's not head office, it's your wife.'

SARAH. So what did he say, you liar?

RONNIE. He said, 'Kahn,' he said, 'as you're so frank and you know too much I'll give you a two-pound rise.'

SARAH. Ronnie, did you get a rise, I asked you?

RONNIE (*kissing her*). No, I did not get a rise.

SARAH. Mad boy, you! I'm going to the meeting.

RONNIE. That's it, Mother. You go to the meeting. At least if you keep on fighting then there's hope for me. (*He helps her on with a coat as he speaks, then she goes. Returning to room*) You want supper, Dad? It's the old dead fish again. I'll lay it for you. (*Moves to kitchen.*)

HARRY. Aren't you going to eat?

RONNIE (*from kitchen*). I'm not hungry. I'll eat later. I must work now. You want me to read the first chapter to you, Dad?

HARRY. Oh, leave me alone, Ronnie — I'm tired.

RONNIE. Tired! You're not tired, Harry — you're just drowning with heritage, mate! (*Re-enters with an assortment of plates, which he lays on the table.*) There, you can wash up after you. I'm going to my room now.

(RONNIE *goes to his room.* HARRY *moves the table and begins to eat. He eats in silence for a few seconds, then stretches out for a newspaper. After glancing through this he turns to the mantelpiece and sees the letter. He looks to Ronnie's room to make sure he is not coming and then moves slowly across to get the letter. First of all he tries to prise it open without tearing anything. Then not succeeding in this he moves to the table to get a knife. As he picks up the knife* RONNIE *enters again.*)

RONNIE. Christ! It's bloody cold in that room: I — now, then, Harry — (*as though playfully scolding a child*) you know you must not read the letter, remember what Mummykins said. (*He moves to take it.*)

HARRY (*retaining it*). I want to see it; it's about me, isn't what's in it.

RONNIE (*making another bid for it*). Use some will-power, Dad; you know the letter is not for you. Now leave it be, there's a good boy.

HARRY (*still retaining it*). I want to see it; it's about me, isn't it? Now leave off, Ronnie.

RONNIE (*snatching it from his father's hand*). No!

HARRY (*banging his hand on the table in rapid succession with the words, like a child in anger, hating to be like a child, and*

127

shrieking). GIVE ME THAT LETTER. GIMME. S'mine. S'mine. I WAN' THAT ENVELOPE. Now. This instant. I — wan' — that — envelope!

(RONNIE *stands there trembling. He had not meant to provoke such anger, and now, having done so, is upset. He is not quite sure what to do. Almost involuntarily he hands over the envelope, and when he has done so he goes to a wall and cries. He is still a boy — he has been frightened.* HARRY *picks up envelope, himself distraught. He does not bother to open it now. Seeing that* RONNIE *is crying he goes over to him and clasps him.*)

HARRY. You shouldn't do these things. I'm a sick man. If I want to open the envelope you shouldn't stop me. You've got no right to stop me. Now you've upset me and yourself — you silly boy.

RONNIE. Can't you see that I can't bear what you are. I don't want to hear your lies all my life. Your weakness frightens me, Harry — did you ever think about that? I watch you and I see myself and I'm terrified.

HARRY (*wandering away from him; he does not know what to say*). What I am — I am. I will never alter. Neither you nor your mother will change me. It's too late now; I'm an old man and if I've been the same all my life so I will always be. You can't alter people, Ronnie. You can only give them some love and hope they'll take it. I'm sorry. It's too late now. I can't help you. (*He shuffles miserably to his room, perceptibly older.*) Don't forget to have supper. Good night.

CURTAIN

ACT THREE

Scene 1

November 1955.

HARRY *has had his second stroke, and now paralysis has made him completely unfit for work. He can only just move around, has difficulty in talking, and is sometimes senile.* SARAH *retains much of her energy but shows signs of age and her troubles — her tone of speaking is compassionate now.*

Evening, in the same L.C.C. flat. HARRY *sits in a chair — huddled by the fireplace, listening to Ravel's 'La Valse' on the radio. He smokes more than ever, it is his one comfort.* SARAH *is sitting by the table struggling to fill out an official Government form — she talks a lot to herself.*

SARAH (*reading form*). Have you an insurance policy for life or death? Name of company. Amount insured for. Annual payments. How should I know the annual payments? I pay one and a penny a week — that's fifty-two shillings and fifty-two pennies. (*Makes mental reckoning.*)

(*The music on the radio has by this time reached a climax and is too loud.* SARAH *goes to turn it off.*)

Oh, shut that off! Classical music! All of a sudden it starts shouting at you.

HARRY. No, no, no, no, I was — I was listening.

SARAH. You *liked* it?

HARRY. I liked it. It reminds me of — of — of — of — it reminds me of Blackfriars Bridge in a fog.

SARAH. Blackfriars Bridge in a fog it reminds you of? Why a fog?

HARRY. Oh, I don't know why a fog. Why a fog?

SARAH. And why Blackfriars Bridge?

HARRY. Because I said so! Och, you're such a silly woman sometimes, Sarah.

129

SARAH (*playing with him*). But if it's in a fog so what difference whether it's Blackfriars Bridge or London Bridge? Ach, I must get these forms done before Bessie and Monty arrive. You remember Bessie and Monty are coming tonight? (SARAH *continues to complete forms.*) If Ronnie were here I'd get him to fill it in for me . . . as if they don't know how many times I was at work this year. Forms! You tell the National Insurance office that you started work on such and such a day so they tell the National Assistance and the National Assistance tells the Income Tax and then there's forms, forms, forms, forms. Oi — such forms. They can't get enough of them into one envelope. (*Writing*) No, I haven't got any property, I haven't got any lodgers, I haven't got a housekeeper. A housekeeper! A housekeeper wouldn't do what I do for you, Harry — washing all those sheets.

(MONTY BLATT *and his wife* BESSIE *appear on the balcony. They knock.* SARAH *jumps up.*)

They're here already. Now Harry, sit up. Do your flies up and brush that cigarette ash off you. And remember — don't let me down — you promised. You want to go now?

(*She takes* HARRY'S *arm but he pushes her away; he doesn't want to go.* SARAH *opens the door to her visitors. Both are richly dressed — over-dressed — and full of bounce and property.*)

MONTY. Sarah — little Sarah. How are you, sweetheart? You remember Bessie?

(*They all shake hands and enter the front room.*)

Harry boy! How's Harry? You're looking well. You feeling well? They haven't changed a bit. Neither of them.

SARAH. Sit down, both of you; I'll get the kettle on. (*Goes off to kitchen.*)

MONTY (*to* BESSIE). Always put the kettle on — that was the first thing Sarah always did. Am I right, Harry? I'm right, aren't I? (*Shouting to* SARAH) Remember, Sarah? It was always a cup of tea first.

SARAH (*coming in*). I remember, I remember.

MONTY (*to* BESSIE). We used to *live* in their old place in the East End, all the boys. Remember Prince and your brother Hymie? How is Hymie? Since we moved to Manchester I've lost contact with everybody, everyeee-body!

SARAH. Hymie's all right. He's got a business. His children are married and he stays at home all the time. Prince works in a second-hand shop.

MONTY. A second-hand shop? But I thought — and Cissie?

SARAH. The union members retired her. She lives on a pension, visits the relatives — you know ...

MONTY. It's all broken up, then?

SARAH. What's broken up about it? They couldn't keep up with the Party — so? The *fight* still goes on.

MONTY (*hastily changing the subject*). And Ada and Dave and Ronnie? Where are they all? Tell me everything. Tell me all the news. I haven't seen you for so long, Sarah — it's so good to see you — isn't it good to see them, Bessie?

SARAH. Ada and Dave are still in the country. They've got two children. Dave is still making furniture by hand —

MONTY. He makes a living?

SARAH. They live! They're not prosperous, but they live.

MONTY. And Ronnie? Ronnie had such ambitions; what's he doing?

SARAH. My Ronnie? He's in Paris.

MONTY. There, I told you he'd go far.

SARAH. As a cook.

MONTY (*not so enthusiastically*). A cook? Ronnie?

BESSIE (*helping them out*). A cook makes good money.

MONTY (*reviving*). Sure a cook makes good money. Ronnie is a smart boy, isn't he, Sarah? Didn't I always say Ronnie was a smart boy? Nobody could understand how an East

End boy could speak with such a posh accent. But cooking!
He likes it? I mean he's happy?

SARAH. I tell you something, Monty. People ask me what is
Ronnie doing and, believe me, I don't know what to answer. He used to throw his arms up in the air and say 'I
want to do something worth while, I want to create.'
Create! So, he's a cook in Paris.

MONTY. Please God he'll be a hotel manager one day.

SARAH. Please God.

MONTY. And Harry? (*He indicates with his head that* HARRY *has
dozed off.*)

SARAH. Poor Harry. He's had two strokes. He won't get any
better. Paralysed down one side. He can't control his
bowels, you know.

BESSIE. Poor man.

SARAH. You think *he* likes it? It's ach a nebish Harry now. It's
not easy for him. But he won't do anything to help himself. I don't know, other men get ill but they fight. Harry's
never fought. Funny thing. There were three men like
this in the flats, all had strokes. And all three of them
seemed to look the same. They walked the same, stooped
the same, and all needing a shave. They used to sit outside
together and talk for hours on end and smoke. Sit and talk
and smoke. That was their life. Then one day one of them
decided he wanted to live so he gets up and finds himself a
job — running a small shoe-mender's — and he's earning
money now. A miracle! Just like that. But the other one —
he wanted to die. I used to see him standing outside in the
rain, the pouring rain, getting all wet so that he could catch
a cold and die. Well, it happened: last week he died.
Influenza! He just didn't want to live. But Harry was not
like either of them. He didn't want to die but he doesn't
seem to care about living. So! What can you do to help a
man like that? I make his food and I buy him cigarettes

132

and he's happy. My only dread is that he will mess himself. When that happens I go mad — I just don't know what I'm doing.

MONTY. It's like that, is it?

SARAH. It's like that. That's life. But how about you, Monty? You still in the Party?

MONTY. No, Sarah — I'm not still in the Party, and I'll tell you why if you want to know —

BESSIE. Now, Monty, don't get on to politics. Sarah, do me a favour and don't get him on to politics.

MONTY. Don't worry, I won't say much —

SARAH. Politics is living, Bessie. I mean everything that happens in the world has got to do with politics.

BESSIE. Listen, Sarah. Monty's got a nice little greengrocer's business in Manchester, no one knows he was ever a member of the Party and we're all happy. It's better he forgets it.

MONTY. No, no — I'll tell her, let me tell her.

BESSIE. I'm warning you, Monty, if you get involved in a political argument I shan't stay. No political argument, you hear me?

MONTY. Listen, Sarah. Remember Spain? Remember how we were proud of Dave and the other boys who answered the call? But did Dave ever tell you the way some of the Party members refused to fight alongside the Trotskyists? And one or two of the Trotskyists didn't come back and they weren't killed in the fighting either? And remember Itzack Pheffer — the Soviet Yiddish writer? We used to laugh because Itzack Pheffer was a funny name — ha, ha. Where's Itzack Pheffer? everyone used to say. Well, we know now, don't we. The great 'leader' is dead now, and we know. The whole committee of the Jewish Anti-Fascist League were shot! Shot, Sarah! In our land of socialism. That was *our* land — what a land that was for us!

133

We didn't believe the stories then; it wasn't possible that it could happen in our one-sixth of the world.

SARAH. And you believe the stories now, Monty?

MONTY (*incredulously*). You don't —

BESSIE. Now, Monty —

MONTY. You don't believe it, Sarah? You won't believe it!

SARAH. And supposing it's true, Monty? So? What should we do, bring back the old days? Is that what you want?

MONTY. I don't know, sweetheart. I haven't got any solutions any more. I've got a little shop up north — I'm not a capitalist by any means — I just make a comfortable living and I'm happy. Bessie — bless her — is having a baby. (*Taps* BESSIE's *belly*.) I'm going to give him all that I can, pay for his education, university if he likes, and then I shall be satisfied. A man can't do anything more, Sarah, believe me. There's nothing more to life than a house, some friends, and a family — take my word.

SARAH. And when someone drops an atom bomb on your family?

MONTY (*pleading*). So what can I do — tell me? There's nothing I can do any more. I'm too small; who can I trust? It's a big, lousy world of mad politicians — I can't trust them, Sarah.

SARAH. The kettle's boiling — I'll make some tea. (*Goes to kitchen.*)

BESSIE. Enough now, Monty, enough.

MONTY (*he has upset himself*). All right, all right. I didn't tell her anything she doesn't know. She's a fine woman is Sarah. She's a fighter. All that worry and she's still going strong. But she has one fault. For her the world is black and white. It you're not white so you must be black. She can't see shades in character — know what I mean? She can't see people in the round. 'They' are all the same bunch. The authorities, the governments, the police, the Post Office —

even the shopkeepers. She's never trusted any of them, always fighting them. It was all so simple. The only thing that mattered was to be happy and eat. Anything that made you unhappy or stopped you from eating was the fault of capitalism. Do you think she ever read a book on political economy in her life? Bless her! Someone told her socialism was happiness so she joined the Party. You don't find many left like Sarah Kahn. I wish you'd have known us in the old days. Harry there used to have a lovely tenor voice. All the songs we sang together, and the strikes and the rallies. I used to carry Ronnie shoulder high to the May Day demonstrations. Everyone in the East End was going somewhere. It was a slum, there was misery, but we were going somewhere. The East End was a big mother.

(SARAH *comes in with the tea.*)
We'll talk about the good times now, shall we, Sarah? Blimey, sweetheart, it's not often that I come to London for a week-end. Here, remember the stall I used to have in Petticoat Lane? I'll take you there tomorrow, Bessie. And Manny the Corn King? Him and his wife used to go to Norwich, to sell phoney corn cures. His wife used to dress up as a nurse and they'd hang letters round the stall from people who were supposed to have been cured.

SARAH. And what about Barney?

MONTY. And Barney, that's it! He used to sell all the old farmers a lucky charm to bring them fortune. Sixpence each he'd sell them for and you know what they were? Haricot beans! Haricot beans dropped in dye to colour them. You could get them for threepence a pound in a grocer's shop and Barney sold them for sixpence each! Sixpence! A pound of beans used to last him for months.

SARAH. Ach! Horrible times! Horrible times — dirty, unclean, cheating!

MONTY. But friendly.

SARAH. Friendly, you call it? You think it was friendly to swindle people?

MONTY. Sweetheart, you take life too seriously. Believe me, those farmers knew very well what they were buying. Nobody swindled anybody because everyone knew.

SARAH. You think so, Monty?

(HARRY *wakes up with a jerk. Something has happened. He tries hurriedly to rise.*)

HARRY. Sarah, quick, help me.

SARAH. What! It's happened? (*She moves quickly to him.*)

MONTY. What is it, Harry boy?

SARAH. It's happened, Harry? Well, quickly then, quickly.

(HARRY, *crippled by paralysis and this attack of incontinence, shuffles, painfully, towards the toilet, with* SARAH *almost dragging him along. He whines and groans pathetically.*)

In front of Monty and Bessie. I'm so ashamed.

(MONTY *attempts to help* HARRY *move.*)

(*Abruptly*) No, leave him. It's all right. I'll manage. Leave him, Monty.

(*They struggle out and into the passage. When they have left the front room,* BESSIE *turns her head away and shudders.*)

BESSIE. Oh, good God!

MONTY. Poor Sarah and Harry. Jesus! It's all come to this?

CURTAIN

Scene 2

December 1956.

The Kahns' room, late one evening. SARAH, PRINCE, HYMIE *and* CISSIE *are sitting round the table playing solo.* HARRY *is by the fire, gazing into it, quite oblivious of what is going on. The cards have just been dealt for a round. Everyone is evaluating his cards in silence. After some seconds:*

PRINCE (*studying his cards*). What time you expecting Ronnie, Sarah?

SARAH (*studying her cards*). He's supposed to arrive at nine thirty tonight.

(*Again silence.*)

HYMIE (*to* CISSIE). Nu? Call!

CISSIE. Misère.

SARAH. How can you call a misère when I want to call a misère?

CISSIE. Please, Sarah — don't give the game away.

PRINCE. Wait a minute, not everybody has passed.

CISSIE. All right then, call!

SARAH. Pass.

PRINCE. Pass.

HYMIE. Pass.

CISSIE. Thank you. Can I start now?

SARAH. Is it your lead? I thought Prince dealt the cards.

CISSIE. What's the matter with you, Sarah? — Hymie dealt them.

PRINCE. I could have sworn Sarah dealt them.

CISSIE. Hymie, who dealt the cards?

HYMIE. We've been so long deciding what to call that I don't know any more. Did I deal them? I don't remember.

(*There is a general discussion as to who dealt them.*)

CISSIE. Now quiet, everybody. Quiet! Every time I come to this house to play solo there's the same confusion. Why don't you pay attention to the game? Now then, what was laid on the table for trumps?

SARAH. The two of spades.

HYMIE. That was the last round. It was the six of diamonds.

SARAH. But I saw it with my own eyes, it was the —

HYMIE. You aren't wearing your glasses, Sarah.

137

PRINCE. It was the six of hearts, I remember now.

CISSIE. Ah, thank God! We've got two people to agree. I also saw the six of hearts on the table. Who's got the six of hearts?

HYMIE. I have.

CISSIE. Which means that you dealt and if you dealt that means that I lead. Everybody happy now? There!

(CISSIE *throws down a card. The others follow. It's* HYMIE'S *trick. He lays down a card and the others follow, but* SARAH *realizes she has made a mistake.*)

SARAH. Wait a minute, wait a minute. I didn't mean to play that card.

CISSIE. Too late; you should watch the game.

SARAH. Ach! fool that I am. But you can see I shouldn't have played that card.

CISSIE. Of course I can see, but I'm glad that you did!

SARAH. Now, Hymie, would I normally play that card?

HYMIE. You aren't wearing your glasses, Sarah: I told you. We can still catch her. Now play.

SARAH. A second, a second. Let me get my glasses. (*Finds her bag, takes out her glasses and proceeds to puff on them and clean them.*) I don't know what's happened to my eyes lately. I went to have my glasses changed the other day — the rims were too big for me, kept slipping into my mouth — so I went to have them changed. The man said he couldn't change them because they were National Health glasses. So you know me, I tell him what for and he says, 'Madam,' he says, 'you want your money back?' So I say, 'Sure I want my money back.' And then I go up to the National Health offices — now listen to this — I go up to the National Health offices and I complain about the small allowance they make me for Harry. So the chap behind the desk — may he wake up dead — he says, 'What do you want, madam, ten pounds a week?' Did you ever hear? So I said, 'Son,' I said, 'when you were still peeing all over the floor I was on strike for better conditions, and don't you be cheeky.' 'Oh dear, you musn't talk to me like that per, per, per, per!'

PRINCE. Come on, Sarah, the game.

(*It is* PRINCE's *lead. The others follow; it is his trick again. Again he leads and the others follow. Now it is for* SARAH *to lead, and she does so.*)

What did you play hearts for? Couldn't you see what suit I was showing you?

SARAH. Prince, let me play my own game. Don't I know what I'm doing?

PRINCE. Well, it doesn't look like it, Sarah, so help me it doesn't. You can't be watching the game. Couldn't you guess she was going to throw off on hearts?

CISSIE. What is this! In the middle of the game!

SARAH. Of course I could see, but how do you know that I can't play anything else?

CISSIE. Are you going to play solo or aren't you going to play solo? No inquests, please.

HYMIE. Prince, play your game.

CISSIE. It's always the same. You can't even get a good game of solo these days!

(PRINCE *plays his card and they all follow.*)

SARAH. Look at him! Now he comes out diamonds and he wants to teach me how to play solo.

(SARAH *leads next time, and after that* CISSIE *lays down her cards and shows that she can't be caught.*)

CISSIE. There! Three-halfpence from everybody, please.

(*Now everybody looks at everybody else's hand to see where everybody else went wrong.*)

SARAH. Well, of course I couldn't catch her, not with my hand.

PRINCE. Why did you come out with hearts when you knew she might be throwing off on them?

SARAH. Because I wanted to give the lead away — *I couldn't* do anything.

HYMIE. But why give the lead away with hearts when you knew she might not have any?

SARAH. How was I to know? It was my smallest card.

CISSIE. You never could play a good game of solo, Sarah.

SARAH. But do me a favour —

CISSIE. Spades! That was the suit to play.

SARAH. Spades? Never!

(*Again everybody starts to speak at once until a loud scream brings them to silence. It comes from the playground below and is followed by a young girl's voice crying.*)

GIRL'S VOICE. Philip! Philip! I want my Philip. Leave me alone — go away.

MAN'S VOICE. Go 'ome, I tell you, 'ome, you silly cow. 'Ome!

GIRL'S VOICE. I won't go till I see Philip. I love him! I love him!

CISSIE. They making a film out there or something?

(*They all go out to the balcony and look down.* SARAH *walks along it off-stage to see what the commotion is all about.*)

Can't see a thing. There's always something happening in these flats. Last week a woman tried to gas herself. Come on, let's go in.

(*They return to room.*)

HARRY. What happened?

PRINCE. Your neighbours are having a party. Sarah's gone to see who's dead.

HYMIE. Why did the woman want to commit suicide?

CISSIE (*raising her skirt to warm her behind*). Who knows why a woman of thirty-two wants to commit suicide? These flats are a world on their own. You live a whole lifetime here and not know your next-door neighbour.

HARRY. I don' — I don' — I don' —

CISSIE. Do you want to write it **down**?

HARRY. I don' know the woman downstairs yet.

140

(*Everyone smiles for him, and having said his piece he returns to gazing at the fire.* SARAH *re-enters.*)

SARAH. Children! They don't know what to do with themselves. Seems she'd just spent the evening watching television with Philip and it was a horror film or something and he kept frightening her. Frightening her! That's all they can do to each other! She got home late and her father started on her so she ran back and started screaming for Philip. The great lover! He came out in his pyjamas to soothe her.

CISSIE (*going to get her coat*). Well, Sarah, I had a nice supper, a nice game of solo, and I'm going before the washing up. It doesn't look as though Ronnie caught that train anyway.

SARAH. I can't understand it. He wrote he was leaving Paris at eight this morning.

HYMIE. Well, it's nearly ten thirty and I must be going as well.

PRINCE. Me too, Sarah.

SARAH. Won't you stay for a cup of tea at least? It's so long since we've played a game of solo. Harry and I don't see many people these days.

HYMIE. It's been a nice evening, Sarah. Why don't you come up to *us* sometimes? I'm always at home.

SARAH. What chance do I get to leave Harry now?

CISSIE. Good night, Sarah.

(HYMIE *kisses* SARAH *and* CISSIE *kisses* HARRY, *and all leave.* SARAH *waves to them from the balcony and returns to the room. She collects the cards and tidies up.*)

SARAH. Harry, you want a cup of tea?

HARRY (*slowly rising*). I'm going to bed.

SARAH. You won't wait up for Ronnie?

HARRY I'll — I'll — I'll —

SARAH. You'll what?

HARRY. See him in the morning.

(SARAH *helps* HARRY *shuffle away to bed, and then settles down in the armchair to read. But she is tired now and lets the paper fall, and dozes.* RONNIE *appears on the balcony with his cases. He gently opens the door and lets himself in. He tiptoes over to* SARAH *and stands looking at her. It is no longer an enthusiastic* RONNIE. *She opens her eyes and after a second of looking at him she jumps up into his arms.*)

SARAH. I fell asleep.

RONNIE. So I saw.

SARAH. I thought you were a dream.

RONNIE. Perhaps I am.

SARAH (*pushing him away to look at him*). I hope not, Ronnie. Oh God, I hope not. Don't go away again. It's been so lonely without you and your friends. I don't mind not having any money, we can always eat, you know that, but I can't bear being on my own. (*Begins to cry.*)

RONNIE. I've only once ever seen you cry.

SARAH. What's the good of crying?

RONNIE. I wish I could cry sometimes. Perhaps if you'd have cried more often it would have been easier.

SARAH. It's just that I can't cope any longer, that's all. Three times a week Daddy has that accident and it gets too much. I'm an old woman now.

RONNIE. What makes you think I shall be able to cope?

SARAH. You? What are you talking about? Of course you'll be able to cope. You're young, aren't you? You're going to settle down.

RONNIE. I — I'm sick, Sarah.

SARAH. Sick?

RONNIE. Oh, not physically. That's why I came home.

SARAH. Didn't you like the place where you worked? You always wrote how happy you were — what an experience it was.

RONNIE. I hated the kitchen.

SARAH. But —

RONNIE. I — hated — the — kitchen! People coming and going and not staying long enough to understand each other. Do you know what I finally discovered — it's all my eye! This notion of earning an honest penny is all my eye. A man can work a whole lifetime and when he is sixty-five he considers himself rich if he has saved a thousand pounds. Rich! A whole lifetime of working in a good, steady, settled, enterprising, fascinating job! For every manager in a restaurant there must be twenty chefs terrified of old age. That's all we are — people terrified of old age, hoping for the football pools to come home. It's all my eye, Sarah.

SARAH. I'll make you some tea. Are you hungry?

RONNIE. No, I don't want anything to eat, thank you — I want to talk to you about something.

SARAH. But you must have to eat, you've been travelling all day.

RONNIE (*categorically*). I do not want to eat — I want to talk.

SARAH. I'll just make some tea, then; the water's boiled. You sit and relax and then you'll go straight to sleep. You'll see, by the morning you'll feel much better. (*Goes to kitchen.*)

RONNIE. Still optimistic, Mother. Food and sleep and you can see no reason why a person should be unhappy.

SARAH (*from the kitchen*). I'd have looked blue all these years if I hadn't've been optimistic.

RONNIE. How's Harry?

SARAH (*entering with two cups of tea*). You'll see him tomorrow; he was too tired to wait up. Want some biscuits? Have a piece of cake. Look, cake I made specially for you — your favourite.

RONNIE (*loudly*). Mother, don't fuss. I'm sorry.

SARAH. Is this how you've come home? You start by shouting? Is this a nice homecoming?

143

RONNIE (*something is obviously boiling in him*). Are you still in the Party?

SARAH (*quizzically*). Yes.

RONNIE. Active?

SARAH. So?

RONNIE (*suddenly*). I don't suppose you've bothered to read what happened in Hungary.

SARAH. Hungary?

RONNIE. Look at me, Mother. Talk to me. Take me by the hand and show me who was right and who was wrong. Point them out. Do it *for* me. I stand here and a thousand different voices are murdering my mind. Do you know, I couldn't wait to come home and accuse you.

SARAH. Accuse me?

RONNIE. You didn't tell me there were any doubts.

SARAH. What doubts? What are you talking about?

RONNIE. Everything has broken up around you and you can't see it.

SARAH (*shouting*). What, what, what, you mad boy? Explain what you mean.

RONNIE. What has happened to all the comrades, Sarah? I even blush when I use that word. Comrade! Why do I blush? Why do I feel ashamed to use words like democracy and freedom and brotherhood? They don't have meaning any more. I have nothing to write about any more. Remember all that writing I did? I was going to be a great socialist writer. I can't make sense of a word, a simple word. You look at me as if I'm talking in a foreign language. Didn't it hurt *you* to read about the murder of the Jewish Anti-Fascist Committee in the Soviet Union?

SARAH. You as well. Monty Blatt came up some months ago and said the same thing. He's also left the Party. He runs a greengrocer shop in Manchester.

RONNIE. And Dave and Ada in the Cotswolds, and Prince

working in a second-hand shop, and Uncle Hymie stuck smugly at home and Auntie Cissie once devoted — once involved — wandering from relative to relative. What's happened to us? Were we cheated or did we cheat ourselves? I just don't know, God in heaven, I just do not know! Can you understand what it is suddenly not to know? (*Collapses into armchair.*) And the terrifying thing is — I don't care either.

(*They sit in silence for some seconds.*)

SARAH. Drink your tea, darling.

(RONNIE *closes his eyes and talks.*)

RONNIE. Do you know what the trouble is, Mother? Can't you guess?

SARAH. You're tired, Ronnie.

RONNIE. You *do* know what the trouble is. You just won't admit it.

SARAH. In the morning you'll feel better.

RONNIE. Think hard. Look at my face. Look at my nose and my deep-set eyes; even my forehead is receding.

SARAH. Why don't you listen to me? Go to bed and —

RONNIE. Political institutions, society — they don't really affect people that much.

SARAH. Ronnie!

RONNIE. Who else was it who hated the jobs he had, who couldn't bear the discipline imposed by a daily routine, couldn't make sense of himself and gave up?

SARAH (*frightened*). Are you mad?

RONNIE. I've lost my faith and I've lost my ambition. Now I understand him perfectly. I wish I hadn't shouted at him as I used to.

SARAH. Mad boy!

RONNIE (*rising, opens his eyes and shouts*). You know that I'm right. *You've* never been right about anything. You wanted everybody to be happy but you wanted them to be

145

happy your way. It was strawberries and cream for everyone — whether they liked it or not. And now look what's
happened. The family you always wanted has disinte-
grated, and the great ideal you always cherished has
exploded in front of your eyes. But you won't face it. You
just refuse to face it. I don't know how you do it but you
do — you just do. (*Louder*) You're a pathological case,
Mother — do you know that? You're still a *communist!*
(*He wants to take back his words but he has lost the power to
express anything any more.*)

SARAH. All right! So I'm still a communist! Shoot me then!
I'm a communist! I've always been one — since the time
when all the world was a communist. You know that?
When you were a baby and there was unemployment and
everybody was thinking so — all the world was a communist. But it's different now. Now the people have forgotten. I sometimes think they're not worth fighting for
because they forget so easily. You give them a few
shillings in the bank and they can buy a television so they
think it's all over, there's nothing more to be got, they
don't have to think any more! Is that what you want? A
world where people don't think any more? Is that what
you want me to be satisfied with — a television set? Look
at him! My son! He wants to die!

RONNIE. Don't laugh at me, Sarah.

SARAH. You want me to cry again? We should all sit down
and cry?

RONNIE. I don't see things in black and white any more. My
thoughts keep going pop, like bubbles. That's my life now
— you know? — a lot of little bubbles going pop.

SARAH. And he calls me a pathological case! Pop! Pop, pop,
pop, pop — shmop! You think it doesn't hurt me — the
news about Hungary? You think I know what happened
and what didn't happen? Do any of us know? Who do I

146

know who to trust now — God, who are our friends now? But all my life I've fought. With your father and the rotten system that couldn't help him. All my life I worked with a party that meant glory and freedom and brotherhood. You want me to give it up now? You want me to move to Hendon and forget who I am? If the electrician who comes to mend my fuse blows it instead, so I should stop having electricity? I should cut off my light? Socialism is my light, can you understand that? A way of life. A man *can* be beautiful. I hate ugly people — I can't bear meanness and fighting and jealousy — I've got to have light. I'm a simple person, Ronnie, and I've got to have light and love.

(RONNIE *looks up at her meaningfully.*)

You think I didn't love your father enough, don't you? I'll tell you something. When Ada had diphtheria and I was pregnant I asked Daddy to carry her to the hospital. He wouldn't. We didn't have money because he didn't care to work and I didn't know what to do. He disappeared. It was Mrs Bernstein who saved her — you remember Mrs Bernstein? No, of course not, she died before you were born. It was Mrs Bernstein's soup. Ada still has that taste in her mouth — chicken soup with barley. She says it is a friendly taste — ask her. That saved her. Not even my brothers had money in those days, and a bit of dry crust with a cup of tea — ah! it was wonderful. But Daddy had the relief money. Someone told me they saw him eating salt-beef sandwiches in Bloom's. He didn't care. Maybe it was his illness *then* — who knows! He was never really a bad man. He never beat us or got drunk or gambled — he wasn't vulgar or coarse and he always had friends. So what was wrong? *I* could never understand him. All I did was fight him because he didn't care. Look at him now. He doesn't care to live. He's never cared to fully undress himself and put on pyjamas; never cared to keep shaved or washed; or be on time or even turn up! And now he walks around with his fly-buttons and his shoelaces undone because he still doesn't care to fight his illness — and the dirt gathers around him. He doesn't care! And so I fought him because he didn't care. I fought everybody who didn't care. All the authorities, the shopkeepers, even today — those stinking assistance officers — I could buy them with my little finger — even now I'm still fighting them. And you want to be like them, like your father? I'll fight you then.

RONNIE. And lose again.

SARAH. But your father was a weak man. Could you do any of the things he did?

RONNIE. I would not be surprised.

SARAH. Ronnie, your father would never have left his mother to go abroad as you did. I don't tell you all this now to pull you down but on the contrary — so you should know, so you should care. Learn from us, for God's sake learn from us. What does it matter if your father was a weakling, or the man you worked with was an imbecile. They're human beings.

RONNIE. That doesn't mean a thing.

SARAH. There will always be human beings and as long as there are there will always be the idea of brotherhood.

RONNIE. Doesn't mean a thing.

SARAH. Despite the human beings.

RONNIE. Not a thing.

SARAH. Despite them!

RONNIE. It doesn't mean ...

SARAH (*exasperated*). All right then! Nothing, then! It all comes down to nothing! People come and people go, wars destroy, accidents kill and plagues starve — it's all nothing, then! Philosophy? You want philosophy? Nothing means anything! There! Philosophy! I know! So? Nothing!

148

Despair — die then! Will that be achievement? To die? (*Softly*) You don't want to do that, Ronnie. So what if it all means nothing? When you know *that* you can start again. Please, Ronnie, don't let me finish this life thinking I lived for nothing. We got through, didn't we? We got scars but we got through. You hear me, Ronnie? (*She clasps him and moans.*) You've got to care, you've got to care or you'll die.

(RONNIE *unclasps her and moves away. He tries to say something — to explain. He raises his arms and some jumbled words come from his lips.*)

RONNIE. I — I can't, not now, it's too big, not yet — it's too big to care for it, I — I ...

(RONNIE *picks up his case and brokenly moves to his room mumbling:* 'Too big, Sarah — too big, too big.')

SARAH (*shouting after him*). You'll die, you'll die — if you don't care you'll die. (*He pauses at door.*) Ronnie, if you don't care you'll die. (*He turns slowly to face her.*)

CURTAIN

ENGLAND ARISE

AS MAN IS ONLY HUMAN

Roots

For
Dusty

CHARACTERS OF THE PLAY

BEATIE BRYANT, *a young woman aged twenty-two,*
a friend of Ronnie Kahn
JENNY BEALES, *her sister*
JIMMY BEALES, *her brother-in-law*
MRS BRYANT, *her mother*
MR BRYANT, *her father*
FRANKIE BRYANT, *her brother*
PEARL BRYANT, *her sister-in-law*
STAN MANN, *a neighbour of the Bealeses*
MR HEALEY, *a manager at the farm*

★

ACT I
An isolated cottage in Norfolk, the house of the Bealeses

ACT II
Scene 1: Two days later at the cottage of Mr and Mrs Bryant,
in the kitchen
Scene 2: The same a couple of hours later

ACT III
Two weeks later in the front room of the Bryants'

★

Time: The present

First presented at the Belgrade Theatre, Coventry, on
25th May 1959

153

This is a play about Norfolk people; it could be a play about any country people and the moral could certainly extend to the metropolis. But as it is about Norfolk people it is important that some attempt is made to find out how they talk. A very definite accent and intonation exists and personal experience suggests that this is not difficult to know. The following may be of great help:

When the word 'won't' is used, the 'w' is left out. It sounds the same but the 'w' is lost.

Double 'ee' is pronounced 'i' as in 'it' — so that 'been' becomes 'bin', 'seen' becomes 'sin', etc.

'Have' and 'had' become 'hev' and 'hed' as in 'head'.

'Ing' loses the 'g' so that it becomes 'in'.

'Bor' is a common handle and is a contraction of neighbour.

Instead of the word 'of' they say 'on', e.g. 'I've hed enough on it' or 'What do you think on it?'

Their 'yes' is used all the time and sounds like 'year' with a 'p' — 'yearp'.

'Blast' is also common usage and is pronounced 'blust', a short sharp sound as in 'gust'.

The cockney 'ain't' becomes 'ent' — also short and sharp.

The 't' in 'what' and 'that' is left out to give 'thaas' and 'whaas', e.g. 'Whaas matter then?'

Other idiosyncrasies are indicated in the play itself.

ACT ONE

A rather ramshackle house in Norfolk where there is no water laid on, nor electricity, nor gas. Everything rambles and the furniture is cheap and old. If it is untidy it is because there is a child in the house and there are few amenities, so that the mother is too overworked to take much care.

An assortment of clobber lies around: papers and washing, coats and basins, a tin wash-tub with shirts and underwear to be cleaned, tilly lamps and primus stoves. Washing hangs on a line in the room. It is September.

JENNY BEALES is by the sink washing up. She is singing a recent pop song. She is short, fat and friendly, and wears glasses. A child's voice is heard from the bedroom crying 'Sweet, Mamma, sweet.'

JENNY (*good-naturedly*). Shut you up Daphne and get you to sleep now. (*Moves to get a dishcloth.*)

CHILD'S VOICE. Daphy wan' sweet, sweet, sweet.

JENNY (*going to cupboard to get sweet*). My word child, Father come home and find you awake he'll be after you. (*Disappears to bedroom with sweet.*) There — now sleep, gal, don't wan' you grumpy wi' me in mornin'.

(*Enter JIMMY BEALES. Also short, chubby, blond though hardly any hair left, ruddy complexion. He is a garage mechanic. Wears blue dungarees and an army pack slung over his shoulder. He wheels his bike in and lays it by the wall. Seems to be in some sort of pain — around his back. JENNY returns.*)

Waas matter wi' you then?

JIMMY. I don' know gal. There's a pain in my guts and one a'tween my shoulder blades I can hardly stand up.

JENNY. Sit you down then an' I'll git you your supper on the table.

JIMMY. Blust gal! I can't eat yit.

155

(JIMMY *picks up a pillow from somewhere and lies down on the sofa holding pillow to stomach.* JENNY *watches him a while.*)

JENNY. Don't you know what 'tis yit?

JIMMY. Well, how should *I* know what 'tis.

JENNY. I told Mother about the pain and she says it's indigestion.

JIMMY. What the hell's indigestion doin' a'tween my shoulder blades then?

JENNY. She say some people get indigestion so bad it go right through their stomach to the back.

JIMMY. Don't be daft.

JENNY. That's what I say. Blust Mother, I say, you don't git indigestion in the back. Don't you tell me, she say, I hed it!

JIMMY. What hevn't she hed.

(JENNY *returns to washing up while* JIMMY *struggles a while on the sofa.* JENNY *hums. No word. Then —*)

JENNY. Who d'you see today?

JIMMY. Only Doctor Gallagher.

JENNY (*wheeling round*). You see who?

JIMMY. Gallagher. His wife driv him up in the ole Armstrong.

JENNY. Well I go t'hell if that ent a rum thing.

JIMMY (*rising and going to table; pain has eased*). What's that then?

JENNY (*moving to get him supper from oven*). We was down at the whist drive in the village and that Judy Maitland say he were dead. 'Cos you know he've hed a cancer this last year and they don't give him no longer'n three weeks don't you?

JIMMY. Ole crows. They don' wan' nothin' less than a death to wake them up.

JENNY. No. No longer'n three weeks.

GIRL'S VOICE (*off*). Yoo-hoo! Yoo-hoo!

JIMMY. There's your sister.

JENNY. That's her.

GIRL'S VOICE (*off*). Yoo-hoo! Anyone home?

JENNY (*calling*). Come you on in gal, don't you worry about yoo-hoo.

(*Enter* BEATIE BRYANT, *an ample, blonde, healthy-faced young woman of twenty-two years. She is carrying a case.*)

JIMMY. Here she is.

JENNY (*with reserve, but pleased*). Hello, Beatrice — how are you?

BEATIE (*with reserve, but pleased*). Hello, Jenny — how are you? What's that lovely smell I smell?

JENNY. Onions for supper and bread for the harvest festival.

BEATIE. Watcha Jimmy Beales, how you doin' bor?

JIMMY. Not so bad gal, how's yourself?

BEATIE. All right you know. When you comin' to London again for a football match?

JIMMY. O blust gal, I don' wanna go to any more o' those things. Ole father Bryant was there in the middle of that crowd and he turn around an' he say (*imitating*), Stop you a-pushin' there, he say, stop you a-pushin'.

JENNY. Where's Ronnie?

BEATIE. He's comin' down at the end of two weeks.

JIMMY. Ent you married yit?

BEATIE. No.

JIMMY. You wanna hurry then gal, a long engagement don't do the ole legs any good.

JENNY. Now shut you up Jimmy Beales and get that food down you. Every time you talk, look, you miss a mouthful! That's why you complain of pain in your shoulder blades.

BEATIE. You bin hevin' pains then Jimmy?

JIMMY. Blust yes! Right a'tween my shoulder blades.

JENNY. Mother says it's indigestion.

BEATIE. What the hell's indigestion doin' a'tween his shoulder blades?

JENNY. Mother reckon some people get indigestion so bad it go right through their stomach to the back.

BEATIE. Don't talk daft!

JENNY. That's what I say. Blust Mother, I say, you don' git indigestion in the back. Don't you tell me, she say, I hed it!

BEATIE. What hevn't she hed. How is she?

JENNY. Still the same you know. How long you staying this time?

BEATIE. Two days here — two weeks at home.

JENNY. Hungry gal?

BEATIE. Watcha got?

JENNY. Watcha see.

BEATIE. Liver? I'll hev it!

(BEATIE *makes herself at home. Near by is a pile of comics. She picks one up and reads.*)

JENNY. We got some ice-cream after.

BEATIE (*absorbed*). Yearp.

JENNY. Look at her. No sooner she's in than she's at them ole comics. You still read them ole things?

JIMMY. She don't change much do she?

BEATIE. Funny that! Soon ever I'm home again I'm like I always was — it don' even seem I bin away. I do the same lazy things an' I talk the same. Funny that!

JENNY. What do Ronnie say to it?

BEATIE. He don't mind. He don't even know though. He ent never bin here. Not in the three years I known him. But I'll tell you (*she jumps up and moves around as she talks*) I used to read the comics he bought for his nephews and he used to get riled —

(*Now* BEATIE *begins to quote Ronnie, and when she does she imitates him so well in both manner and intonation that in fact as the play progresses we see a picture of him through her.*)

'Christ, woman, what can they give you that you can *be* so absorbed?' So you know what I used to do? I used to get

158

a copy of the *Manchester Guardian* and sit with that wide open — and a comic behind!

JIMMY. *Manchester Guardian?* Blimey Joe — he don' believe in hevin' much fun then?

BEATIE. That's what I used to tell him. 'Fun?' he say, 'fun? Playing an instrument is fun, painting is fun, reading a book is fun, talking with friends is fun — but a comic? A comic? for a young woman of twenty-two?'

JENNY (*handing out meal and sitting down herself*). He sound a queer bor to me. Sit you down and eat gal.

BEATIE (*enthusiastically*). He's alive though.

JIMMY. Alive? Alive you say? What's alive about someone who can't read a comic? What's alive about a person that reads books and looks at paintings and listens to classical music?

(*There is a silence at this, as though the question answers itself — reluctantly.*)

JIMMY. Well, it's all right for some I suppose.

BEATIE. And then he'd sneak the comic away from me and read it his-self!

JENNY. Oh, he didn't really mind then?

BEATIE. No — 'cos sometimes I read books as well. 'There's nothing wrong with comics,' he'd cry — he stand up on a chair when he want to preach but don't wanna sound too dramatic.

JIMMY. Eh?

BEATIE. Like this, look. (*Stands on a chair.*) 'There's nothing wrong with comics only there's something wrong with comics all the time. There's nothing wrong with football, only there's something wrong with *only* football. There's nothing wrong with rock 'n' rolling, only God preserve me from the girl that can do nothing else!' (*She sits down and then stands up again, remembering something else.*) Oh yes, 'and there's nothing wrong with talking about the

weather, only don't talk to me about it!' (*Sits down.*)
(JIMMY *and* JENNY *look at each other as though she, and no
doubt Ronnie, is a little barmy.* JIMMY *rises and begins to
strap on boots and gaiters ready for going out to an
allotment.*)

JENNY. He never really row with you then?

BEATIE. We used to. There was a time when he handled all
official things for me you know. Once I was in between
jobs and I didn't think to ask for my unemployment
benefit. *He* told me to. But when I asked they told me I
was short on stamps and so I wasn't entitled to benefit. *I*
didn't know what to say but he did. He went up and argued
for me — he's just like his mother, she argues with everyone — and I got it. I didn't know how to talk see, it was all
foreign to me. Think of it! An English girl born and bred
and I couldn't talk the language — except for to buy food
and clothes. And so sometimes when he were in a black
mood he'd start on me. 'What can you talk of?' he'd ask.
'Go on, pick a subject. Talk. Use the language. Do you
know what language is?' Well, I'd never thought before —
hev you? — it's automatic to you isn't it, like walking?
'Well, language is words,' he'd say, as though he were
telling me a secret. 'It's bridges, so that you can get safely
from one place to another. And the more bridges you
know about the more places you can see!' (*To* JIMMY)
And do *you* know what happens when you can see a place
but you don't know where the bridge is?

JIMMY (*angrily*). Blust gal, what the hell are you on about.

BEATIE. Exactly! You see, you hev a row! Still, rows is all
right. I like a row. So then he'd say: 'Bridges! bridges!
bridges! Use your bridges woman. It took thousands of
years to build them, use them!' And that riled me. 'Blust
your bridges,' I'd say. 'Blust you and your bridges — I
want a row.' Then he'd grin at me. 'You want a row?' he'd

160

ask. 'No bridges this time?' 'No bridges,' I'd say — and
we'd row. Sometimes he hurt me but then, slowly, he'd
build the bridge up *for* me — and then we'd make love!
(*Innocently continues her meal.*)

JENNY. You'd what, did you say?

BEATIE. Make love. Love in the afternoon gal. Ever had it?
It's the only time *for* it. Go out or entertain in the evenings;
sleep at night, study, work and chores in the mornings;
but love — alert and fresh, when you got most energy —
love in the afternoon.

JIMMY. I suppose you take time off from work every afternoon
to do it?

BEATIE. I'm talking about week-ends and holidays — daft.

JENNY. Oh, Beatie, go on wi' you!

BEATIE. Well, go t'hell Jenny Beales, you're blushin'. Ent you
never had love in the afternoon? Ask Jimmy then.

JENNY (*rising to get sweet*). Shut you up gal and get on wi' your
ice-cream. It's strawberry flavour. Want some more
James?

JIMMY (*taking it in the middle of lacing up boots*). Yes please,
vanilla please. (*Eating*) Good cream ent it? Made from the
white milk of a Jersey cow.

BEATIE. This is good too — made from pink milk ent it?
(*Pause.*)

JIMMY. Yearp! (*Pause.*) Come from a pink cow!
(*Pause. They are all enjoying the cream.*)

JENNY (*eating*). You remember Dickie Smart, Beatie?

BEATIE (*eating*). Who?

JENNY (*eating*). We had a drink wi' him in the Storks when
you was down last.

BEATIE (*eating*). Yearp.

JENNY (*eating*). Well, he got gored by a bull last Thursday.
His left ear was nearly off, his knee were gored, his ribs
bruised, and the ligaments of his legs torn.

161

(*Pause as they finish eating.*)

BEATIE (*euphemistically*). He had a rough time then!

JENNY. Yearp. (*To* JIMMY) You off now?

JIMMY. Mm.

(JENNY *collects dishes.*)

BEATIE. Still got your allotment Jimmy?

JIMMY. Yearp.

BEATIE. Bit heavy going this weather.

JIMMY. That ent too bad just yit — few more weeks an' the old mowld'll cling.

BEATIE. Watcha got this year?

JIMMY. Had spuds, carrots, cabbages you know. Beetroot, lettuces, onions, and peas. But me runners let me down this year though.

JENNY. I don't go much on them old things.

BEATIE. You got a fair owle turn then?

JIMMY. Yearp.

(JIMMY *starts to sharpen a reap hook.*)

BEATIE (*jumping up*). I'll help you wash.

JENNY. That's all right gal.

BEATIE. Where's the cloth?

JENNY. Here 'tis.

(BEATIE *helps collect dishes from table and proceeds to help wash up. This is a silence that needs organizing. Throughout the play there is no sign of intense living from any of the characters —* BEATIE's *bursts are the exception. They continue in a routine rural manner. The day comes, one sleeps at night, there is always the winter, the spring, the autumn, and the summer — little amazes them. They talk in fits and starts mainly as a sort of gossip, and they talk quickly too, enacting as though for an audience what they say. Their sense of humour is keen and dry. They show no affection for each other — though this does not mean they would not be upset were one of them to die. The silences are*

162

important — as important as the way they speak, if we are to know them.)

JENNY. What about that strike in London? Waas London like wi'out the buses?

BEATIE. Lovely! No noise — and the streets, you should see the streets, flowing with people — the city looks human.

JIMMY. They wanna call us Territorials out — we'd soon break the strike.

BEATIE. That's a soft thing for a worker to say for his mates.

JIMMY. Soft be buggered, soft you say? What they earnin' those busmen, what they earnin'? And what's the farm worker's wage? Do you know it gal?

BEATIE. Well, let the farm workers go on strike too then! It don't help a farm labourer if a busman don't go on strike do it now?

JENNY. You know they've got a rise though. Father Bryant's go up by six and six a week as a pigman, and Frank goes up seven 'n' six a week for driving a tractor.

JIMMY. But you watch the Hall sack some on 'em.

JENNY. Thaas true Beatie. They're such sods, honest to God they are. Every time there's bin a rise someone get sacked. Without fail. You watch it — you ask father Bryant when you get home, ask him who's bin sacked since the rise.

BEATIE. One person they 'ont sack is him though. They 'ont find many men 'd tend to pigs seven days a week and stay up the hours he do.

JENNY. Bloody fool! (*Pause.*) Did Jimmy tell you he've bin chosen for the Territorials' Jubilee in London this year?

BEATIE. What's this then? What'll you do there?

JIMMY. Demonstrate and parade wi' arms and such like.

BEATIE. Won't do you any good.

JIMMY. Don't you reckon? Gotta show we can defend the country you know. Demonstrate arms and you prevent war.

BEATIE (*she has finished wiping up*). Won't demonstrate any-thing bor. (*Goes to undo her case.*) Present for the house! Have a hydrogen bomb fall on you and you'll find them things silly in your hands. (*Searches for other parcels.*)

JIMMY. So you say gal? So you say? That'll frighten them other buggers though.

BEATIE. Frighten yourself y'mean. (*Finds parcels.*) Presents for the kid.

JIMMY. And what do you know about this all of a sudden?

JENNY (*revealing a tablecloth*). Thank you very much Beatie. Just what I need.

BEATIE. You're not interested in defending your country Jimmy, you just enjoy playing soldiers.

JIMMY. What did I do in the last war then — *sing* in the trenches?

BEATIE (*explaining — not trying to get one over on him*). Ever heard of Chaucer, Jimmy?

JIMMY. No.

BEATIE. Do you know the M.P. for this constituency?

JIMMY. What you drivin' at gal — don't give me no riddles.

BEATIE. Do you know how the British Trade Union Move-ment started? And do you believe in strike action?

JIMMY. No to both those.

BEATIE. What you goin' to war to defend then?

JIMMY (*he is annoyed now*). Beatie — you bin away from us a long time now — you got a boy who's educated an' that and he's taught you a lot maybe. But don't you come pushin' ideas across at us — we're all right as we are. You can come when you like an' welcome but don't bring no discussion of politics in the house wi' you 'cos that'll only cause trouble. I'm telling you. (*He goes off.*)

JENNY. Blust gal, if you hevn't touched him on a sore spot. He live for them Territorials he do — that's half his life.

BEATIE (*she is upset now*). What's he afraid of talking for?

JENNY. He ent afraid of talking Beatie — blust he can do that, gal.

BEATIE. But not talk, not really talk, not use bridges. I sit with Ronnie and his friends sometimes and I listen to them talk about things and you know I've never heard half of the words before.

JENNY. Don't he tell you what they mean?

BEATIE. I get annoyed when he keep tellin' me — and he want me to ask. (*Imitates him half-heartedly now*). 'Always ask, people love to tell you what they know, always ask and people will respect you.'

JENNY. And do you?

BEATIE. No! I don't! An' you know why? Because I'm stubborn, I'm like Mother, I'm stubborn. Somehow I just can't bring myself to ask, and you know what? I go mad when I listen to them. As soon as they start to talk about things I don't know about or I can't understand I get mad. They sit there, casually talking, and suddenly they turn on you, abrupt. 'Don't you think?' they say. Like at school, pick on you and ask a question you ent ready for. Sometimes I don't say anything, sometimes I go to bed or leave the room. Like Jimmy — just like Jimmy.

JENNY. And what do Ronnie say to that then?

BEATIE. He get mad too. 'Why don't you ask me woman, for God's sake why don't you ask me? Aren't I dying to tell you about things? Only ask!'

JENNY. And he's goin' to marry you?

BEATIE. Why not?

JENNY. Well I'm sorry gal, you mustn't mind me saying this, but it don't seem to me like you two got much in common.

BEATIE (*loudly*). It's not true! We're in love!

JENNY. Well, you know.

BEATIE (*softly*). No, I don't know. I won't know till he come here. From the first day I went to work as waitress in the

165

Dell Hotel and saw him working in the kitchen I fell in love — and I thought it was easy. I thought everything was easy. I chased him for three months with compliments and presents until I finally give myself to him. He never said he love me nor I didn't care but once he had taken me he seemed to think he was responsible for me and I told him no different. I'd *make* him love me I thought. I didn't know much about him except he was different and used to write most of the time. And then he went back to London and I followed him there. I've never moved far from home but I did for him and he felt all the time he couldn't leave me and I didn't tell him no different. And then I got to know more about him. He was interested in all the things I never even thought about. About politics and art and all that, and he tried to teach me. He's a socialist and he used to say you couldn't bring socialism to a country by making speeches, but perhaps you could pass it on to someone who was near you. So I pretended I was interested — but I didn't understand much. All the time he's trying to teach me but I can't take it Jenny. And yet, at the same time, I want to show I'm willing. I'm not used to learning. Learning was at school and that's finished with.

JENNY. Blust gal, you don't seem like you're going to be happy then. Like I said.

BEATIE. But I love him.

JENNY. Then you're not right in the head then.

BEATIE. I couldn't have any other life now.

JENNY. Well, I don't know and that's a fact.

BEATIE (*playfully mocking her*). Well I don't know and that's a fact! (*Suddenly*) Come on gal, I'll teach you how to bake some pastries.

JENNY. Pastries?

BEATIE. Ronnie taught me.

JENNY. Oh, you learnt that much then?

BEATIE. But he don't know. I always got annoyed when he tried to teach me to cook as well — Christ! I had to know something — but it sank in all the same.

(*By this time it has become quite dark and* JENNY *proceeds to light a tilly lamp.*)

JENNY. You didn't make it easy then?

BEATIE. Oh don't you worry gal, it'll be all right once we're married. Once we're married and I got babies I won't need to be interested in half the things I got to be interested in now.

JENNY. No you won't will you! Don't need no education for babies.

BEATIE. Nope. Babies is babies — you just have 'em.

JENNY. Little sods!

BEATIE. You gonna hev another Jenny?

JENNY. Well, course I am. What you on about? Think Jimmy don't want none of his own?

BEATIE. He's a good man Jenny.

JENNY. Yearp.

BEATIE. Not many men 'd marry you after you had a baby.

JENNY. No.

BEATIE. He didn't ask you any questions? Who was the father? Nor nothing?

JENNY. No.

BEATIE. You hevn't told no one hev you Jenny?

JENNY. No, that I hevn't.

BEATIE. Well, that's it gal, don't you tell me then!

(*By this time the methylated spirit torch has burned out and* JENNY *has finished pumping the tilly lamp and we are in brightness.*)

JENNY (*severely*). Now Beatie, stop it. Every time you come home you ask me that question and I hed enough. It's finished with and over. No one don't say nothing and no one know. You hear me?

BEATIE. Are you in love with Jimmy?

JENNY. Love? I don't believe in any of that squit — we just got married, an' that's that.

BEATIE (*suddenly looking around the room at the general chaos*). Jenny Beales, just look at this house. Look at it!

JENNY. I'm looking. What's wrong?

BEATIE. Let's clean it up.

JENNY. Clean what up?

BEATIE. Are you going to live in this house all your life?

JENNY. You gonna buy us another?

BEATIE. Stuck out here in the wilds with only ole Stan Mann and his missus as a neighbour and sand pits all around. Every time it rain look you're stranded.

JENNY. Jimmy don't earn enough for much more 'n we got.

BEATIE. But it's so untidy.

JENNY. You don' wan' me bein' like sister Susan do you? 'Cos you know how clean she is don' you — she's so bloody fussy she's gotten to polishing the brass overflow pipe what leads out from the lavatory.

BEATIE. Come on gal, let's make some order anyway — I love tidying up.

JENNY. What about the pastries? Pastries? Oh my sainted aunt, the bread! (*Dashes to the oven and brings out a most beautiful-looking plaited loaf of bread. Admiring it.*) Well, no one wanna complain after that. Isn't that beautiful Beatie?

BEATIE. I could eat it now.

JENNY. You hungry again?

BEATIE (*making an attack upon the clothes that are lying around*). I'm always hungry again. Ronnie say I eat more 'n I need. 'If you get fat woman I'll leave you — without even a discussion!'

JENNY (*placing bread on large oval plate to put away*). Well, there ent nothin' wrong in bein' fat.

BEATIE. You ent got no choice gal. (*Seeing bike*) A bike!

What's a bike doin' in a livin' room — I'm putting it outside.

JENNY. Jimmy 'ont know where it is.

BEATIE. Don't be daft, you can't miss a bike. (*Wheels it outside and calls from there.*) Jenny! Start puttin' the clothes away.

JENNY. Blust gal, I ent got nowhere to put them.

BEATIE (*from outside*). You got drawers — you got cupboards.

JENNY. They're full already.

BEATIE (*entering — energy sparks from her*). Come here — let's look. (*Looks.*) Oh, go away — you got enough room for ten families. You just bung it all in with no order, that's why. Here — help me.

(*They drag out all manner of clothes from the cupboard and begin to fold them up.*)

BEATIE. How's my Frankie and Pearl?

JENNY. They're all right. You know she and Mother don't talk to each other?

BEATIE. What, again? Who's fault is it this time?

JENNY. Well, Mother she say it's Pearl's fault and Pearl she say it's Mother.

BEATIE. Well, they wanna get together quick and find whose fault it is 'cos I'm going to call the whole family together for tea to meet Ronnie.

JENNY. Well, Susan and Mother don't talk neither so you got a lot of peace-making to do.

BEATIE. Well go t'hell, what's broken them two up?

JENNY. Susan hev never bin struck on her mother, you know that don't you — well, it seems that Susan bought something off the club from Pearl and Pearl give it to Mother and Mother sent it to Susan through the fishmonger what live next door her in the council houses. And of course Susan were riled 'cos she didn't want her neighbours to know that she bought anything off the club. So they don't speak.

BEATIE. Kids! It make me mad.

JENNY. And you know what 'tis with Pearl don't you — it's 'cos Mother hev never thought she was good enough for her son Frankie.

BEATIE. No more she wasn't neither!

JENNY. What's wrong wi' her then? I get on all right.

BEATIE. Nothing's wrong wi' her, she just wasn't good enough for our Frankie, that's all.

JENNY. Who's being small-minded now?

BEATIE. Always wantin' more'n he can give her.

JENNY. An' I know someone else who always wanted more'n she got.

BEATIE (sulkily). It's not the same thing.

JENNY. Oh yes 'tis.

BEATIE. 'Tent.

JENNY. 'Tis my gal. (Mimicking the child BEATIE) I wan' a 'nana, a 'nana, a 'nana. Frankie's got my 'nana, 'nana, 'nana.

BEATIE. Well, I liked bananas.

JENNY. You liked anything you could get your hands on and Mother used to give in to you 'cos you were the youngest. Me and Susan and Frankie never got nothing 'cos o' you — 'cept a clout round the ear.

BEATIE. 'Tent so likely. You got everything and I got nothing.

JENNY. All we got was what we pinched out the larder and then you used to go and tell tales to Mother.

BEATIE. I never did.

JENNY. Oh, didn't you my gal? Many's the time I'd've willingly strangled you — with no prayers — there you are, no prayers whatsoever. Strangled you till you was dead.

BEATIE. Oh go on wi' you Jenny Beales.

(By now they have finished folding the clothes and have put away most of the laundry and garments that have till this moment cluttered up the room. BEATIE says 'There,' stands

170

up and looks around, finds some coats sprawled helter-skelter, and hangs them up behind the door.)

BEATIE. I'll buy you some coat hangers.

JENNY. You get me a couple o' coats to hang on 'em first please.

BEATIE (*looking around*). What next. Bottles, jars, nicknacks, saucepans, cups, papers — everything anywhere. Look at it! Come on!

(BEATIE *attempts to get these things either into their proper places or out of sight.*)

JENNY. You hit this place like a bloody whirlwind you do, like a bloody whirlwind. Jimmy'll think he've come into the wrong house and I shan't be able to find a thing.

BEATIE. Here, grab a broom. (*She is now gurgling with sort of animal noises signifying excitement. Her joy is childlike.*) How's Poppy?

JENNY. Tight as ever.

BEATIE. What won't he give you now?

JENNY. 'Tent nothing wi' me gal. Nothing he do don't affect me. It's Mother I'm referring to.

BEATIE. Don't he still give her much money?

JENNY. Money? She hev to struggle and skint all the time — *all* the time. Well it ent never bin no different from when we was kids hev it?

BEATIE. No.

JENNY. I tell you what. It wouldn't surprise me if Mother were in debt all the time, that it wouldn't. No. It wouldn't surprise me at all.

BEATIE. Oh, never.

JENNY. Well, what do you say that for Beatie — do you know how much he allow her a week look?

BEATIE. Six pounds?

JENNY. Six pound be buggered. Four pounds ten! An' she hev to keep house *an'* buy her own clothes out of that.

BEATIE. Still, there's only two on 'em.

JENNY. You try keepin' two people in food for four pound ten. She pay seven an' six a week into Pearl's club for clothes, two and six she hev on the pools, and a shilling a week on the Labour Tote. (*Suddenly*) Blust! I forgot to say. Pearl won the Tote last week.

BEATIE. A hundred pounds?

JENNY. A hundred pounds! An' ole Mrs Dyson what used to live Startson way, she come up second wi' five pounds and seventy.

BEATIE. Well no one wrote me about it.

JENNY. 'Cos you never wrote no one else.

BEATIE. What she gonna do wi' it — buy a TV?

JENNY. TV? Blust no. You know she hevn't got electricity in that house. No, she say she's gonna get some clothes for the kids.

> (*There is a sound now of a drunk old man approaching, and alongside of it the voice of* JIMMY. *The drunk is singing:* 'I come from Bungay Town, I calls I Bungay Johnnie.')
> Well I go t'hell if that ent Stan Mann drunk again. And is that Jimmy wi' him? (*Listens.*)

BEATIE. But I thought Stan Mann was paralysed.

JENNY. That don't stop him getting paralytic drunk. (*Listens again.*) That's Jimmy taking him into the house I bet. A fortune that man hev drunk away — a whole bleedin' fortune. Remember the fleet of cars he used to run and all that land he owned, and all them cattle he had and them fowl? Well, he've only got a few acres left and a few ole chickens. He drink it all away. Two strokes he've had from drinking and now he's paralysed down one side. But that don't stop him getting drunk — no it don't.

> (JIMMY *enters and throws his jacket on the couch, takes off his boots and gaiters, and smiles meanwhile.*)

JIMMY. Silly ole bugger.

JENNY. I was just telling Beatie how he've drunk a fortune away hevn't he?

JIMMY. He wanna drink a little more often and he'll be finished for good.

JENNY. Didn't he hev all them cows and cars and land Jimmy? And didn't he drink it all away bit by bit?

JIMMY. Silly ole sod don't know when to stop.

JENNY. I wished I had half the money he drink.

JIMMY. He messed his pants.

JENNY. He what? Well where was this then?

JIMMY. By the allotment.

JENNY. Well, what did *you* do then?

JIMMY. He come up to me — 'course I knowed he were drunk the way he walk — he come up to me an' he say, "Evenin' Jimmy Beales, thaas a fine turnover you got there.' An' I say, 'Yearp 'tis.' An' then he bend down to pick a carrot from the ground an' then he cry, 'Oops, I done it again!' An' 'course, soon ever he say 'done it again' I knowed what'd happened. So I took his trousers down and ran the ole hose over him.

BEATIE. Oh, Jimmy, you never did.

JIMMY. I did gal. I put the ole hose over him and brought him home along the fields with an ole sack around his waist.

BEATIE. He'll catch his death.

JIMMY. Never — he's strong as an ox.

JENNY. What'd you do with his trousers and things?

JIMMY. Put it on the compost heap — good for the land!

(*Now* STAN MANN *enters. He's not all that drunk. The cold water has sobered him a little. He is old — about seventy-five — and despite his slight stoop one can see he was a very strong upright man He probably looks like everyman's idea of a farmer — except that he wears no socks or boots at this moment and he hobbles on a stick.*)

STAN. Sorry about that ole son.

173

JIMMY. Don't you go worrying about that my manny — get you along to bed.

JENNY. Get some shoes on you too Stan, or you'll die of cold *and* booze.

STAN (*screwing up his eyes across the room*). Is that you Jenny? Hello ole gal. How are you?

JENNY. It's you you wanna worry about now ole matey. I'm well enough.

STAN (*screwing his eyes still more*). Who's that next to you?

JENNY. Don't you recognize her? It's our Beatie, Stan.

STAN. Is that you Beatie? Well blust gal, you gotten fatter since I seen you last. You gonna be fat as Jenny here? Come on over an' let's look at you.

BEATIE (*approaching*). Hello Stan Mann, how are you?

STAN (*looking her up and down*). Well enough gal, well enough. You married yit?

BEATIE. No.

STAN. You bin courtin' three years. Why ent you married yit?

BEATIE (*slightly embarrassed*). We ent sure yit.

STAN. You ent sure you say? What ent you sure of? You know how to do it don't you?

JENNY. Go on wi' you to bed Stan Mann.

STAN. Tell your boy he don't wanna waste too much time or I'll be hevin' yer myself for breakfast — on a plate.

JENNY. Stan Mann, I'm sendin' you to your bed — go on now, off wi' you, you can see Beatie in the mornin'.

STAN (*as he is ushered out — to* BEATIE). She's fat ent she? I'm not sayin' she won't do mind, but she's fat. (*As he goes out*) All right ole sweetheart, I'm goin'. I'm just right for bed. Did you see the new bridge they're building? It's a rum ole thing isn't it ... (*out of sound*)

JIMMY. Well, I'm ready for bed.

BEATIE. I can't bear sick men. They smell.

JIMMY. Ole Stan's all right — do anythin' for you.

174

BEATIE. I couldn't look after one you know.

JIMMY. Case of hevin' to sometimes.

BEATIE. Ronnie's father's paralysed like that. I can't touch him.

JIMMY. Who see to him then?

BEATIE. His mother. She wash him, change him, feed him. Ronnie help sometimes. I couldn't though. Ronnie say, 'Christ, woman, I hope you aren't around when I'm ill.' (*Shudders.*) Ole age terrify me.

JIMMY. Where you sleepin' tonight gal?

BEATIE. On the couch in the front room I suppose.

JIMMY. You comfortable sleepin' on that ole thing? You wanna sleep with Jenny while you're here?

BEATIE. No thanks, Jimmy. (*She is quite subdued now.*) I'm all right on there.

JIMMY. Right, then I'm off. (*Looking around*) Where's the *Evening News* I brought in?

JENNY (*entering*). You off to bed?

JIMMY. Yearp. Reckon I've had 'nough of this ole day. Where's my *News?*

JENNY. Where d'you put it Beatie?

JIMMY (*suddenly seeing the room*). Blust, you movin' out?

BEATIE. Here you are Jimmy Beales. (*Hands him paper.*) It's all tidy now.

JIMMY. So I see. Won't last long though will it? 'Night. (*Goes to bed.*)

JENNY. Well I'm ready for my bed too — how about you Beatie?

BEATIE. Yearp.

JENNY (*taking a candle in a stick and lighting it*). Here, take this with you. Your bed's made. Want a drink before you turn in?

BEATIE. No thanks gal.

JENNY (*picking up tilly lamp and making towards one door*). Right then. Sleep well gal.

175

BEATIE (*going to other door with candle*). Good night Jenny. (*She pauses at her door. Loud whispers from now on.*) Hey Jenny.

JENNY. What is it?

BEATIE. I'll bake you some pastries when I get to Mother's.

JENNY. Father won't let you use his electricity for me, don't talk daft.

BEATIE. I'll get Mother on to him. It'll be all right. Your ole ovens weren't big 'nough anyways. Good night.

JENNY. Good night.

BEATIE (*an afterthought*). Hey Jenny.

JENNY. What now?

BEATIE. Did I tell you I took up painting?

JENNY. Painting?

BEATIE. Yes — on cardboard and canvases with brushes.

JENNY. What kind of painting?

BEATIE. Abstract painting — designs and patterns and such like. I can't do nothing else. I sent two on 'em home. Show you when you come round — if Mother hevn't thrown them out.

JENNY. You're an artist then?

BEATIE. Yes. Good night.

JENNY. Good night.

(*They enter their bedrooms, leaving the room in darkness.*[1] *Perhaps we see only the faint glow of moonlight from outside, and then*)

THE CURTAIN FALLS

[1] It might be better for Jenny to have previously made up Beatie's bed in the couch on the set. Then Beatie would not have to leave the stage at all.

ACT TWO

Scene 1

Two days have passed. BEATIE *will arrive at her own home, the home of her parents. This is a tied cottage on a main road between two large villages. It is neat and ordinary inside. We can see a large kitchen — where most of the living is done — and attached to it is a large larder; also part of the front room and a piece of the garden where some washing is hanging.*

MRS BRYANT *is a short, stout woman of fifty. She spends most of the day on her own, and consequently when she has a chance to speak to anybody she says as much as she can as fast as she can. The only people she sees are the tradesmen, her husband, the family when they pop in occasionally. She speaks very loudly all the time so that her friendliest tone sounds aggressive, and she manages to dramatize the smallest piece of gossip into something significant. Each piece of gossip is a little act done with little looking at the person to whom it is addressed. At the moment she is at the door leading to the garden, looking for the cat.*

MRS BRYANT. Cossie, Cossie, Cossie, Cossie, Cossie, Cossie! Here Cossie! Food Cossie! Cossie, Cossie, Cossie! Blust you cat, where the hell are you. Oh hell on you then, I ent wastin' my time wi' you now.

(*She returns to the kitchen and thence the larder, from which she emerges with some potatoes. These she starts peeling. STAN MANN appears round the back door. He has a handkerchief to his nose and is blowing vigorously, as vigorously as his paralysis will allow. MRS BRYANT looks up, but continues her peeling.*)

STAN. Rum thing to git a cold in summer, what you say Daphne?

MRS BRYANT. What'd you have me say my manny. Sit you down bor and rest a bit. Shouldn't wear such daf' clothes.

177

STAN. Daf' clothes? Blust woman! I got on half a cow's hide,
what you sayin'! Where's the gal?

MRS BRYANT. Beatie? She 'ent come yit. Didn't *you* see her?

STAN. Hell, I was up too early for her. She always stay the
week-end wi' Jenny 'fore comin' home?

MRS BRYANT. Most times.

(STAN *sneezes.*)

What you doin' up this way wi' a cold like that then? Get
you home to bed.

STAN. Just come this way to look at the vicarage. Stuff's
comin' up for sale soon.

MRS BRYANT. You still visit them things then?

STAN. Yearp. Pass the ole time away. Pass the ole time.

MRS BRYANT. Time drag heavy then?

STAN. Yearp. Time drag heavy. She do that. Time drag so
slow, I get to thinkin' it's Monday when it's still Sunday.
Still, I had my day gal I say. Yearp. I had that all right.

MRS BRYANT. Yearp. You had that an' a bit more ole son. I
shant grumble if I last as long as you.

STAN. Yearp. I hed my day. An' I'd do it all the same again,
you know that? Do it all the same I would.

MRS BRYANT. Blust! All your drinkin' an' that?

STAN. Hell! Thaas what kep' me goin' look. Almost anyways.
None o' them young 'uns'll do it, hell if they will. There
ent much life in the young 'uns. Bunch o' weak-kneed
ruffians. None on 'em like livin' look, none on 'em! You
read in them ole papers what go on look, an' you wonder
if they can see. You do! Wonder if they got eyes to look
around them. Think they know where they live? 'Course
they don't, they don't you know, not one. Blust! the
winter go an' the spring come on after an' they don't see
buds an' they don't smell no breeze an' they don't see gals,
an' when they see gals they don't know whatta do wi' 'em.
They don't!

MRS BRYANT. Oh hell, they know *that* all right.

STAN. Gimme my young days an' I'd show 'em. Public demonstrations I'd give!

MRS BRYANT. Oh shut you up Stan Mann.

STAN. Just gimme young days again Daphne Bryant an' I'd mount you. But they 'ont come again will they gal?

MRS BRYANT. That they 'ont. My ole days working in the fields with them other gals, thems 'ont come again, either.

STAN. No, they 'ont that! Rum ole things the years ent they? (*Pause.*) Them young 'uns is all right though. Long as they don't let no one fool them, long as they think it out theirselves. (*Sneezes and coughs.*)

MRS BRYANT (*moving to help him up*). Now get you back home Stan Mann. (*Good-naturedly*) Blust, I aren't hevin' no dead 'uns on me look. Take a rum bor, take a rum an' a drop o' hot milk and get to bed. What's Mrs Mann thinking of lettin' you out like this.

(*She pulls the coat round the old man and pushes him off. He goes off mumbling and she returns, also mumbling, to her peeling.*)

STAN. She's a good gal, she's right 'nough, she don't think I got it this bad. I'll pull this ole scarf round me. Hed this scarf a long time, hed it since I started wi' me cars. *She* bought it me. Lasted a long time. Shouldn't need it this weather though ... (*Exits.*)

MRS BRYANT (*mumbling same time as* STAN). Go on, off you go. Silly ole bugger, runnin' round with a cold like that. Don't know what 'e's doin' half the time. Poor ole man. Cossie? Cossie? That you Cossie? (*Looks through door into front room and out of window at* STAN.) Poor ole man.

(*After peeling some seconds she turns the radio on, turning the dial knob through all manner of stations and back again until she finds some very loud dance music which she leaves blaring* **on.** *Audible to us, but not to* MRS BRYANT, *is the call of*

179

'Yoo-hoo Mother, yoo-hoo'. BEATIE *appears round the garden and peers into the kitchen.* MRS BRYANT *jumps.*)

MRS BRYANT. Blust, you made me jump.

BEATIE (*toning radio down*). Can't you hear it? Hello, Mother. (*Kisses her.*)

MRS BRYANT. Well, you've arrived then.

BEATIE. Didn't you get my card?

MRS BRYANT. Came this morning.

BEATIE. Then you knew I'd arrive.

MRS BRYANT. 'Course I did.

BEATIE. My things come?

MRS BRYANT. One suitcase, one parcel in brown paper —

BEATIE. My paintings.

MRS BRYANT. And one other case.

BEATIE. My pick-up. D'you see it?

MRS BRYANT. I hevn't touched a thing.

BEATIE. Bought myself a pick-up on the H.P.

MRS BRYANT. Don't you go telling that to Pearl.

BEATIE. Why not?

MRS BRYANT. She'll wanna know why you didn't buy off her on the club.

BEATIE. Well, hell, Mother, I weren't gonna hev an ole pick-up sent me from up north somewhere when we lived next door to a gramophone shop.

MRS BRYANT. No. Well, what bus you come on — the half-past-ten one?

BEATIE. Yearp. Picked it up on the ole bridge near Jenny's.

MRS BRYANT. Well I looked for you on the half-past-nine bus and you weren't on that so I thought to myself I bet she come on the half-past-ten and you did. You see ole Stan Mann?

BEATIE. Was that him just going up the road?

MRS BRYANT. Wearin' an ole brown scarf, that was him.

BEATIE. I see him! Just as I were comin' off the bus. Blust!

180

Jimmy Beales give him a real dowsin' down on his allotment 'cos he had an accident.

MRS BRYANT. What, another?

BEATIE. Yearp.

MRS BRYANT. Poor ole man. Thaas what give him that cold then. He come in here sneezin' fit to knock hisself down.

BEATIE. Poor ole bugger. Got any tea Ma? I'm gonna unpack. (BEATIE *goes into front room with case. We see her take out frocks, which she puts on hangers, and underwear and blouses, which she puts on couch.*)

MRS BRYANT. Did you see my flowers as you come in? Got some of my hollyhocks still flowering. Creeping up the wall they are — did you catch a glimpse on 'em? And my asters and geraniums? Poor ole Joe Simonds gimme those afore he died. Lovely geraniums they are.

BEATIE. Yearp.

MRS BRYANT. When's Ronnie coming?

BEATIE. Saturday week — an' Mother, I'm heving all the family along to meet him when he arrive so you patch your rows wi' them.

MRS BRYANT. What you on about gal? What rows wi' them?

BEATIE. You know full well what rows I mean — them ones you hev wi' Pearl and Susan.

MRS BRYANT. 'Tent so likely. They hev a row wi' me gal but I give 'em no heed, that I don't. (*Hears van pass on road.*) There go Sam Martin's fish van. He'll be calling along here in an hour.

BEATIE (*entering with very smart dress*). Like it Mother?

MRS BRYANT. Blust gal, that's a good 'un ent it! Where d'you buy that then?

BEATIE. Swan and Edgar's.

MRS BRYANT. Did Ronnie choose it?

BEATIE. Yearp.

MRS BRYANT. He've got good taste then.

BEATIE. Yearp. Now listen Mother, I don't want any on you to let me down. When Ronnie come I want him to see we're proper. I'll buy you another bowl so's you don't wash up in the same one as you wash your hands in and I'll get some more tea cloths so's you 'ont use the towels. And no swearin'.

MRS BRYANT. Don't he swear then?

BEATIE. He swear all right, only I don't want him to hear *you* swear.

MRS BRYANT. Hev you given it up then?

BEATIE. Mother, I've never swore.

MRS BRYANT. Go to hell, listen to her!

BEATIE. I never did, now! Mother, I'm *telling* you, listen to me. Ronnie's the best thing I've ever had and I've tried hard for three years to keep hold of him. I don't care what you do when he's gone but don't show me up when he's here.

MRS BRYANT. Speak to your father gal.

BEATIE. Father too. I don't want Ronnie to think I come from a small-minded family. 'I can't bear mean people,' he say. 'I don't care about their education, I don't care about their past as long as their minds are large and inquisitive, as long as they're generous.'

MRS BRYANT. Who say that?

BEATIE. Ronnie.

MRS BRYANT. He *talk* like that?

BEATIE. Yearp.

MRS BRYANT. Sounds like a preacher.

BEATIE (*standing on a chair*). 'I don't care if you call me a preacher, I've got something to say and I'm going to say it. I don't care if you don't like being told things — we've come to a time when you've got to say this is right and this is wrong. God in heaven, have we got to be wet all the time? Well, have we?' Christ, Mother, you've got them ole wasps still flying around. (*She waves her arms in the air flaying the wasps.*) September and you've still got wasps. Owee! shoo-shoo! (*In the voice of her childhood*) Mammy, Mammy, take them ole things away. I doesn't like the — ooh! Nasty things.

(BEATIE *jumps off chair and picks up a coat hanger. Now both she and her mother move stealthily around the room 'hunting' wasps. Occasionally* MRS BRYANT *strikes one dead or* BEATIE *spears one against the wall.* MRS BRYANT *conducts herself matter-of-fact-like but* BEATIE *makes a fiendish game of it.*)

MRS BRYANT. They're after them apples on that tree outside. Go on! Off wi' you! Outside now! There — that's got 'em out, but I bet the buggers'll be back in a jiffy look.

BEATIE. Oh yes, an' I want to have a bath.

MRS BRYANT. When d'you want that then?

BEATIE. This morning.

MRS BRYANT. You can't hev no bath this morning, that copper won't heat up till after lunch.

BEATIE. Then I'll bake the pastries for Jenny this morning and you can put me water on now. (*She returns to sort her clothes.*)

MRS BRYANT. I'll do that now then. I'll get you the soft water from the tank.

(MRS BRYANT *now proceeds to collect bucket and move back and forth between the garden out of view and the copper in the kitchen. She fills the copper with about three buckets of water and then lights the fire underneath it. In between buckets she chats.*)

(*Off* — *as she hears lorry go by*) There go Danny Oakley to market. (*She returns with first bucket.*)

BEATIE. Mother! I dreamt I died last night and heaven were at the bottom of a pond. You had to jump in and sink and you know how afeared I am of water. It was full of film stars and soldiers and there were two rooms. In one room they was playing skiffle and — and — I can't remember what were goin' on in the other. Now who was God? I can't remember. It was someone we knew, a she. (*Returns to unpacking.*)

MRS BRYANT (*entering with second bucket; automatically*). Yearp. (*Pause.*) You hear what happened to the headache doctor's patient? You know what they say about him — if you've got a headache you're all right but if you've got something more you've had it! Well he told a woman not to worry about a lump she complained of under her breast and you know what that were? That turned out to be thrombosis! There! Thrombosis! She had that breast off. Yes, she did. Had to hev it cut off. (*Goes for next bucket.*)

BEATIE (*automatically*). Yearp. (*She appears from front room with two framed paintings. She sets them up and admires them. They are primitive designs in bold masses, rather well-balanced shapes and bright poster colours — red, black, and yellow — see Dusty Bicker's work.*) Mother! Did I write and tell you I've took up painting? I started five months ago. Working in gouache. Ronnie says I'm good. Says I should carry on and maybe I can sell them for curtain designs. 'Paint girl,' he say. 'Paint! The world is full of people who don't do the things they want so you paint and give us all hope!'

(MRS BRYANT *enters.*)

BEATIE. Like 'em?

MRS BRYANT (*looks at them a second*). Good colours ent they. (*She is unmoved and continues to empty a third bucket while* BEATIE *returns paintings to other room.*) Yes gal, I ent got no row wi' Pearl but I ask her to change my Labour Tote man 'cos I wanted to give the commission to Charlie Gorleston and she didn't do it. Well, if she can be like that I can be like that too. You gonna do some baking you say?

BEATIE (*enters from front room putting on a pinafore and carrying a*

parcel). Right now. Here y'are Daphne Bryant, present for you. I want eggs, flour, sugar, and marg. I'm gonna bake a sponge and give it frilling. (*Goes to larder to collect things.*)

MRS BRYANT (*unpacking parcel; it is a pinafore*). We both got one now.

(MRS BRYANT *continues to peel potatoes as* BEATIE *proceeds to separate four eggs, the yolks of which she starts whipping with sugar. She sings meanwhile a ringing folk song.*)

BEATIE.

Oh a dialogue I'll sing you as true as me life.
Between a coal owner and poor pitman's wife
As she was a-walking along the highway
She met a coal owner and to him did say
        Derry down, down, down Derry down.
Whip the eggs till they're light yellow he says.

MRS BRYANT. Who says?

BEATIE. Ronnie.

Good morning Lord Firedamp the good woman said
I'll do you no harm sir so don't be afraid
If you'd been where I'd been for most of my life
You wouldn't turn pale at a poor pitman's wife
        Singing down, down, down Derry down.

MRS BRYANT. What song's that?

BEATIE. A coalmining song.

MRS BRYANT. I tell you what I reckon's a good song, that 'I'll wait for you in the heavens blue'. I reckon that's a lovely song I do. Jimmy Samson he sing that.

BEATIE. It's like twenty other songs, it don't mean anything and it's sloshy and sickly.

MRS BRYANT. Yes, I reckon that's a good song that.

BEATIE (*suddenly*). Listen Mother, let me see if I can explain something to you. Ronnie always say that's the point of knowing people. 'It's no good having friends who scratch

185

each other's back,' he say. 'The excitement in knowing people is to hand on what you know and to learn what you don't know. Learn from me,' he say, 'I don't know much but learn what I know.' So let me try and explain to you what he explain to me.

MRS BRYANT (*on hearing a bus*). There go the half-past-eleven bus to Diss — blust that's early. (*Puts spuds in saucepan on oven and goes to collect runner beans, which she prepares.*)

BEATIE. Mother, I'm *talking* to you. Blust woman it's not often we get together and really talk, it's nearly always me listening to you telling who's dead. Just listen a second.

MRS BRYANT. Well go on gal, but you always take so long to say it.

BEATIE. What are the words of that song?

MRS BRYANT. I don't know all the words.

BEATIE. I'll tell you.

(*Recites them.*)

> I'll wait for you in the heavens blue
> As my arms are waiting now.
> Please come to me and I'll be true
> My love shall not turn sour.
> I hunger, I hunger, I cannot wait longer,
> My love shall not turn sour.

There! Now what do that mean?

MRS BRYANT (*surprised*). Well, don't you know what that mean?

BEATIE. I mean what do they do to you? How do the words affect you? Are you moved? Do you find them beautiful?

MRS BRYANT. Them's as good words as any.

BEATIE. But do they make you feel better?

MRS BRYANT. Blust gal! That ent meant to be a laxative!

BEATIE. I must be mad to talk with you.

MRS BRYANT. Besides it's the tune I like. Words never mean anything.

BEATIE. All right, the tune then! What does *that* do to you? Make your belly go gooey, your heart throb, make your head spin with passion? Yes, passion, Mother, know what it is? Because you won't find passion in that third-rate song, no you won't!

MRS BRYANT. Well all right gal, so it's third-rate you say. Can you say why? What make that third-rate and them frilly bits of opera and concert first-rate? 'Sides, did I write that song? Beatie Bryant, you do go up and down in your spirits, and I don't know what's gotten into you gal, no I don't.

BEATIE. I don't know either, Mother. I'm worried about Ronnie I suppose. I have that same row with him. I ask him exactly the same questions — what make a pop song third-rate. And he answer and I don't know what he talk about. Something about registers, something about commercial world blunting our responses. 'Give yourself time woman,' he say. 'Time! You can't learn how to live overnight. *I* don't even know,' he say, 'and half the world don't know but we got to try. Try,' he say, ''cos we're still suffering from the shock of two world wars and we don't know it. Talk,' he say, 'and look and listen and think and ask questions.' But Jesus! I don't know what questions to ask or *how* to talk. And he gets so riled — and yet sometimes so nice. 'It's all going up in flames,' he say, 'but I'm going to make bloody sure I save someone from the fire.'

MRS BRYANT. Well I'm sure *I* don't know what he's on about. Turn to your baking gal look and get you done, Father'll be home for his lunch in an hour.

(*A faint sound of an ambulance is heard.* MRS BRYANT *looks up but says nothing.* BEATIE *turns to whipping the eggs again and* MRS BRYANT *to cleaning up the runner beans. Out of this pause* MRS BRYANT *begins to sing* 'I'll wait for you in the heavens blue', *but on the second line she hums the tune incorrectly.*)

BEATIE (*laughs*). No, no, hell Mother, it don't go like that. It's —

(BEATIE *corrects her and in helping her mother she ends by singing the song, with some enthusiasm, to the end.*)

MRS BRYANT. Thank God you come home sometimes gal — you do bring a little life with you anyway.

BEATIE. Mother, I ent never heard you express a feeling like that.

MRS BRYANT (*she is embarrassed*). The world don't want no feelings gal. (*Footsteps are heard.*) Is that your father home already?

(MR BRYANT *appears at the back door and lays a bicycle against the wall. He is a small shrivelled man wearing denims, a peaked cap, boots, and gaiters. He appears to be in some pain.*)

BEATIE. Hello poppy Bryant.

MR BRYANT. Hello Beatie. You're here then.

MRS BRYANT. What are you home so early for?

MR BRYANT. The ole guts ache again. (*Sits in armchair and grimaces.*)

MRS BRYANT. Well, what is it?

MR BRYANT. Blust woman, I don't know what 'tis n'more'n you, do I?

MRS BRYANT. Go to the doctor man I keep telling you.

BEATIE. What is it father Bryant?

MRS BRYANT. He got guts ache.

BEATIE. But what's it from?

MR BRYANT. I've just said I don't know.

MRS BRYANT. Get you to a doctor man, don't be so soft. You don't want to be kept from work do you?

MR BRYANT. That I don't, no I don't. Hell, I just see ole Stan Mann picked up an' thaas upset me enough.

MRS BRYANT. Picked up you say?

MR BRYANT. Well, didn't you hear the ambulance?

MRS BRYANT. There! I hear it but I didn't say narthin'. Was that for Stan Mann then?

MR BRYANT. I was cycling along wi' Jack Stones and we see this here figure on the side o' the road there an' I say, thaas a rum shape in the road Jack, and he say, blust, that's ole Stan Mann from Heybrid, an' 'twere. 'Course soon ever he see what 'twere, he rushed off for 'n ambulance and I waited alongside Stan.

BEATIE. But he just left here.

MRS BRYANT. I see it comin'. He come in here an' I shoved him off home. Get you to bed and take some rum an' a drop o' hot milk, I tell him.

BEATIE. Is he gonna die?

MR BRYANT. Wouldn't surprise me, that it wouldn't. Blust, he look done in.

MRS BRYANT. Poor ole fellah. Shame though ent it?

MR BRYANT. When d'you arrive Beatie?

MRS BRYANT. She come in the half-past-ten bus. I looked for her on the nine-thirty bus and she weren't on that, so I thought to myself I bet she come on the half-past-ten. She did.

MR BRYANT. Yearp.

MRS BRYANT. You gonna stay away all day?

MR BRYANT. No I aren't. I gotta go back 'cos one of the ole sows is piggin'. 'Spect she'll be hevin' them in a couple of hours. (To BEATIE) Got a sow had a litter o' twenty-two. (Picks up paper to read.)

BEATIE. Twenty-two? Oh Pop, can I come see this afternoon?

MR BRYANT. Yearp.

MRS BRYANT. Thought you was hevin' a bath.

BEATIE. Oh yes, I forgot. I'll come tomorrow then.

MR BRYANT. They'll be there. What you doin' gal?

MRS BRYANT. She's baking a sponge, now leave her be.

MR BRYANT. Oh, you learnt something in London then.

BEATIE. Ronnie taught me.

MR BRYANT. Well where *is* Ronnie then?

MRS BRYANT. He's comin' on Saturday a week an' the family's goin' to be here to greet him.

MR BRYANT. All on 'em?

MRS BRYANT *and* BEATIE. All on 'em!

MR BRYANT. Well that'll be a rum gatherin' then.

MRS BRYANT. And we've to be on our best behaviour.

MR BRYANT. No cussin' and swearin'?

MRS BRYANT *and* BEATIE. No.

MR BRYANT. Blust, I shan't talk then.

(*A young man,* MR HEALEY, *appears round the garden — he is the farmer's son, and manager of the estate* BRYANT *works for.*)

MRS BRYANT (*seeing him first*). Oh, Mr Healey, yes. Jack! It's Mr Healey.

(MR BRYANT *rises and goes to the door.* HEALEY *speaks in a firm, not unkind, but business-is-business voice. There is that apologetic threat even in his politeness.*)

MR HEALEY. You were taken ill.

MR BRYANT. It's all right, sir, only guts ache, won't be long goin'. The pigs is all seen to, just waiting for the ole sow to start.

MR HEALEY. What time you expecting it?

MR BRYANT. Oh, she 'ont come afore two this afternoon, no she 'ont be much afore that.

MR HEALEY. You're sure you're well, Jack? I've been thinking that it's too much for you carting those pails round the yard.

MR BRYANT. No, that ent too heavy, sir, 'course 'tent. You don't wanna worry, I'll be along after lunch. Just an ole guts ache that's all — seein' the doctor tonight — eat too fast probably.

MR HEALEY. If you're sure you're all right, then I'll put young

Daniels off. You can manage without him now we've fixed the new pump in.

MR BRYANT. I can manage, sir — 'course I can.

MR HEALEY (*moving off outside*). All right then, Jack. I'll be with you around two o'clock. I want to take the old one out of number three and stick her with the others in seventeen. The little ones won't need her, will they? Then we'll have them sorted out tomorrow.

MR BRYANT. That's right, sir, they *can* go on their own now, they can. I'll see to it tomorrow.

MR HEALEY. Right then, Jack. Oh — you hear Stan Mann died?

MR BRYANT. He died already? But I saw him off in the ambulance no more'n half-hour ago.

MR HEALEY. Died on the way to hospital. Jack Stones told me. Lived in Heybrid, didn't he?

MR BRYANT. Alongside my daughter.

MR HEALEY (*calling*). Well, good morning, Mrs Bryant.

MRS BRYANT (*calling*). Good morning, Mr Healey.

(*The two men nod to each other. MR HEALEY goes off. MR BRYANT lingers a second.*)

MRS BRYANT (*to* BEATIE). That was Mr Healey, the new young manager.

BEATIE. I know it Mother.

MR BRYANT (*returning slowly*). He's dead then.

MRS BRYANT. Who? Not Stan Mann!

MR BRYANT. Young Healey just tell me.

MRS BRYANT. Well I go t'hell. An' he were just here look, just here alongside o' me not more'n hour past.

MR BRYANT. Rum ent it?

BEATIE (*weakly*). Oh hell, I hate dying.

MRS BRYANT. He were a good ole bor though. Yes he was. A good ole stick. There!

BEATIE. Used to ride me round on his horse, always full o' life

191

an' jokes. 'Tell your boy he wanna hurry up and marry you,' he say to me, 'or I'll hev you meself on a plate.'

MRS BRYANT. He were a one for smut though.

BEATIE. I was talkin' with him last night. Only last night he was tellin' me how he caught me pinchin' some goose-berries off his patch an' how he gimme a whole apron full and I went into one o' his fields near by an' ate the lot. 'Blust,' he say, 'you had the ole guts ache,' an' he laugh, sat there laughin' away to hisself.

MRS BRYANT. I can remember that. Hell, Jenny'll miss him — used always to pop in an' out o' theirs.

BEATIE. Seem like the whole world gone suddenly dead don' it?

MR BRYANT. Rum ent it?

(*Silence.*)

MRS BRYANT. You say young Healey tell you that? *He's* a nice man Mr Healey is, yes he is, a good sort, I like him.

BEATIE. Sound like he were threatening to sack Father; don't know about being nice.

MR BRYANT. That's what I say see, get a rise and they start cutting down the men or the overtime.

MRS BRYANT. The Union magazine's come.

MR BRYANT. I don't want that ole thing.

BEATIE. Why can't you do something to stop the sackings?

MR BRYANT. You can't, you can't — that's what I say, you can't. Sharp as a pig's scream they are — you just *can't* do nothin'.

BEATIE. Mother, where's the bakin' tin?

MR BRYANT. When we gonna eat that?

BEATIE. You ent! It's for Jenny Beales.

MR BRYANT. You aren't making that for Jenny are you?

BEATIE. I promised her.

MR BRYANT. Not with my electricity you aren't.

BEATIE. But I promised, Poppy.

MR BRYANT. That's no matters. I aren't spendin' money on electricity bills so's you can make every Tom, Dick 'n' Harry a sponge cake, that I aren't.

MRS BRYANT. Well, don't be so soft man, it won't take more'n half-hour's bakin'.

MR BRYANT. I don't care what it'll take I say. I aren't lettin' her. Jenny wants cakes, she can make 'em herself. So put that away Beatie and use it for something else.

MRS BRYANT. You wanna watch what you're sayin' of 'cos I live here too.

MR BRYANT. I know all about that but I pay the electricity bill and I says she isn't bakin'.

BEATIE. But Poppy, one cake.

MR BRYANT. No I say.

BEATIE. Well, Mummy, do something — how can he be so mean.

MRS BRYANT. Blust me if you ent the meanest ole sod that walks this earth. Your own daughter and you won't let her use your oven. You bloody ole hypercrite.

MR BRYANT. You pay the bills and then you call names.

MRS BRYANT. What I ever seen in you God only knows. Yes! an' he never warn me. Bloody ole hypercrite!

MR BRYANT. You pay the bills and then you call names I say.

MRS BRYANT. On four pounds ten a week? You want me to keep you *and* pay bills? Four pound ten he give me. God knows what he do wi' the rest. I don't know how much he've got. I don't, no I don't. Bloody ole hypercrite.

MR BRYANT. Let's hev grub and not so much o' the lip woman.
(BEATIE *begins to put the things away. She is on the verge of the tears she will soon let fall.*)

MRS BRYANT. That's how he talk to me — when he do talk. 'Cos you know he don't ever talk more'n he hev to, and when he do say something it's either 'how much this cost' or 'lend us couple o' bob.' He've got the money but sooner than break into that he borrow off me. Bloody old miser. (*To* BEATIE) What you wanna cry for gal? 'Tent worth it. Blust, you don't wanna let an ole hypercrite like him upset you, no you don't. I'll get my back on you my manny, see if I don't. You won't get away with no tricks on me.

(BEATIE *has gone into the other room and returned with a small packet.*)

BEATIE (*throwing parcel in father's lap*). Present for you.

MRS BRYANT. I'd give him presents that I would! I'd walk out and disown him! Beatie, now stop you a-cryin' gal — blust, he ent worth cryin' for, that he ent. Stop it I say and we'll have lunch. Or you lost your appetite gal?

(BEATIE *sniffs a few tears back, pauses, and* —)

BEATIE. No — no, that I ent. Hell, I can eat all right!

CURTAIN

Scene 2

Lunch has been eaten. MR BRYANT *is sitting at the table rolling himself a cigarette.* MRS BRYANT *is collecting the dishes and taking them to a sink to wash up.* BEATIE *is taking things off the table and putting them into the larder — jars of sauce, plates of sliced bread and cakes, butter, sugar, condiments, and bowl of tinned fruit.*

MRS BRYANT (*to* BEATIE). Ask him what he want for his tea.

MR BRYANT. She don't ever ask me before, what she wanna ask me now for?

MRS BRYANT. Tell him it's his stomach I'm thinking about — I don't want him complaining to me about the food I cook.

MR BRYANT. Tell her it's no matters to me — I ent got no pain now besides.

BEATIE. Mother, is that water ready for my bath?

MRS BRYANT. Where you hevin' it?

194

BEATIE. In the kitchen of course.

MRS BRYANT. Blust gal, you can't bath in this kitchen during the day, what if someone call at the door?

BEATIE. Put up the curtain then, I shan't be no more'n ten minutes.

MR BRYANT. 'Sides, who want to see her in her dickey suit.

BEATIE. I know men as 'ould pay to see me in my dickey suit. (*Posing her plump outline*) Don't you think I got a nice dickey suit?

(MR BRYANT *makes a dive and pinches her bottom.*)

Ow! Stoppit Bryants, stoppit!

(*He persists.*)

Daddy, stop it now!

MRS BRYANT. Tell him he can go as soon as he like, I want your bath over and done with.

BEATIE. Oh Mother, stop this nonsense do. If you want to tell him something tell him — not me.

MRS BRYANT. *I* don't want to speak to him, hell if I do.

BEATIE. Father, get the bath in for me please. Mother, where's them curtains.

(MR BRYANT *goes off to fetch a long tin bath — wide at one end, narrow at the other — while* MRS BRYANT *leaves washing up to fish out some curtains which she hangs from one wall to another concealing thus a corner of the kitchen. Anything that is in the way is removed.* BEATIE *meanwhile brings out a change of underwear, her dressing-gown, the new frock, some soap, powder, and towel. These she lays within easy reach of the curtain.*)

BEATIE. I'm gonna wear my new dress and go across the fields to see Frankie and Pearl.

MRS BRYANT. Frankie won't be there, what you on about? He'll be gettin' the harvest in.

BEATIE. You makin anything for the harvest festival?

MR BRYANT (*entering with bath, places it behind curtain*). Your

mother don't ever do anything for the harvest festival —
don't you know that by now.

BEATIE. Get you to work father Bryant, I'm gonna plunge in
water and I'll make a splash.

MRS BRYANT. Tell him we've got kippers for tea and if he don'
want none let him say now.

BEATIE. She says it's kippers for tea.

MR BRYANT. Tell her I'll eat kippers. (*Goes off collecting bike on
the way.*)

BEATIE. He says he'll eat kippers. Right now, Mother, you get
cold water an' I'll pour the hot.

(*Each now picks up a bucket. MRS BRYANT goes off out to
collect the cold water and BEATIE plunges bucket into boiler to
retrieve hot water. The bath is prepared with much childlike
glee. BEATIE loves her creature comforts and does with
unabashed, almost animal, enthusiasm that which she enjoys.
When the bath is prepared, BEATIE slips behind the curtain to
undress and enter.*)

MRS BRYANT. You hear about Jimmy Skelton? They say he've
bin arrested for accosting some man in the village.

BEATIE. Jimmy Skelton what own the pub?

MRS BRYANT. That's him. I know all about Jimmy Skelton
though. He were a young boy when I were a young girl.
I always partner him at whist drives. He's been to law
before you know. Yes! An' he won the day too! Won the
day he did. I don't take notice though, him and me gets on
all right. What do Ronnie's mother do with her time?

BEATIE. She've got a sick husband to look after.

MRS BRYANT. She an educated woman?

BEATIE. Educated? No. She's a foreigner. Nor ent Ronnie
educated neither. He's an intellectual, failed all his exams.
They read and things.

MRS BRYANT. Oh, they don't do nothing then?

BEATIE. Do nothing? I'll tell you what Ronnie do, he work

till all hours in a hot ole kitchen. An' he teach kids in a club to act and jive and such. And he don't stop at week-ends either 'cos then there's political meetings and such and I get breathless trying to keep up wi' him. OOOhh, Mother it's hot ...

MRS BRYANT. I'll get you some cold then.

BEATIE. No — ooh — it's lovely. The water's so soft Mother.

MRS BRYANT. Yearp.

BEATIE. It's so soft and smooth. I'm in.

MRS BRYANT. Don't you stay in too long gal. There go the twenty-minutes-past-one bus.

BEATIE. Oh Mother, me bath cubes. I forgot me bath cubes. In the little case by me pick-up.

(MRS BRYANT *finds bath cubes and hands them to* BEATIE.)

MRS BRYANT (*continuing her work*). I shall never forget when I furse heard on it. I was in the village and I was talking to Reggie Fowler. I say to him, there've bin a lot o' talk about Jimmy ent there? Disgustin', I say. Still, there's somebody wanna make some easy money, you'd expect that in a village wouldn't you? Yes, I say to him, a lot of talk. An' he stood there, an' he were a-lookin' at me an' a-lookin' as I were a-talkin' and then he say, missus, he say, I were one o' the victims! Well, you could've hit me over the head wi' a hammer. I was one o' the victims, he say.

BEATIE. Mother, these bath cubes smell beautiful. I could stay here all day.

MRS BRYANT. Still, Jimmy's a good fellow with it all — do anything for you. I partner him at whist drives; he bin had up scores o' times though.

BEATIE. Mother, what we gonna make Ronnie when he come?

MRS BRYANT. Well, what do he like?

BEATIE. He like trifle and he like steak and kidney pie.

MRS BRYANT. We'll make that then. So long as he don't com-plain o' the guts ache. Frankie hev it too you know.

BEATIE. Know why? You all eat too much. The Londoners think we live a healthy life but they don't know we stuff ourselves silly till our guts ache.

MRS BRYANT. But you know what's wrong wi' Jimmy Beales? It's indigestion. He eat too fast.

BEATIE. What the hell's indigestion doin' a'tween his shoulder blades?

MRS BRYANT. 'Cos some people get it so bad it go right through their stomach to the back.

BEATIE. You don't get indigestion in the back Mother, what you on about?

MRS BRYANT. Don't you tell me gal, I hed it!

BEATIE. Owee! The soap's in me eyes — Mother, towel, the towel, quickly the towel!

(MRS BRYANT *hands in towel to* BEATIE. *The washing up is probably done by now, so* MRS BRYANT *sits in a chair, legs apart and arms folded, thinking what else to say.*)

MRS BRYANT. You heard that Ma Buckley hev been taken to Mental Hospital in Norwich? Poor ole dear. If there's one thing I can't abide that's mental cases. They frighten me — they do. Can't face 'em. I'd sooner follow a man to a churchyard than the mental hospital. That's a terrible thing to see a person lose their reason — that 'tis. Well, I tell you what, down where I used to live, down the other side of the Hall, years ago we moved in next to an old woman. I only had Jenny and Frank then — an' this woman she were the sweetest of people. We used to talk and do errands for each other — Oh she was a sweet ole dear. And then one afternoon I was going out to get my washin' in and I saw her. She was standin' in a tub o' water up to her neck. She was! Up to her neck. An' her eyes had that glazed, wonderin' look and she stared straight at me she did. Straight at me. Well, do you know what? I was struck *dumb*. I was *struck* dumb wi' shock. What wi' her bein' so nice all this while, the sudden comin' on her like that in the tub fair upset me. It did! And people tell me afterwards that she's bin goin' in an' out o' hospital for years. Blust, that scare me. That scare me so much she nearly took me round the bend wi' her.

(BEATIE *appears from behind the curtain in her dressing-gown, a towel round her head.*)

BEATIE. There! I'm gonna hev a bath every day when I'm married.

(BEATIE *starts rubbing her hair with towel and fiddles with radio. She finds a programme playing Mendelssohn's Fourth Symphony, the slow movement, and stands before the mirror, listening and rubbing.*)

BEATIE (*looking at her reflection*). Isn't your nose a funny thing, and your ears. And your arms and your legs, aren't they funny things — sticking out of a lump.

MRS BRYANT (*switching off radio*). Turn that squit off!

BEATIE (*turning on her mother violently*). *Mother!* I could kill you when you do that. No wonder I don't know anything about anything. I never heard nothing but dance music because you always turned off the classics. I never knowed anything about the news because you always switched off after the headlines. I never read any good books 'cos there was never any in the house.

MRS BRYANT. What's gotten into you now gal?

BEATIE. God in heaven Mother, you live in the country but you got no — no — no majesty. You spend your time among green fields, you grow flowers and you breathe fresh air and you got no majesty. Your mind's cluttered up with nothing and you shut out the world. What kind of a life did you give me?

MRS BRYANT. Blust gal, I weren't no teacher.

BEATIE. But you hindered. You didn't open one door for me. Even his mother cared more for me than what you did.

Beatie, she say, Beatie, why don't you take up evening
classes and learn something other than waitressing. Yes,
she say, you won't ever regret learnin' things. But did you
care what job I took up or whether I learned things? You
didn't even think it was necessary.

MRS BRYANT. I fed you. I clothed you. I took you out to the
sea. What more d'you want. We're only country folk you
know. We ent got no big things here you know.

BEATIE. Squit! Squit! It makes no difference country or town.
All the town girls I ever worked with were just like me. It
makes no difference country or town — that's squit. Do
you know when I used to work at the holiday camp and I
sat down with the other girls to write a letter we used to
sit and discuss what we wrote about. An' we all agreed, all
on us, that we started: 'Just a few lines to let you know',
and then we get on to the weather and then we get stuck
so we write about each other and after a page an' half of
big scrawl end up: 'Hoping this finds you as well as it
leaves me.' There! We couldn't say any more. Thousands
of things happening at this holiday camp and we couldn't
find words for them. All of us the same. Hundreds of girls
and one day we're gonna be mothers, and you *still* talk to
me of Jimmy Skelton and the ole woman in the tub. Do
you know I've heard that story a dozen times. A dozen
times. Can't you hear yourself Mother? Jesus, how can I
bring Ronnie to this house.

MRS BRYANT. Blust gal, if Ronnie don't like us then he —

BEATIE. Oh, he'll like you all right. He like people. He'd've
loved ole Stan Mann. Ole Stan Mann would've understood everything Ronnie talk about. Blust! That man
liked livin'. Besides, Ronnie say it's too late for the old
'uns to learn. But he says it's up to us young 'uns. And them
of us that know hev got to teach them of us as don't know.

MRS BRYANT. I bet he hev a hard time trying to change you gal!

200

BEATIE. He's *not* trying to change me Mother. You can't change people, he say, you can only give them some love and hope they'll take it. And he's tryin' to teach me and I'm tryin' to understand — do you see that Mother?

MRS BRYANT. I don't see what that's got to do with music though.

BEATIE. Oh my God! (*Suddenly*) I'll show you. (*Goes off to front room to collect pick-up and a record.*) Now sit you down gal and I'll show you. Don't start ironing or reading or nothing, just sit there and be prepared to learn something. (*Appears with pick-up and switches on.*) You aren't too old, just you sit and listen. That's the trouble you see, we ent ever prepared to learn anything, we close our minds the minute anything unfamiliar appear. *I* could never listen to music. I used to like some on it but then I'd lose patience, I'd go to bed in the middle of a symphony, or my mind would wander 'cos the music didn't mean anything to me so I'd go to bed or start talking. 'Sit back woman,' he'd say, 'listen to it. Let it happen to you and you'll grow as big as the music itself.'

MRS BRYANT. Blust he talk like a book.

BEATIE. An' sometimes he talk as though you didn't know where the moon or the stars was. (BEATIE *puts on record of Bizet's L'Arlésienne Suite.*) Now listen. This is a simple piece of music, it's not highbrow but it's full of living. And that's what he say socialism is. 'Christ,' he say. 'Socialism isn't talking all the time, it's living, it's singing, it's dancing, it's being interested in what go on around you, it's being concerned about people and the world.' Listen Mother. (*She becomes breathless and excited.*) Listen to it. It's simple isn't it? Can you call that squit?

MRS BRYANT. I don't say it's all squit.

BEATIE. You don't have to frown because it's alive.

MRS BRYANT. No, not all on it's squit.

BEATIE. See the way the other tune comes in? Hear it? Two simple tunes, one after the other.

MRS BRYANT. I aren't saying it's all squit.

BEATIE. And now listen, listen, it goes together, the two tunes together, they knit, they're perfect. Don't it make you want to dance? (*She begins to dance a mixture of a cossack dance and a sailor's hornpipe.*)

(*The music becomes fast and her spirits are young and high.*) Listen to that Mother. Is it difficult? Is it squit? It's light. It make me feel light and confident and happy. God, Mother, **we** could all be so much more happy and alive. Wheeeee ...

(BEATIE *claps her hands and dances on and her* MOTHER *smiles and claps her hands and —*)

THE CURTAIN FALLS

ACT THREE

Two weeks have passed. It is Saturday, the day Ronnie is to arrive. One of the walls of the kitchen is now pushed aside and the front room is revealed. It is low-ceilinged, and has dark brown wooden beams. The furniture is not typical country farmhouse type. There may be one or two windsor-type straight-back chairs, but for the rest it is cheap utility stuff. Two armchairs, a table, a small bamboo table, wooden chairs, a small sofa, and a swivel bookcase. There are a lot of flowers around — in pots on the window ledge and in vases on the bamboo table and swivel case.

It is three in the afternoon, the weather is cloudy — it has been raining and is likely to start again. On the table is a spread of food (none of this will be eaten). There are cakes and biscuits on plates and glass stands. Bread and butter, butter in a dish, tomatoes, cheese, jars of pickled onions, sausage rolls, dishes of tinned fruit — it is a spread! Round the table are eight chairs. BEATIE's paintings are hanging on the wall. The room is empty because BEATIE is upstairs changing and MRS BRYANT is in the kitchen. BEATIE —until she descends — conducts all her conversation shouting from upstairs.)

BEATIE. Mother! What you on at now?

MRS BRYANT (*from kitchen*). I'm just puttin' these glass cherries on the trifle.

BEATIE. Well come on look, he'll be here at four thirty.

MRS BRYANT (*from kitchen*). Don't you fret gal, it's another hour 'n' half yet, the postman hevn't gone by. (*Enters with an enormous bowl of trifle.*) There! He like trifle you say?

BEATIE. He love it.

MRS BRYANT. Well he need to 'cos there's plenty on it. (*To herself, surveying the table*) Yes, there is, there's plenty on it. (*It starts to rain.*) Blust, listen to that weather.

BEATIE. Rainin' again!

MRS BRYANT (*looking out of window*). Raining? It's rainin' fit to drowned you. (*Sound of bus.*) There go the three-o'clock.

BEATIE. Mother get you changed, come on, I want us ready in time.

MRS BRYANT. Blust you'd think it were the bloody Prince of Egypt comin'. (*Goes upstairs.*)

(*The stage is empty again for a few seconds. People are heard taking off their macs and exclaiming at the weather from the kitchen. Enter* FRANK *and* PEARL BRYANT. *He is pleasant and dressed in a blue pin-striped suit, is ruddy-faced and blond-haired. An odd sort of shyness makes him treat everything as a joke. His wife is a pretty brunette, young, and ordinarily dressed in plain, flowered frock.*)

FRANK (*calling*). Well, where are you all? Come on — I'm hungry.

PEARL. Shut you up bor, you only just had lunch.

FRANK. Well I'm hungry again. (*Calling*) Well, where is this article we come to see?

BEATIE. He ent arrived.

FRANK. Well, he want to hurry, 'cos I'm hungry.

BEATIE. You're always hungry.

FRANK. What do you say he is — a strong socialist?

BEATIE. Yes.

FRANK. And a Jew boy?

BEATIE. Yes.

FRANK (*to himself*). Well, that's a queer mixture then.

PEARL (*calling*). I hope he don't talk politics all the time.

FRANK. Have you had a letter from him yet?

PEARL. Stop it Frank, you know she hevn't heard.

FRANK. Well that's a rum boy friend what don't write. (*Looks at paintings, pauses before one of them and growls.*)

PEARL. Watch out or it'll bite you back.

(BEATIE *comes down from upstairs. She is dressed in her new frock and looks happy, healthy, and radiant.*)

FRANK. Hail there, sister! I was then contemplating your masterpiece.

BEATIE. Well don't contemplate too long 'cos you aren't
hevin' it.

FRANK. Blust! I'd set my ole heart on it.

PEARL. That's a nice frock Beatie.

FRANK. Where's the rest of our mighty clan?

BEATIE. Jenny and Jimmy should be here soon and Susie and
Stan mightn't come.

FRANK. What's wrong wi' them?

BEATIE. Don't talk to me about it 'cos I hed enough! Susie
won't talk to Mother.

PEARL. That make nearly eighteen months she hevn't spoke.

BEATIE. Why ever did *you* and Mother fall out Pearl?

FRANK. 'Cos Mother's so bloody stubborn that's why.

PEARL. Because one day she said she wanted to change her
Labour Tote man, that's why, and she asked me to do it
for her. So I said all right, but it'll take a couple of weeks;
and then she get riled because she said I didn't want to
change it for her. And then I ask her why didn't she
change him herself and she say because she was too ill to
go all the way to see John Clayton to tell him, and then
she say to me, why, don't you think I'm ill? And I say
— I know this were tactless o' me — but I say, no Mother,
you don't look ill to me. And she didn't speak to me since.
I only hope she don't snub me this afternoon.

BEATIE. Well, she tell me a different story.

FRANK. Mother's always quarrelling.

PEARL. Well I reckon there ent much else she *can* do stuck in
this ole house on her own all day. And father Bryant he
don't say too much when he's home you know.

FRANK. Well blust, she hevn't spoke to her own mother for
three years, not since Granny Dykes took Jenny in when
she had that illegitimate gal Daphne.

BEATIE. Hell! What a bloody family!

FRANK. A mighty clan I say.

(JIMMY *and* JENNY BEALES *now enter.*)

JENNY. Hello Frankie, hello Pearl, hello Beatie.

FRANK. And more of the mighty clan.

JENNY. Mighty clan you say? Mighty bloody daft you mean. Well, where is he?

FRANK. The mysterious stranger has not yet come — we await.

JENNY. Well, I aren't waitin' long 'cos I'm hungry.

PEARL. That's all this family of Bryants ever do is think o' their guts.

FRANK (*to* JIMMY). Have you formed your association yit?

JENNY. What association is this?

FRANK. What! Hevn't he told you?

JIMMY. Shut you up Frank Bryant or you'll get me hung.

FRANK. Oh, a mighty association — a mighty one! I'll tell ye. One day you see we was all sittin' round in the pub — Jimmy, me, Starkie, Johnny Oats, and Bonky Dawson — we'd hed a few drinks and Jimmy was feelin' — well, he was feelin' — you know what, the itch! He hed the itch! He started complaining about ham, ham, ham all the time. So then Bonky Dawson say, blust, he say, there must be women about who feel the same. And Starkie he say, well 'course they are, only how do you tell? And then we was all quiet a while thinkin' on it when suddenly Jimmy says, we ought to start an association of them as need a bit now and then and we all ought to wear a badge he say, and when you see a woman wearin' a badge you know she need a bit too.

JIMMY. Now that's enough Frank or I'll hit you over the skull.

FRANK. Now, not content wi' just that, ole Jimmy then say, and we ought to have a password to indicate how bad off you are. So listen what he suggest. He suggest you go up to any one o' these women what's wearin' a badge and you say, how many lumps of sugar do you take in your tea? And if she say 'two' then you know she ent too badly off, but she's willin'. But if she say 'four' then you know she's in as bad a state as what you are, see?

(*Long pause.*)

JENNY. He'd hev a fit if she said she took sixteen lumps though wouldn't he?

(*Pause.*)

PEARL. Where's mother Bryant?

BEATIE. Upstairs changin'.

PEARL. Where's father Bryant?

BEATIE. Tendin' the pigs.

FRANK. You're lucky to hev my presence you know.

BEATIE. Oh?

FRANK. A little more sun and I'd've bin gettin' in the harvest.

PEARL. Well, what did you think of that storm last night? All that thunder 'n' lightnin' and it didn't stop once.

BEATIE. Ronnie love it you know. He sit and watch it for bloody hours.

FRANK. He's a queer article then.

JENNY. He do sound a rum 'un don't he?

BEATIE. Well you'll soon see.

JIMMY. Hev he got any sisters?

BEATIE. One married and she live not far from here.

PEARL. She live in the country? A town girl? Whatever for?

BEATIE. Her husband make furniture by hand.

PEARL. Can't he do that in London?

BEATIE. Ronnie say they think London's an inhuman place.

JIMMY. So 'tis, so 'tis.

BEATIE. Here come father Bryant.

(MR BRYANT *enters. He is in denims and raincoat, tired, and stooped slightly.*)

FRANK. And this be the male head of the mighty Bryant clan!

MR BRYANT. Blust, you're all here soon then.

BEATIE. Get you changed quick Father — he'll be along any minute look.

MR BRYANT. Shut you up gal, I'll go when I'm ready, I don't want you pushin' me.

(MRS BRYANT *comes from upstairs. She looks neat and also wears a flowered frock.*)

FRANK. And this be the female head o' the mighty Bryant clan!

MRS BRYANT. Come on Bryant, get you changed — we're all ready look.

MR BRYANT. Blust, there go the other one. Who is he this boy, that's what I wanna know.

MRS BRYANT. He's upset! I can see it! I can tell it in his voice. Come on Bryants, what's the matters.

MR BRYANT. There ent much up wi' me, what you on about woman. (*Makes to go.*) Now leave me be, you want me changed look.

MRS BRYANT. If there ent much up wi' you, I'll marry some other.

FRANK. Healey bin at you Pop?

BEATIE. The pigs dyin'?

MRS BRYANT. It's something serious or he wouldn't be so happy lookin'.

MR BRYANT. I bin put on casual labour.

JENNY. Well isn't that a sod now.

MRS BRYANT. Your guts I suppose.

MR BRYANT. I tell him it's no odds, that there's no pain. That don't matters Jack, he says, I aren't hevin' you break up completely on me. You go on casual, he say, and if you gets better you can come on to the pigs again.

MRS BRYANT. That's half pay then?

BEATIE. Can't you get another job?

FRANK. He've bin wi' them for eighteen years.

BEATIE. But you must be able to do something else — what about cowman again?

MR BRYANT. Bill Waddington do that see. He've bin at it this last six 'n' half years.

JENNY. It's no good upsettin' yourself Beatie. It happen all the time gal.

JIMMY. Well, we told her when she was at ours didn't we.

MRS BRYANT (*to* MR BRYANT). All right, get you on up, there ent nothin' we can do. We'll worry on it later. We always manage. It's gettin' late look.

MR BRYANT. Can he swim? 'Cos he bloody need to. It's rainin' fit to drowned you. (*Goes off upstairs.*)

MRS BRYANT. Well, shall we have a little cup o' tea while we're waitin'? I'll go put the kettle on. (*Goes to kitchen.*)
(*Everyone sits around now.* JENNY *takes out some knitting and* JIMMY *picks up a paper to read. There is a silence. It is not an awkward silence, just a conversationless room.*)

PEARL (*to* JENNY). Who's lookin' after your children?

JENNY. Ole mother Mann next door.

PEARL. Poor ole dear. How's she feelin' now?

JENNY. She took it bad. (*Nodding at* JIMMY) Him too. He think he were to blame.

PEARL. Blust that weren't his fault. Don't be so daft Jimmy Beales. Don't you go fretting yourself or you'll make us all feel queer look. You done nothin' wrong bor — he weren't far off dying 'sides.

FRANK. They weren't even married were they?

JENNY. No, they never were — she started lookin' after him when he had that first stroke and she just stayed.

JIMMY. Lost her job 'cos of it too.

FRANK. Well, yes, she would, wouldn't she — she was a State Registered Nurse or something weren't she? (*To* BEATIE) Soon ever the authorities got to hear o' that they told her to pack up livin' wi' him or quit her job, see?

JENNY. Bloody daft I reckon. What difference it make whether she married him or not.

PEARL. I reckon you miss him Jenny?

JENNY. Hell yes — that I do. He were a good ole bor — **always** joking and buying the kid sweets. Well, do you know I cry when I heard it? I did. Blust, that fair shook me — that it did, there!

JIMMY. Who's lookin' after *your* kid then, Pearl?

PEARL. Father.

(*Pause.*)

JIMMY (*to* FRANK). Who do you think'll win today?

FRANK. Well Norwich won't.

JIMMY. No.

(*Pause.* MRS BRYANT *enters and sits down.*)

MRS BRYANT. Well the kettle's on.

PEARL (*to* BEATIE). Hev his sister got any children?

BEATIE. Two boys.

JIMMY. She wanna get on top one night then they'll hev girls.

JENNY. Oh shut you up Jimmy Beales.

MRS BRYANT. Hed another little win last night.

JENNY. When was this?

MRS BRYANT. The fireman's whist drive. Won seven 'n' six in the knockout.

JENNY. Yearp.

FRANK (*reading the paper*). I see that boy what assaulted the ole woman in London got six years.

MRS BRYANT. Blust! He need to! I'd've given him six years and a bit more. Bloody ole hooligans. Do you give me a chance to pass sentence and I'd soon clear the streets of crime, that I would. Yes, that I would.

BEATIE (*springing into activity*). All right Mother — we'll give you a chance. (*Grabs* JIMMY's *hat and umbrella. Places hat on mother's head and umbrella in her arms.*) There you are, you're a judge. Now sum up and pass judgment.

MRS BRYANT. I'd put him in prison for life.

FRANK. You gotta sum up though. Blust, you just can't stick a man in prison and say nothing.

MRS BRYANT. Goodbye, I'd say.

BEATIE. Come on Mother, speak up. Anybody can say 'go to prison', but *you* want to be a judge. Well, you show a judge's understanding. Talk! Come on Mother, talk!
(*Everyone leans forward eagerly to hear Mother talk. She looks startled and speechless.*)

MRS BRYANT. Well I — I — yes I — well I — Oh, don't be so soft.

FRANK. The mighty head is silent.

BEATIE. Well yes, she would be wouldn't she.

MRS BRYANT. What do you mean, I would be? You don't expect me to know what they say in courts do you? I aren't no judge.

BEATIE. Then why do you sit and pass judgment on people? If someone do something wrong you don't stop and think why. No discussin', no questions, just (*snap of fingers*) — off with his head. I mean look at Father getting less money. I don't see the family sittin' together and discussin' it. It's a problem! But which of you said it concerns you?

MRS BRYANT. Nor don't it concern them. I aren't hevin' people mix in my matters.

BEATIE. But they aren't just people — they're your family for hell's sake!

MRS BRYANT. No matters, I aren't hevin' it!

BEATIE. But Mother I —

MRS BRYANT. Now shut you up Beatie Bryant and leave it alone. I shall talk when I hev to and I never shall do, so there!

BEATIE. You're so stubborn.

MRS BRYANT. So you keep saying.

(MR BRYANT *enters, he is clean and dressed in blue pin-striped suit*)

MR BRYANT. You brewed up yit?

MRS BRYANT (*jumping up and going to kitchen*). Oh hell, yes — I forgot the tea look.

MR BRYANT. Well, now we're all waitin' on him.

JENNY. Don't look as if Susie's comin'.

BEATIE. Stubborn cow!

(*Silence.*)

JENNY. Hev you seen Susie's television set yit?

BEATIE. I seen it.

FRANK. Did you know also that when they first hed it they took it up to bed wi' them and lay in bed wi' a dish of chocolate biscuits?

PEARL. But now they don't bother — they say they've had it a year now and all the old programmes they saw in the beginning they're seein' again.

MRS BRYANT (*entering with tea*). Brew's up!

BEATIE. Oh, for Christ's sake let's stop gossiping.

PEARL. I aren't gossiping. I'm making an intelligent observation about the state of television, now then.

MR BRYANT. What's up wi' you now?

BEATIE. You weren't doin' nothin' o' the sort — you was gossiping.

PEARL. Well that's a heap sight better'n quotin' all the time.

BEATIE. I don't quote all the time, I just tell you what Ronnie say.

FRANK. Take it easy gal — he's comin' soon — don't need to go all jumpin' an' frantic.

BEATIE. Listen! Let me set you a problem.

JIMMY. Here we go.

BEATIE. While we're waitin' for him I'll set you a moral problem. You know what a moral problem is? It's a problem about right and wrong. I'll get you buggers thinking if it's the last thing I do. Now listen. There are four huts —

FRANK. What?

BEATIE. Huts. You know — them little things you live in. Now there are two huts on one side of a stream and two huts on the other side. On one side live a girl in one hut and a wise man in the other. On the other side live Tom in one hut and Archie in the other. Also there's a ferryman what run a boat across the river. Now — listen, concentrate — the girl loves Archie but Archie don't love the girl. And Tom love the girl but the girl don't go much on Tom.

JIMMY. Poor bugger.

BEATIE. One day the girl hears that Archie — who don't love her, remember — is going to America, so she decides to try once more to persuade him to take her with him. So listen what she do. She go to the ferryman and ask him to take her across. The ferryman say, I will, but you must take off all your clothes.

MRS BRYANT. Well, whatever do he wanna ask that for?

BEATIE. It don't matters why — he do! Now the girl doesn't know what to do so she ask the wise man for advice, and he say, you must do what you think best.

FRANK. Well that weren't much advice was it!

BEATIE. No matters — he give it. So the girl thinks about it and being so in love she decides to strip.

PEARL. Oh I say!

MR BRYANT. Well, this is a rum ole story ent it?

BEATIE. Shut up Father and listen. Now, er — where was I?

MR BRYANT. She was strippin'.

BEATIE. Oh yes! So, the girl strips and the ferryman takes her over — he don't touch her or nothing — just takes her over and she rushes to Archie's hut to implore him to take her with him and to declare her love again. Now Archie promises to take her with him and so she sleeps with him the night. But when she wake up in the morning he've gone. She's left alone. So she go across to Tom and explain her plight and ask for help. But soon ever he knowed what she've done, he chuck her out see? So there she is. Poor little gal. Left alone with no clothes and no friends and no hope of staying alive. Now — this is the question, think

213

about it, don't answer quick — who is the person most
responsible for her plight?

JIMMY. Well, can't she get back?

BEATIE. No, she can't do anything. She's finished. She've hed
it! Now, who's to blame?

(*There is a general air of thought for the moment and* BEATIE
looks triumphant and pleased with herself.)

MRS BRYANT. Be you a-drinkin' on your tea look. Don't you
worry about no naked gals. The gal won't get cold but the
tea will.

PEARL. Well I say the girl's most responsible.

BEATIE. Why?

PEARL. Well, she made the choice didn't she?

FRANK. Yes, but the old ferryman made her take off her clothes.

PEARL. But she didn't hev to.

FRANK. Blust woman, she were in love!

BEATIE. Good ole Frank.

JENNY. Hell if I know.

BEATIE. Jimmy?

JIMMY. Don't ask me gal — I follow decisions. I aren't makin'
none.

BEATIE. Father?

MR BRYANT. I don't know what you're on about.

BEATIE. Mother?

MRS BRYANT. Drink you your tea gal — never you mind what
I think.

(*This is what they're waiting for.*)

PEARL. Well — what do Ronnie say?

BEATIE. He say the gal is responsible only for makin' the
decision to strip off and go across and that she do that
because she's in love. After that she's the victim of two
phoney men — one who don't love her but take advantage
of her and one who say he love her but don't love her
enough to help her, and that the man who say he love her

214

but don't do nothin' to help her is most responsible because he were the last one she could turn to.

JENNY. He've got it all worked out then!

BEATIE (*jumping on a chair thrusting her fist into the air like Ronnie, and glorying in what is the beginning of a hysteric outburst of his quotes*). 'No one do that bad that you can't forgive them.'

PEARL. He's sure of himself then?

BEATIE. 'We can't be sure of everything but certain basic things we must be sure about or we'll die.'

FRANK. He think everyone is gonna listen then?

BEATIE. 'People *must* listen. It's no good talking to the converted. *Everyone* must argue and think or they will stagnate and rot and the rot will spread.'

JENNY. Hark at that then.

BEATIE (*her strange excitement growing; she has a quote for everything*). 'If wanting the best things in life means being a snob then glory hallelujah I'm a snob. But I'm not a snob Beatie, I just believe in human dignity and tolerance and co-operation and equality and —'

JIMMY (*jumping up in terror*). He's a communist!

BEATIE. 'I'm a socialist!'

(*There is a knock on the front door.*)

BEATIE (*jumping down joyously as though her excited quotes have been leading to this one moment*). He's here, he's here! (*But at the door it is the* POSTMAN, *from whom she takes a letter and a parcel.*) Oh, the silly fool, the fool. Trust him to write a letter on the day he's coming. Parcel for you Mother.

PEARL. Oh, that'll be your dress from the club.

MRS BRYANT. What dress is this then? I didn't ask for no dress from the club.

PEARL. Yes you did, you did ask me, didn't she ask me Frank? Why, we were looking through the book together Mother.

MRS BRYANT. No matters what we was doin' together I aren't hevin' it.

PEARL. But Mother you distinctly —

MRS BRYANT. I aren't hevin' it so there now!

(BEATIE *has read the letter — the contents stun her. She cannot move. She stares around speechlessly at everyone.*)

MRS BRYANT. Well, what's the matter wi' you gal? Let's have a read. (*Takes letter and reads contents in a dead flat but loud voice — as though it were a proclamation.*) 'My dear Beatie. It wouldn't really work would it? My ideas about handing on a new kind of life are quite useless and romantic if I'm really honest. If I were a healthy human being it might have been all right but most of us intellectuals are pretty sick and neurotic — as you have often observed — and we couldn't build a world even if we were given the reins of government — not yet any-rate. I don't blame you for being stubborn, I don't blame you for ignoring every suggestion I ever made — I only blame myself for encouraging you to believe we could make a go of it and now two weeks of your not being here has given me the cowardly chance to think about it and decide and I —'

BEATIE (*snatching letter*). Shut up!

MRS BRYANT. Oh — so we know now do we?

MR BRYANT. What's this then — ent he comin'?

MRS BRYANT. Yes, we know now.

MR BRYANT. Ent he comin' I ask?

BEATIE. *No he ent comin'.*

(*An awful silence ensues. Everyone looks uncomfortable.*)

JENNY (*softly*). Well blust gal, didn't you know this was going to happen?

(BEATIE *shakes her head.*)

MRS BRYANT. So *we're* stubborn are we?

JENNY. Shut you up Mother, the girl's upset.

MRS BRYANT. Well I can see that, I can see that, he ent coming,

216

I can see that, and we're here like bloody fools, I can see that.

PEARL. Well did you quarrel all that much Beatie?

BEATIE (*as if discovering this for the first time*). He always wanted me to help him but I never could. Once he tried to teach me to type but soon ever I made a mistake I'd give up. I'd give up every time! I couldn't bear making mistakes. I don't know why, but I couldn't bear making mistakes.

MRS BRYANT. Oh — so we're hearin' the other side o' the story now are we?

BEATIE. He used to suggest I start to copy real objects on to my paintings instead of only abstracts and I never took heed.

MRS BRYANT. Oh, so you never took heed.

JENNY. Shut you up I say.

BEATIE. He gimme a book sometimes and I never bothered to read it.

FRANK (*not maliciously*). What about all this discussion we heard of?

BEATIE. I *never* discussed things. He used to beg me to discuss things but I never saw the point on it.

PEARL. And he got riled because o' that?

BEATIE (*trying to understand*). I didn't have any patience.

MRS BRYANT. Now it's coming out.

BEATIE. I couldn't help him — I never knew patience. Once he looked at me with terrified eyes and said, 'We've been together for three years but you don't know who I am or what I'm trying to say — and you don't care do you?'

MRS BRYANT. And there she was tellin' me.

BEATIE. I never knew what he wanted — I didn't think it mattered.

MR BRYANT. And there she were gettin' us to solve the moral problem and now we know she didn't even do it herself. That's a rum 'un, ent it?

217

MRS BRYANT. The apple don't fall far from the tree — that it don't.

BEATIE (*wearily*). So you're proud on it? You sit there smug and you're proud that a daughter of yours wasn't able to help her boy friend? Look at you. All of you. You can't say anything. You can't even help your own flesh and blood. Your daughter's bin ditched. It's your problem as well isn't it? I'm part of your family aren't I? Well, help me then! Give me words of comfort! Talk to me — for God's sake, someone talk to me. (*She cries at last.*)

MR BRYANT. Well, what do we do now?

MRS BRYANT. We sit down and we eat that's what we do now.

JENNY. Don't be soft Mother, we can't leave the girl crying like that.

MRS BRYANT. Well, blust, 'tent my fault she's cryin'. I did what I could — I prepared all this food, I'd've treated him as my own son if he'd come but he hevn't! We got a whole family gathering specially to greet him, all on us look, but he hevn't come. So what am I supposed to do?

BEATIE. My God, Mother, I hate you — the only thing I ever wanted and I weren't able to keep him, I didn't know how. I hate you, I hate ...

(MRS BRYANT *slaps* BEATIE'S *face. Everyone is a little shocked at this harsh treatment.*)

MRS BRYANT. There! I hed enough!

MR BRYANT. Well what d'you wanna do that for?

MRS BRYANT. I hed enough. All this time she've bin home she've bin tellin' me I didn't do this and I didn't do that and I hevn't understood half what she've said and I've hed enough. She talk about bein' part o' the family but she've never lived at home since she've left school look. Then she go away from here and fill her head wi' high-class squit and then it turn out she don't understand any on it herself. It turn out she do just the same things she say I do. (*Into*

BEATIE's *face*) Well, am I right gal? I'm right ent I? When you tell me I was stubborn, what you mean was that *he* told you *you* was stubborn — eh? When you tell me I don't understand you mean *you* don't understand isn't it? When you tell me I don't make no effort you mean *you* don't make no effort. Well, what you blaming me for? Blaming me all the time! I haven't bin responsible for you since you left home — you bin on your own. She think I like it, she do! Thinks I like it being cooped up in this house all day. Well I'm telling you my gal — I don't! There! And if I had a chance to be away working somewhere the whole lot on you's could go to hell — the lot on you's. All right so I am a bloody fool — all right! So I know it! A whole two weeks I've bin told it. Well, so then I can't help you my gal, no that I can't, and you get used to that once and for all.

BEATIE. No you can't Mother, I know you can't.

MRS BRYANT. I suppose doin' all those things for him weren't enough. I suppose he weren't satisfied wi' goodness only.

BEATIE. Oh, what's the use.

MRS BRYANT. Well, don't you sit there an' sigh gal like you was Lady Nevershit. I ask you something. Answer me. You do the talking then. Go on — you say you know something we don't so *you* do the talking. Talk — go on, talk gal.

BEATIE (*despairingly*). I can't Mother, you're right — the apple don't fall far from the tree do it? You're right, I'm like you. Stubborn, empty, wi' no tools for livin'. I got no roots in nothing. I come from a family o' farm labourers yet I ent got no roots — just like town people — just a mass o' nothin'.

FRANK. Roots, gal? What do you mean, roots?

BEATIE (*impatiently*). Roots, roots, roots! Christ, Frankie, you're in the fields all day, you should know about growing things. Roots! The things you come from, the things that feed you. The things that make you proud of yourself — roots!

MR BRYANT. You got a family ent you?

BEATIE. I am not talking about family roots — I mean — the — I mean — Look! Ever since it begun the world's bin growin' hasn't it? Things hev happened, things have bin discovered, people have bin thinking and improving and inventing but what do we know about it all?

JIMMY. What is she on about?

BEATIE (*various interjection*). What do you mean, what am I on about? I'm talking! Listen to me! I'm tellin' you that the world's bin growing for two thousand years and we hevn't noticed it. I'm telling you that we don't know what we are or where we come from. I'm telling you something's cut us off from the beginning. I'm telling you we've got no roots. Blimey Joe! We've all got large allotments, we all grow things around us so we should know about roots. You know how to keep your flowers alive don't you Mother? Jimmy — you know how to keep the roots of your veges strong and healthy. It's not only the corn that need strong roots, you know, it's us too. But what've we got? Go on, tell me, what've we got? We don't know where we push up from and we don't bother neither.

PEARL. Well, I aren't grumbling.

BEATIE. You say you aren't — oh yes, you say so, but look at you. What've you done since you come in? Hev you said anythin'? I mean really said or done anything to show you're alive? Alive! Blust, what do it mean? Do you know what it mean? Any of you? Shall I tell you what Susie said when I went and saw her? She say she don't care if that ole atom bomb drop and she die — that's what she say. And you know why she say it? I'll tell you why, because if she had to care she'd have to do something about it and she find *that* too much effort. Yes she do. She can't be bothered — she's too bored with it all. That's what we all are — we're all too bored.

MRS BRYANT. Blust woman — bored you say, bored? You say Susie's bored, with a radio and television an' that? I go t'hell if she's bored!

BEATIE. Oh yes, we turn on a radio or a TV set maybe, or we go to the pictures — if them's love stories or gangsters — but isn't that the easiest way out? Anything so long as we don't have to make an effort. Well, am I right? You know I'm right. Education ent only books and music — it's asking questions, all the time. There are millions of us, all over the country, and no one, not one of us, is asking questions, we're all taking the easiest way out. Everyone I ever worked with took the easiest way out. We don't fight for anything, we're so mentally lazy we might as well be dead. Blust, we are dead! And you know what Ronnie say sometimes? He say it serves us right! That's what he say — it's our own bloody fault!

JIMMY. So that's us summed up then — so we know where *we* are then!

MRS BRYANT. Well if he don't reckon we count nor nothin', then it's as well he didn't come. There! It's as well he didn't come.

BEATIE. Oh, *he* thinks we count all right — living in mystic communion with nature. Living in mystic bloody communion with nature (indeed). But us count? Count Mother? I wonder. Do we? Do you think we really count? You don' wanna take any notice of what them ole papers say about the workers bein' all-important these days — that's all squit! 'Cos we aren't. Do you think when the really talented people in the country get to work they get to work for us? Hell if they do! Do you think they don't know we 'ont make the effort? The writers don't write thinkin' we can understand, nor the painters don't paint expecting us to be interested — that they don't, nor don't the composers give out music thinking we can appreciate it. 'Blust,' they say, 'the masses is too stupid for us to come down to them. Blust,' they say, 'if they don't make no effort why should we bother?' So you know who come along? The slop singers and the pop writers and the film makers and women's magazines and the Sunday papers and the picture strip love stories — that's who come along, and you don't have to make no effort for them, it come easy. 'We know where the money lie,' they say, 'hell we do! The workers've got it so let's give them what they want. If they want slop songs and film idols we'll give 'em that then. If they want words of one syllable, we'll give 'em that then. If they want the third-rate, *blust!* We'll give 'em *that* then. Anything's good enough for them 'cos they don't ask for no more!' The whole stinkin' commercial world insults us and we don't care a damn. Well, Ronnie's right — it's our own bloody fault. We want the third-rate — we got it! We got it! We got it! We ...

(*Suddenly* BEATIE *stops as if listening to herself. She pauses, turns with an ecstatic smile on her face —*)

D'you hear that? D'you hear it? Did you listen to me? I'm talking. Jenny, Frankie, Mother — I'm not quoting no more.

MRS BRYANT (*getting up to sit at table*). Oh hell, I hed enough of her — let her talk a while she'll soon get fed up.

(*The others join her at the table and proceed to eat and murmur.*)

BEATIE. Listen to me someone. (*As though a vision were revealed to her*) God in heaven, *Ronnie!* It does work, it's happening to me, I can feel it's happened, I'm beginning, on my own two feet — I'm beginning ...

(*The murmur of the family sitting down to eat grows as* BEATIE'*s last cry is heard. Whatever she will do they will continue to live as before. As* BEATIE *stands alone, articulate at last* —)

THE CURTAIN FALLS

'I'LL WAIT FOR YOU IN THE HEAVENS BLUE'

I'm Talking about Jerusalem

CHARACTERS OF THE PLAY

RONNIE KAHN
ADA SIMMONDS, *his sister*
SARAH KAHN, *their mother*
DAVE SIMMONDS, *Ada's husband*
1ST REMOVAL MAN
2ND REMOVAL MAN
LIBBY DOBSON, *wartime friend of Dave*
COLONEL DEWHURST, *Dave's employer*
SAMMY, *Dave's apprentice*
DANNY SIMMONDS
ESTHER KAHN }
CISSIE KAHN } *aunts of Ronnie and Ada*

★

ACT I
September 1946

ACT II
Scene 1: July 1947
Scene 2: Autumn 1953
Scene 3: Autumn 1957

ACT III
1959

★

First presented at the Belgrade Theatre, Coventry, on
4th April 1960

227

ACT ONE

Norfolk. A house in the middle of fields. We see the large kitchen of the house, the garden, and the end part of an old barn.

September 1946. DAVE and ADA SIMMONDS are just moving in. Boxes and cases are strewn around. DAVE and two REMOVAL MEN are manœuvring a large wardrobe, 1930 type, from a lorry off stage. ADA is unpacking one of the cases. SARAH KAHN, her mother, is buttering some bread on a table, and from a portable radio comes a stirring part of Beethoven's Ninth Symphony. RONNIE KAHN, Ada's brother, is standing on a box conducting both the music and the movement of people back and forth. DAVE — unlike ADA and RONNIE —· speaks with a slight cockney accent.

RONNIE. Gently now. Don't rush it. You're winning.

DAVE. Instead of standing there and giving orders why don't you give a bloody hand?

RONNIE. You don't need any more hands. I'm organizing you, I'm inspiring you.

DAVE. Jesus Christ it's heavy, it's heavy. Drop it a minute.

RONNIE. Lower it gently — mind the edges, it's a work of art.

DAVE. I'll work of art you. And turn that radio off — I can cope with Beethoven but not both of you.

RONNIE (*turns off radio*). What are you grumbling for? I've been shlapping things to and fro up till now, haven't I? Only as it's the last piece I thought I'd exercise my talents as a foreman. Don't I make a good foreman? (*Calling*) Hey, Mother, don't I make a good foreman?

SARAH (*coming from the kitchen*). What've you lost?

RONNIE. Listen to her! What've you lost! She's just like her daughter, she can't hear a thing straight. Watch this. Hey, Ada! The sea's not far away you know.

ADA. You can't have any because I haven't put the kettle on yet.

RONNIE. Lunatic family.

229

DAVE. Come on. We'll never get done. Ready?
(*They bend to lift the wardrobe.* SARAH *returns to kitchen.*)
RONNIE. Heave — slowly — don't strain — heave.
IST R.M. Where's it going?
DAVE. Through the kitchen and upstairs.
RONNIE. You won't get through the kitchen, go round the back.
DAVE. We'll manage.
(RONNIE *goes on ahead and pushes* ADA, *the box and* SARAH *and table out of their path.*)
RONNIE. Make way, make way — the army is marching on its stomach. (DAVE *and the two men are bent forward in effort.*) You see, I can't help, there's not enough room for four to get round that door.
(*They stop at other end of the kitchen and lower the wardrobe.*)
DAVE. We have to get round here and along the passage.
2ND R.M. Never. You can't bend wardrobes.
IST R.M. Could saw it in half.
RONNIE (*pretending to be offended*). Good God man! An original twentieth-century piece and you want to saw it in half? Ahhhhhhhhh. (*Weeps upon it.*)
IST R.M. You still at school?
RONNIE. So?
IST R.M. Talk a lot don't you.
RONNIE. What's that got to do with school?
IST R.M. Should've thought they'd taught you manners.
SARAH (*coming into battle*). Don't you think he's got manners then?
2ND R.M. But he talks so don't he?
ADA (*joining battle*). Sooner he talked than he remained silent.
RONNIE. My lunatic family comes to my rescue.
IST R.M. I'd've clipped him round the ear if he'd've called me lunatic.
DAVE. We'll have to take it back and use the front entrance.

RONNIE. What's the good of me being a foreman if you don't listen to me.

(RONNIE *again pushes back table and box which women had returned.*)

RONNIE. Make way, make way. The retreat! (*Opens radio again and conducts them and symphony out of kitchen.*)

SARAH. Everything he makes into a joke.

(*The men raise the wardrobe and struggle back, this time going round the back of the house.* RONNIE *pauses and surveys the scene.*)

RONNIE. Nineteen forty-six! The war is really over isn't it, eh, Mother? Aren't you proud that your children are the first to pick up the ruins?

SARAH. I'm proud, yes! (*Pushes radio lid closed*).

RONNIE. Of course proud! We just put a Labour Party in power didn't we? It's right they should be the pioneers — good! Ever-y-bo-dy is building. Out go the slums, whist! And the National Health Service comes in. The millennium's come and you're still grumbling. What's the matter, you don't like strawberries and cream?

SARAH (*looking around*). Strawberries and cream?

RONNIE. All right, so it's shmultz herring and plum pudding for the meanwhile. But it's a great saga you're witnessing. The wandering Jews strike again! None of the easy life for them, none of the comforts of electricity —

SARAH. They're madmen!

RONNIE. They don't need roads, give them a muddy lane —

SARAH. Tell me Ada, how are you going to get to the village? Not even a road here there isn't. Just fields — a house in the middle of nowhere.

ADA. Ronnie, go and get some water for tea.

RONNIE. And none of the joys of running water for these brave people, a well! A biblical well. I can see you Ada, like Miriam at the well and Dave will come like Moses and drive away the strangers and draw water for you and you shall love him and marry him, and you shall bear him a son and he will be called Adam and the son shall grow strong and the land of Israel shall grow mighty around him —

SARAH. Yes, here!

(SARAH *moves to throw something on a dustheap out of hearing.*)

ADA. It was Zipporah and Moses anyway.

RONNIE. Zipporah. What a beautiful name. I've always wanted to write the Bible. Ada, haven't you ever felt you've wanted to sit down and write something that's already written? God, how many times I've felt like composing the 'Autumn Journal'.

(SARAH *returns in time to hear this.*)

ADA. What?

RONNIE. You know — Louis MacNeice —

> Sleep, my past and all my sins,
> In distant snow or dried roses
> Under the moon for night's cocoon will open
> When day begins.

ADA. I know what you mean.

SARAH (*surprised*). It's wonderful, Ronnie.

RONNIE. Isn't it beautiful Mother? It's a poetry I can talk, I don't have to recite it.

(*As if telling* her *something*).

> Sleep to the noises of running water
> Tomorrow to be crossed, however deep;
> This is no river of the dead or Lethe,
> Tonight we sleep
> On the banks of the Rubicon — the die is cast;
> There will be time to audit
> The accounts later, there will be sunlight later
> And the equation will come out at last.

My God, I want to write it again and again.

SARAH. But Ronnie, you've never read me that one before. Now that one, *that* one you try and get published.

(*At this,* ADA *and* RONNIE *break into uncontrollable laughter.* SARAH *cannot understand why.*)

SARAH. So what's funny?

RONNIE. Oh, Mother I love you, love you. (*He cuddles her.*)

SARAH (*pushing him away because he tends to smother her*). All right so you love me, love me, but what's funny?

RONNIE (*picking up pail and going to get water*). My mother encourages me — get it published she says! (*Goes off laughing.*)

SARAH. Is he gone mad or something?

ADA. Oh, Mummy, you are funny — he was quoting a poem by a famous poet.

SARAH. How did I get such clever children?

RONNIE (*off*). Hey, Ada! How do I get the water out of this well?

ADA (*shouting*). Lift up the lid and hook the bucket on and just let it down.

RONNIE (*after a second*). Hey Ada! There's no water in this well.

ADA (*shouting*). Of course there is, you idiot.

RONNIE. But I can't see it.

ADA. It's a long way down.

RONNIE. You can die of thirst before you get to the bottom.

SARAH (*sighing*). Ada, Ada. You're both mad.

ADA. Next time you come down, we'll have lots of improvements.

SARAH. I don't understand it, I just don't see why you have to come out here. Is London so bad? Millions of people live there!

ADA. Thank you.

SARAH. All of a sudden they pick up and go away.

ADA (*calling*). Dave, where's the paraffin?

233

DAVE (*off*). I put it in the corner.

ADA. I see it. (*Picks up paraffin and proceeds to fill and light primus stove.*)

SARAH. A primus stove! What's the point? All this heavy work. No roads, no electricity, no running water, no proper lavatory. It's the Middle Ages. Tell me why you want to go back to the Middle Ages?

ADA. We'll get a calor gas stove in time.

SARAH. Progress!

ADA. Mummy, please, ple-ease help us. It's not easy this move, for any of us. Doesn't it occur to you that we desperately need your blessing, please —

SARAH. I'm here aren't I? Silly girl. But how can I bless — ? I brought up two nice children, and I want to see them round me — that's wrong? But all right, so you want to go away, so you want to build a life of your own, but here? Why here? Explain it to me, maybe I'll be happier. Why here?

RONNIE (*off, shouting*). Hey, Dave — how you managing?

DAVE (*off*). We're managing. Just a few more stairs.

RONNIE. That's right boys — heave, heave!

DAVE. I'll heave this bloody thing on top of your head if you don't shut up. Go away and make some tea.

RONNIE (*entering*). The men want tea. Feed the workers. Hey Addie — you know what I discovered by the well? You can shout! It's marvellous. You can shout and no one can hear you.

ADA (*triumphantly*). Of course!

SARAH (*derisively*). Of course.

RONNIE. Of course — listen. (*Goes into garden and stands on a tea chest and shouts.*) *Down with capitalism! Long live the workers' revolution! You see? And long live Ronnie Kahn too!* (*Waits for a reply.*) No one argues with you. No one says anything. Freedom! You can jump about. (*Jumps off chest.*) You can spin in the air. (*Jumps and spins with arms akimbo.*) You can do somersaults ... (*He rolls on the grass shouting 'wheeeee'.*) You can bang the earth. (*He thumps the ground with his fists with utter joy.*) My God — it's wonderful — you can go mad all on your own and no one'll say anything. (*Sits up wide-eyed.*)

SARAH. He's not my son. I'll swear he's not my son.

RONNIE (*crawling on all fours up to the kitchen door*). Of course I'm not your son. My real mother was a gipsy and lived in a caravan, and one day she came to your door and instead of buying flowers from her you bought me. And everyone believed us. They used to look at you, and then at me and say no — no, it's true, he doesn't look like you does he?

SARAH. Make the tea.

RONNIE (*springing up*). Where's the kettle?

ADA. In one of the boxes.

RONNIE. It's like camping.

SARAH. Camping!

ADA. Finished the bread Mummy?

SARAH. I've finished the bread. What about the soup?

ADA. Soup?

RONNIE. She made a chicken soup last night and put it in bottles. She puts everything in bottles. (*Looks in Sarah's bag.*)

SARAH. And a meat pie too I made.

ADA. Oh Mummy, you shouldn't have.

SARAH. I shouldn't have, I shouldn't have! Everything I shouldn't have. Did *you* think about what you were going to eat when you came here?

ADA. I brought bread and tomatoes and fruit and cheese.

RONNIE. Cheese!

SARAH. As if I didn't know what you'd bring!

RONNIE. She always offers me cheese when I'm hungry.

ADA. You're both mad.

SARAH. *We're* mad! My children and they still don't know how
to organize their lives.

RONNIE (*holding up jar*). Bottled Chicken Soup. It looks like —
er — hum — yes, well, I hope it tastes different.

ADA. We've only one primus so you'll have to wait until the
water's boiled. Get out a table-cloth Ronnie.

RONNIE. A table-cloth? What, here? Now?

ADA. This place may be a shambles but I don't intend living
as though it's one.

(DAVE *and the* REMOVAL MEN *have returned by this time
and* RONNIE *throws out a cloth assisted by* SARAH.)

1ST R.M. Got a problem living here haven't you?

2ND R.M. Ain't very modern is it, Jim?

RONNIE. Got the wardrobe in place?

2ND R.M. We got it through the door.

DAVE. You can help me manœuvre it later, Ronnie.

1ST R.M. What made you move here, mate? Not being nosey
or anything, but you can't say it's everybody's choice of a
new home.

DAVE. It's a long story.

2ND R.M. Couldn't you find a better place? More convenience?
I mean it's not very sanitary, is it?

DAVE. Not easy to find the right place with little cash. Saw the
job advertised, a cheap house for sale near by—grabbed it!

SARAH. Hard! Everything has to be hard for them.

1ST R.M. Still, they're young, missus, ain't they? Gotta admit
it's fresh out here.

2ND R.M. Too bleedin' fresh if you ask me.

RONNIE. Come on, Dave. Give them an answer. It's a golden
opportunity this. The world has asked you why you've
come here. There stands the world (*To* R. MEN) and here
stand you two. You're on trial comrade.

ADA. Don't arse around Ronnie, the men want their tea.

RONNIE. But I'm serious, girl. I want to know too. You've

236

always been my heroes, now you've changed course. You've left communism behind — what now?

1ST R.M. Communist, are you?

2ND R.M. That's a dirty word, ain't it?

1ST R.M. Not during the war it wasn't.

RONNIE. The world is waiting, Dave.

DAVE. I'm not going to make speeches, Ronnie.

SARAH. Is a reason a speech?

DAVE. You can't talk about reasons, Sarah, just like that. A decision grows, slowly — you discover it.

RONNIE. But where did this one start?

ADA. Ceylon —

DAVE. — When I was stationed out there. I was with Air Sea Rescue, boat building.

1ST R.M. We was in India. That's where Ted and me met. Decided on this game out there.

DAVE. I was in India for a bit. Where were you?

2ND R.M. Bombay.

DAVE. Karachi, me. That's where I met Libby Dobson, Ada — remember? I always wrote to you about Libby Dobson? Me and him were going to do everything together when we got back to Civvy Street. Like you two. But *that* was a ship in the night.

ADA. He made a great impression on you, though.

RONNIE. Taught me a lot. When we get straight we'll have him down here — shouldn't be difficult to trace him. He always wanted to do something like this with me. This'll please him this move, old Libby Dobson'd get a kick out of coming here.

1ST R.M. What was Ceylon like?

DAVE. Beautiful island. Being a carpenter I used to watch the local carpenters at work. They used to make their own tools and sometimes they'd show me. They'd sit out on the beach fashioning the boats or outside their houses planing and chiselling away at their timber, and they let me sit with them once they knew I was also building boats. And you know, one day, as I watched, I made a discovery — the kind of discovery you discover two or three times in a lifetime. I discovered an old truth: that a man is made to work and that when he works he's giving away something of himself, something very precious —

2ND R.M. We didn't see anything precious about living in mud huts and working in disease.

DAVE. No, no. You miss the point — I'm talking about the *way* they worked, not the conditions. I know about disease, I know about the mud huts, but what I was trying to say —

ADA. It's no good trying to explain. We're here and let's —

SARAH (*angrily*). Ada stop it! Stop it! Impatience! What's the matter with you all of a sudden. Don't explain! Nothing she wants to explain. No more talking. Just a cold, English you-go-your-way-and-I'll-go-mine! Why?

ADA. Because language isn't any use! Because we talk about one thing and you hear another that's why.

RONNIE. Come on, Dave, you haven't said enough. The world doesn't believe you —

ADA. The world!

RONNIE. Explain more.

ADA. Explain what? We've moved house, what's there to explain? What's so exceptional?

SARAH (*posing the real question*). What's wrong with socialism that you have to run to an ivory tower?

DAVE. Nothing's wrong with socialism Sarah, only we want to live it — not talk about it.

SARAH. Live it? Here?

ADA. Oh the city is paradise I suppose!

SARAH. The city is human beings. What's socialism without human beings tell me?

238

DAVE. I know the city Sarah. Believe me sweetheart! Since being demobbed I've worked in a factory turning out doors and window frames and I've seen men hating themselves while they were doing it. Morning after morning they've come in with a cold hatred in their eyes, brutalized! All their humanity gone. These you call men? All their life they're going to drain their energy into something that will give them nothing in return. Why do you think these two (*the* R.M.*s*) decided to set up on their own? Eh? I'll tell you —

SARAH. But this isn't a socialist society yet —

ADA. What the hell difference do you think that'll make? All anyone talks about is taking over capitalist society, but no one talks about really changing it.

2ND R.M. And you're going to change it?

1ST R.M. On your own, cock?

DAVE. No of course we can't change it. But you see that barn out there? I'll work as a chippy on the Colonel's farm here for a year and then in a year's time that barn'll be my workshop. There I shall work and here, ten yards from me, where I can see and hear them, will be my family. And they will share in my work and I shall share in their lives. I don't want to be married to strangers. I've seen the city make strangers of husbands and wives, but not me, not me and my wife.

SARAH. Words, words.

ADA. *Not* words. At last something more than just words.
    (*Pause. Their defiance sinks in.*)

RONNIE (*to the* R.M.*s*). So now *you* (*to* ADA *and* DAVE) and now the *world* knows. And the world — will watch you.

1ST R.M. Come on China. It's time to set off. These socialists can't even make us a cup of tea.
    (*At which point the whole Kahn family swing into action with regrets and apologies and thrust sandwiches and fruit into the arms of the startled lorry drivers.*)

2ND R.M. Oi, oi! Whoa! Merry Christmas!

1ST R.M. Think of us poor city sods won't you? Good luck!

> (*The R.M.s go off to the lorry. We hear the lorry start, it revs and slowly moves off in gear. The family stands and watches, and waves and calls 'Goodbye,' listening till the sound dies away.*
> *Silence.*
> *Each feels that with the going of the lorry has gone the last of the old life.*
> *It is getting dark.*)

RONNIE. Well — you're here. You've come. Welcome to the Shambles.

> (DAVE *moves to* ADA *and kisses her.* RONNIE *watches.* SARAH *sits unhappily in a chair away from them all.*)

DAVE. We've got a house.

ADA. We've got a house.

DAVE. Tired darling?

ADA. A bit.

DAVE. It's not *such* a mess.

ADA. I know.

DAVE. It looks it but it's not such a mess.

ADA. I know, angel.

DAVE. Are you in control?

ADA. I'm in control.

DAVE. I love you very much.

ADA. I love you very much.

RONNIE (*moving to* SARAH). And I love you too sweetheart. (*His arm round her*) Look at my sister — (*with mock passion*) isn't she beautiful?

SARAH. I don't understand what went wrong, I don't understand how she can be like that.

ADA (*breaking away from* DAVE). I'm not like anything Mummy, only like your daughter. (*Kisses* SARAH.) You can come and visit us. Look — (*waving arms around with mock majesty*) a country house. Aren't you pleased your daughter's got a country house? We can entertain in grand style! Everyone can come for a holiday — we'll have the maiden aunts down! Aunty Cissie and Aunt Esther can come and pull up weeds for us.

RONNIE. They're really very bourgeois these idealists you know.

SARAH. So far away.

ADA. Only a hundred miles.

SARAH. A hundred miles! You can say it easily. And what if Harry gets worse? It doesn't stop at one stroke, your father's never been very strong.

DAVE. I'm going to unpack some of the things upstairs.

ADA. Light the tilly lamp for me darling before you go up. Supper won't be long. (DAVE *does so.*)

RONNIE. I'm going to look over the district. I bet there are hidden treasures and secret hideouts.

SARAH. Take your raincoat. (RONNIE *does so.*)

DAVE. I suppose *I'll* have to take a candle up with me.

ADA. Come on Mummy. Let's get some supper ready.

SARAH. Do you have to work any more Dave? Can't you rest a little?

DAVE. I'll prepare some beds and take out some of the clothes and hang them. We'll get straight bit by bit. No sense in rushing it. They're good things these lamps. There! It's alight. (*A soft glow covers part of the kitchen.*)

ADA. A lovely light.

SARAH. It took someone all this time to discover electricity — he shouldn't have bothered!

(DAVE *smiles, shakes his head and goes off upstairs. The women busy themselves. They tidy the general mess and then lay plates and knives and forks on the table.* ADA's *movements are slow and calm.* SARAH *is volatile and urgent, though somehow she manages to speak slowly and with deliberation — softly. The atmosphere sinks in. Then —*)

241

SARAH. And Dave doesn't like me — you know that?

(ADA *doesn't reply. Silence. They continue moving around.*)
I don't know why it should be that he doesn't like me.
I don't think I've ever done anything to hurt him. (*Pause.*)
Perhaps that's why he's taking you away, because he
doesn't like me. Who knows!

(*Still* ADA *does not reply — instead she very softly starts
humming.*)
He's changed you. Dave's changed a lot from the old days,
Ada. (*Pause.*) Or perhaps he hasn't, perhaps it's me. Who
knows. I know he fought in Spain, he's really a wonderful
boy but — Ach! children! You bring them up, you teach
them this you teach them that, you do what you think is
right and still it's no good. They grow up and they grow
away and you're left with — with — ! Where do their
madnesses come from? Who knows. *I* don't know why
Dave doesn't like me.

(*Still no word from* ADA. *She hums perhaps a little louder.*)
SARAH. What you humming for? Humming! All of a sudden
she does this humming when I talk to her. A new madness.
Stop it Ada. Stop it! Silly girl.

(*An elderly gentleman appears. He is* COLONEL DEWHURST,
*the farmer for whom Dave will be working. He comes
from the path and knocks on the kitchen door just as* SARAH
finishes.)
COLONEL (*as door is opened to him*). Mrs Simmonds? I'm
Colonel Dewhurst.
ADA. Oh hello, come in please, we're still unpacking so
forgive —
COLONEL. But I understand, ma'am, I just thought —
ADA. This is my mother. Mother, Colonel Dewhurst, Dave's
employer.
COLONEL (*shaking hands*). How do you do, ma'am. You must
be very tired. Come a long way today, haven't you?

ADA (*calling*). Dave! Dave! Colonel Dewhurst.

DAVE. I'm coming down, a second.

ADA. Do sit down please.

COLONEL. I was telling your mother you've come a long way today.

ADA. Yes, we have.

COLONEL. It must seem strange.

SARAH. It seems very strange.

ADA. My mother thinks we're mad Colonel.

COLONEL. To come to the country? A fine life, a fine life.

SARAH. With no sanitation or electricity?

COLONEL. Thousands of places like that, thousands! But it's a large house, fresh air —

SARAH. There are parks in London.

COLONEL. *I* wouldn't change now.

SARAH. Maybe you've got some amenities my children haven't?

COLONEL. But they're young, aren't they? It's good they start off with a struggle, makes them appreciate life —

SARAH (*to* ADA). We brought you up with riches I suppose?

DAVE (*appearing and shaking hands*). Hello Colonel Dewhurst.

COLONEL. I thought I'd drop over and see you were arriving safely.

DAVE. That's very good of you.

COLONEL. It won't take you long to get used to it. It's a bracing life in the country.

DAVE. We're not rushing things. I think we'll manage.

COLONEL. Of course you will, yes, I'm sure. When do you think you'll be able to start — er — you know, when can I expect —

DAVE. Well I hoped you wouldn't mind giving us a few days to settle in and get our bearings.

COLONEL. Yes, well, there's no need to come in tomorrow, I think that'll be all right, yes, that'll be all right. But my foreman is waiting to start some fencing — want to get a few more sows in. He's been waiting a long time for a carpenter. No, no need to come in tomorrow — early start the next day'll do, do perfectly.

DAVE. Thanks.

COLONEL. Yes, well, thought I'd pop over and see you were arriving safely. Come at a good time — we've had some rain but it's gone. Doesn't do to have too much rain.

ADA (*not really knowing the reply*). No it doesn't does it?

COLONEL. Talking of rain, Simmonds, I'd advise you to buy yourself a tank to catch the soft water. Good stuff, that. Save you work, too. Not so much to pull up from the well. Buy one with a tap — easier. Don't drink it, though. Use it for washing and things.

DAVE. Thank you for telling us.

COLONEL. I'll see you right. (*Walks out into the garden.* DAVE *and* ADA *follow to doorway.*) You'll learn lots of things as you go along. (*Looks around.*) Good garden here. Grow your own veges. Apple tree there. Prune it a bit. Sturdy barn too, couple hundred years old. Use it for chickens, build a run inside it. You could do that, couldn't you? Build yourself a chicken run?

DAVE. I expect so. A little bit of intelligence can build you anything.

COLONEL (*suddenly become the employer*). Eight o'clock on Wednesday morning, then, Simmonds. Good night to you both. (*Goes off.*)

(DAVE *and* ADA *stand a second and look at each other.*)

SARAH. That's the man you're working for?

ADA (*to* DAVE). He didn't give you much time to settle in did he?

DAVE. No, he didn't did he?

SARAH. You won't have time to scratch yourself, I'm telling you.

ADA. Well perhaps he needs you.

DAVE (*certain*). I'm sure he does. (*Not so certain*) But I reckon he could have given us a couple of days to settle in.

ADA. Yes he could have.

DAVE. We're still rushing —

ADA. Seems like it.

(*They are disappointed.* SARAH *watches them sadly.*)

SARAH. Oh my children, children! Straight away they want to walk into paradise. Perhaps it's a good thing you should start work so soon, you'll settle in the house gradually and working will get you into a stride, a routine. Always have a routine.

ADA (*brightening at this*). Perhaps Mum is right darling. Perhaps it's better to get stuck in straight away.

DAVE. No moping you mean?

ADA. I mean have no time to think we've done the wrong thing.

DAVE. *You* don't think we've done the wrong thing do you darling.

ADA. No — I do not.

DAVE. I do love you. (*Kisses her briefly.*)

ADA. Come on, let's get this food over with. Where's Ronnie?

SARAH. Looking for hidden treasure.

DAVE. He's what?

SARAH. He's gone out exploring — in the mountains there. (*Waves vaguely.*)

ADA. There aren't any mountains in Norfolk Mother.

SARAH. I'm very surprised.

DAVE. What's that fire there?

(*They all look at a red glow coming from behind the barn.* DAVE *and* ADA *rush off to one side of the barn.*)

DAVE. I hope the bloody fool hasn't been up to any of his tricks.

(SARAH *stands looking in the direction they've gone. After a*

245

few seconds RONNIE *strolls in from the other side of the barn. He walks in a kind of daze, clutching a branch, gazing into space.*)

RONNIE. You can build fires under the night sky.

SARAH. What've you been up to you mad boy?

RONNIE. There's bracken in every hedge and you can make fires with them.

SARAH. Have you set the barn on fire?

RONNIE. It's beautiful.

SARAH. For God's sake stop playing the fool and answer me.

RONNIE (*looking around him*). It's all very beautiful.

(ADA *and* DAVE *appear*).

ADA. Ronnie, you are a nitwit, you could have set the whole place alight.

RONNIE. Oh no. I know about these things.

SARAH. What did he do? I can't get any sense out of him.

DAVE. It's all right — he made a camp fire, don't panic, nothing's burning. Let's eat.

(*They settle down to eat except* RONNIE, *who for the moment leans against a box, still enraptured.*)

SARAH. He's so mad. I get so angry sometimes. Look at him, in a daze. Take your raincoat off and sit down and eat.

(RONNIE *sits down at the table but doesn't take off his raincoat.*)

ADA. What are you sitting down in your raincoat for?

RONNIE. Somehow I feel, I feel — I ... (*unable to explain*)

ADA. Yes, yes, but why are you eating with your raincoat on?

SARAH. Another madness! Every so often he gets a madness into his head and you can't shake him out of it. I get so annoyed. Ronnie, take your raincoat off!

DAVE. What are you getting upset for, both of you. The boy wants to eat in his raincoat let him eat in his raincoat.

ADA. He's not normal!

DAVE. All right so he's not normal, why should you worry.

ADA. I do worry. I'm not going to sit at the table with him while he's wearing a raincoat. Ronnie take your raincoat off!

(RONNIE *continues eating.*)

SARAH. I don't know what makes him like this. Ronnie take your raincoat off!

ADA. He's so bloody stubborn. *Ronnie!*

DAVE. You and your mother, you're both the same. Why don't you leave the boy alone. What harm is he doing in a raincoat.

ADA. Because it annoys me that's why! (*to* DAVE) Don't side with him Dave because if you side with him he knows he can get away with it.

(SARAH *rises at this point and goes to a corner of the room where she finds an umbrella.*)

DAVE. Now look at us! Here we are quarrelling among ourselves just because your brother is sitting down at the table wearing a macintosh. Have you ever heard such lunacy? What's your mother up to?

(SARAH *sits at the table and opens the umbrella over her and proceeds to eat. Everyone looks at her in amazement. Suddenly* RONNIE *bursts out laughing, jumps up from the chair, kisses her, and takes off his raincoat.* DAVE *sees what has happened and laughs also. There is great merriment.*)

DAVE. Well if you Kahns aren't the most lunatic family I know.

(*They all begin to eat.* SARAH *twists the umbrella once on her shoulders, sticks her hand out to see if the 'rain' has finished, and then folds up the umbrella and eats.*)

SARAH. Don't I know my children!

DAVE. You're all so much alike, that's why.

(*They eat on in silence for a moment until suddenly* SARAH *gets up from the table and moves quickly out from the kitchen to the garden where she takes a handkerchief from her apron. She weeps a little.* RONNIE *rises and goes to the door.*)

RONNIE. Sarah?

SARAH. It's all right, I'm all right, leave me, go back inside and finish eating.

(RONNIE *returns.*)

RONNIE. Tears again.

ADA. I guessed this might happen. Perhaps she shouldn't have come.

DAVE. Can you blame her darling? Ronnie, sit down and let's finish this food.

RONNIE. I'm not really hungry. (*Half annoyed*) She always makes it seem like the end of the world when she cries.

SARAH (*from the garden*). You know, it reminds me of Hungary, where I was born —

ADA. There, she's better again.

SARAH. There used to be high mountains and a river and a waterfall; my brother Hymie once fell into the river and I saved him. He nearly drowned. The mountains had snow on them.

RONNIE (*calling to her*). But there aren't any mountains or waterfalls here Mother.

SARAH (*after a pause, petulantly*). It still reminds me of Hungary.

ADA. Everything reminds her of Hungary. We were listening to Beethoven the other night and she swore black and blue it was based on a Hungarian folk song.

RONNIE. I'll wash up.

DAVE. Come on, let's finish unpacking.

(RONNIE *takes what remains of the water in the kettle and pours it into a basin, shakes some soap powder into it and begins to wash up.* ADA *and* DAVE *stand by one of the boxes, take out the contents one by one, unwrap them and lay them aside.* SARAH *enters, takes a dishcloth and begins to wipe up what* RONNIE *washes. As they do this* SARAH *begins to sing a soft and melodic Yiddish folk song. She can't remember past the first line.* RONNIE *picks up and reminds her. They sing together.* RONNIE *indicates to* ADA *to join in, she does so and in turn brings in* DAVE. *The new life has started and some of the old has come with them, and* —)

THE CURTAIN FALLS

ACT TWO

Scene 1

July 1947.
Everything is more in order now. Twelve months have passed and with it their first winter.

A signpost saying 'Y.H.A.', with an arrow, leans against a wall, waiting to be knocked into the ground.

The stage is empty. DAVE *appears singing 'Linden Lea' and carrying a roll of linoleum, which he lays down by the back door. He has just returned from work. At the door he pauses and looks out, surveying the countryside. From a room upstairs,* ADA *calls out.*

ADA. Dave?

DAVE. Yes sweetheart.

ADA. My God, what time is it?

DAVE. About five fifteen. Is Libby here?

ADA. No, he'll be back soon. I'm just finishing this letter.

DAVE. It's all right, don't rush.

ADA. Dave — when did we arrive here?

DAVE. Roughly twelve months ago.

> (DAVE *stays by door and begins to unbutton his tall boots. After some seconds* ADA *appears. She is pregnant. She greets* DAVE *with a kiss and then he nods his head towards the view. They both gaze at it a while and inhale deeply.*)

ADA. The corn is yellow now.

DAVE. Colours for each season. The children will love it.

ADA. We'll teach the children to look at things won't we Dave? I shall make it into a sort of game for them. Teach them to take notice. (*With mock pomp*) Don't let the world pass you by, I shall tell them — (*breathing deeply*) breathe, I shall say, breathe deeply and fill your lungs and open your eyes. For the sun, I shall say, open your eyes for that laaaarge sun.

DAVE. Not long ago that field was brown. What does Libby say to it all, now he's had a chance to look around? We didn't get much of a chance to talk last night because he arrived so late.

ADA. A very strange fish your friend Libby Dobson. He doesn't quite fit the picture you painted of him does he?

DAVE. No he doesn't does he? What's he been up to all day?

ADA. I packed him up some sandwiches and he went out for a day's walking. God knows where. He stood out here and he looked around and he said 'It's all sky isn't it?' and then he stalked off with a 'see you'.

DAVE. He looked very sad and worn old Libby — never thought he'd end up a — what does he call himself?

ADA. A business consultant.

DAVE. He was a bloody fine mechanic in the RAF.

ADA. You're disappointed aren't you darling?

DAVE. Yes I am — daft, but I am. You know there's always one person you want to show your life to — show what you've done — and I've thought Libby Dobson was the bloke — should've thought he'd've understood. Blimey! the man had a hand in shaping my ideas — people! Well that's people I suppose.

ADA. Maybe he'll be better after a day's walk. Get me some water look or he'll come and nothing'll be ready and then he will be riled.

DAVE. Riled! You're a real Norfolk girl already. (*Holding her*) Let's pretend he's not here and let's go to bed and just lie there.

ADA. Let's get this one over first.

DAVE. We'll leave a note for old Dobson and he can get his own supper.

ADA. Darling the water.

DAVE. He's a big boy — he can look to himself.

ADA. Besides *I'm* — we're — hungry.

DAVE. Water.

(*He goes off singing 'Linden Lea' and* ADA *goes in to lay a salad.* DAVE *begins to talk to her from the back of the house.*)

DAVE (*off*). Darling we must start making new plans.

ADA. I'm making a salad for supper.

DAVE. What?

ADA. Salad!

DAVE. Plans!

ADA. What?

DAVE. Plans!

ADA. No, salad!

(DAVE *appears at window to kitchen.*)

DAVE. Let's get together — what are *you* talking about?

ADA. I said I'm making a salad for supper.

DAVE. Oh. And I said we must start making new plans. We'll start again. (*Returns to well.*)

ADA (*waits, then calls*). What plans?

DAVE (*off*). I want to build a chicken hut —

ADA. Lovely —

DAVE. And then I want to start laying a concrete floor in the barn so that I can build a proper workshop.

ADA. Have you ever laid a concrete floor before?

DAVE. I hadn't ever made a piece of furniture before had I? You learn. You think about it and you learn. How many more buckets of water do you want for Christ's sake?

ADA. Just fill the copper.

DAVE. But I filled it this morning.

ADA. And I used it this morning.

(DAVE *enters, puffed out, carrying a bucket of water.*)

ADA. Here, put the spare one in the jug.

(ADA *draws a jug from under the sink.*)

DAVE. And that's another thing. I've got to take a pipe from the sink to the well and run it into a drain outside.

ADA. A plumber too.

DAVE. And then we must start thinking about buying a soft water tank, that'll save arms at the well.

ADA. Darling, I need storage space. The one cupboard you built there isn't enough.

DAVE. In time my darling, all in good time. We've made our garden grow haven't we? We've made our garden grow and we've stopped our roof from leaking. I've boarded the old stables up and laid by timber ready to work. The rooms are painted white and nearly all the windows have curtains, and in three months' time I reckon I can start on my own. Look, only the hedges are wild. All in good time my darling.

ADA. And Mummy asks us what we do with our time. They're mad.

DAVE. Think we'll stick it out?

ADA. What the hell kind of question is that —

DAVE. Relax Ada — you've gone all tense — you'll give birth to a poker.

ADA. Dave, and that's another thing. I'm worried about the baby. I've been reading that —

DAVE. Whatever you've been reading forget it! Look at you, you're so healthy. Your belly is high and the baby is probably so big that he's bored with it all. (*Puts his ear to her stomach and has a conversation with the baby.*) Listen, he's talking.

ADA. You're mad darling.

DAVE. I tell you he's talking. Yes. Yes, I can hear you — sounds like a dozen drains emptying — what's that? You don't want to come out? But you've got to come out, I don't care how comfortable it is you'll get cramp. No I'm not going to send a bloody taxi for you — you'll walk. Now you listen to me, you come out when you're told or I'll plug you in there for life — you hear me?

ADA. Dave, for God's sake, don't be crude.

253

DAVE (*snuggling up to her*). Yes, let's be crude.

ADA. In the middle of fields?

DAVE. Right in the middle of fields, one night, at full moon. (*At this moment* LIBBY DOBSON *appears. He's stocky, about 30 years old, and looks as though he wants to be a fisherman and can only be one on holidays.*)

DOBSON. Quite a hideout you've got here, haven't you?

DAVE (*hopefully*). What do you think of it now you've seen it Libby?

DOBSON. You're going to turn it into a youth hostel?

DAVE. Got to make some spare cash somehow mate.

DOBSON. These places really do cater for the hale and bloody hearty, don't they? There — (*puts two bottles on the table*) wine for the table and the whisky's for me. I'm going up to change. (*Goes off.*)

DAVE. Well, I wonder what sort of evening this is going to be?

ADA (*picking up a bucket of waste from under sink and throwing it outside back door*). It'll be all right Dave. People aren't ever as you remember them — you'll just have to get to know each other again.

(*Outside* ADA *notices the rolls of linoleum. Puts down bucket and undoes them.*)

ADA. What's this darling?

DAVE. Some old lino the Colonel threw away. We can use that in the hallway.

ADA. Threw away?

DAVE. Well I saw it lying around in the shed. It's been there for months.

ADA. Did you ask him?

DAVE. But it's been lying around for ages.

ADA. Dave I'm not very moral about taking odd things from employers but I'd hate to have him —

DAVE. It's all right sweetheart I tell you.

ADA. You say it's all right but —

DAVE. Ada, the supper. Libby's hungry and so am I. I want to wash. (*Pours himself water into bowl and strips to the waist to wash, as* ADA *proceeds to lay the table.*)

ADA. Shall I bring out the wine glasses?

DAVE. Bring out the wine glasses.

ADA. Darling don't be cross.

DAVE. But you go on so.

ADA. I don't want things to go wrong.

DAVE. Well a lot will go wrong — so? Are you going to get upset each time?

ADA. Will you light the lamp when you've finished please?

DAVE. I mean a lot *is* going to go wrong isn't it?

ADA. This is different, I —

(DOBSON *returns at this point and sits down, waiting for the next move. Remember, he has already caught them embracing.* DAVE *and* ADA *glance at each other,* DAVE *shrugs his shoulders.* ADA *proceeds to lay out a clean shirt for* DAVE, *he is drying himself. The rest of this scene happens while* ADA *prepares a salad. They never get round to eating it.*)

ADA. Don't forget the lamp when you've done please Dave.

DOBSON. Tilly lamps — the lot. You two have really taken your backward march seriously, eh? Dead serious — cor!

DAVE. Libby — what is it mate, come on, out with it — what's nettled you?

DOBSON. Oh no, Simmonds, please. No old chums and their war memories — I'm on holiday. I'll help you chop your wood — I'll even dance round the may-pole with you — but no heart-searching, I'm a tired man.

(*Throughout an awkward silence the lamp is lit. During this next scene* DOBSON *drinks his whisky, becoming more and more tipsy; just now he stares at the sky.*)

DOBSON. The countryside smells like a cow with diarrhoea.

ADA. Perhaps your nose is still full of smoke and petrol fumes.

DOBSON. Jesus! I could've recognized that remark a mile off.

If I hadn't known, it would have told me your whole story.
Our horrible industrial civilization. We hate the large,
inhuman cities. Eh? Back to nature, boys.

(*An embarrassed silence.*)

ADA (*to* DAVE). I had a letter from Ronnie today.

DAVE. What does your mad brother say?

ADA. You remember his girl friend Jacqueline? The one he
told us knew it all? Well he's come to the dramatic conclusion that people who are similar aren't much good to
each other so he's going to marry a prostitute!

DOBSON. Oh God! I bet your mother's in the Salvation Army.

(ADA *and* DAVE *laugh uproariously at this.*)

ADA. Can you imagine Sarah in the Salvation Army? 'Comrades, Jesus Christ was the first communist to be born
among us.'

DOBSON. Now the picture is complete. Two ex-communists!
There's nothing more pathetic than the laughter of people
who have lost their pet faith.

(*The laughter is dead. That was a bomb.*)

DAVE. What the hell *is* the matter with you Libby? Within a
few minutes you've called us idealists as if you were swearing at us, and then you express disgust because you think
we've lost our faiths.

ADA. Let's have some of your wine shall we?

DOBSON. Yes, let's.

DAVE. You're being offensive Libby.

DOBSON (*wearily*). Oh, come off it! I'm a cynic. You can
recognize a cynic, can't you? You should be using me,
sharpening your ideas on me. The more sceptical I become the higher your ideals should soar, shouldn't they?
Eh? Well, soar then — soar! Be heroic! There's nothing
wrong with idealism, only when it's soft and flabby. The
smell of petrol in my nose! So what! You can't change
the world because it smells of petrol.

ADA. Who's talking about changing the world?

DOBSON. Then go home. Be good children and go home, because you'll never make the beautiful, rustic estate.

ADA. My God darling — it's come to something when we're sneered at for wanting beautiful things.

DOBSON. Because it's a lie. Outdated! Because it's not new!

DAVE. New! New! Everything has to be new! Contemporary! You could walk around on your hands all day — that's new — but it wouldn't be achieving much would it?

DOBSON. That's better — you're bristling, you're bristling. Soon you'll be able to devour me. That's what a cynic's for, Davey mate, to be devoured, gobbled up.

DAVE (to ADA). I don't understand it darling. Everyone accuses us of something or other — rustics, escapists, soft-headed. (To DOBSON) You think there aren't problems here?

ADA. There isn't a servant to draw our water, you know?

DAVE. Or a gardener to grow our vegetables.

ADA. Do you think I'm going to have a nanny to see to my child?

DAVE. Or that there's a private income somewhere?

ADA. In London you waste your time solving the wrong problems.

DAVE. Leaving early to catch the bus! Is that living?

ADA. But God forbid we should ever imagine that we're changing that world by living here.

DOBSON. Then there's not much point in doing this sort of thing, is there?

DAVE. Not even on an individual level?

DOBSON. What do you mean, 'an individual level'?

DAVE. For God's sake stop asking us what we mean by perfectly simple phrases.

DOBSON. That's just it! They are simple phrases. Simple, inane and irresponsible! Individual level! Have you ever taken your ideas to their logical conclusion? Well, have you?

Hasn't a worker in a factory ever looked at you as though you were mad — a little potty, you know? Would you have the world do without cars, planes, electricity, houses, roads? Because *that's* the logical conclusion. If no man should be tied to turning out screws all his life, then that's what it means. No screws — no transport! No labourers — no roads! No banks or offices — no commercial market! No humdrum jobs, then no anything! There you are, solve it! Go on. Think about it. Reorganize the world so's everyone's doing a job he enjoys, so everyone's 'expressing' himself. Go on. Universal happiness? Get it!

DAVE. Now who's being wet? Happiness? (*Mimicking*) What do you mean by happiness? It's the *doing*, the doing! Do you think we care that the city was large or smelt of petrol? It was the boredom man — the sheer boredom. Nine to five! Mass production! Remember? It numbed us, made us soggy and soft. There! *That's* being soggy and soft! Happiness! My God, you cynics are the soggiest.

DOBSON. Nicely, nicely, Davey. Look, only my head and arms are left.

ADA. You sound as though you really believe in Jerusalem.

DOBSON. Shrewd girl. Of course I believe in Jerusalem, only *I* personally can't measure up to it.

ADA. Because your type always tries to win with words that's why — but you never *do* anything, you're never at peace long enough.

DOBSON (*the harshness gone*). The idyll was really broken, wasn't it? I could see it in your faces. Dave's old blood brother has sold his soul. But what do you really know about me, that you think you can say that?

DAVE. We hadn't much of a chance had we comrade? You weren't exactly inviting were you?

DOBSON. I've tried it, Dave — listen to me and go home — I've tried it and failed. Socialism? I didn't sell out that easily. You've gone back to William Morris, but I went back to old Robert Owen. Five thousand pound my old man left me, and I blushed when I heard it. But I still hung on. It's not mine, I decided — the profits of exploitation, I said. Right! Give it back! So I worked out a plan. I found four other young men who were bright mechanics like myself and who were wasting their talents earning ten pounds a week in other men's garages, and I said 'Here's a thousand pounds for each of you — no strings, no loans, it's yours! Now let's open our own garage and exploit no one but ourselves. There's only one provision, I said, 'only one: as soon as there is an excess profit of another thousand pounds, we find someone else to inherit it and we expand that way!' See the plan? A chain of garages owned and run by the workers themselves, the real thing, and I will build it myself. Can you imagine what a bloody fool they must have thought me? Can you guess the hell of a time they had planning to buy me out? Democracy, mate? I spit it! Benevolent dictatorship for me. You want Jerusalem? Order it with an iron hand — no questions, no speeches for and against — bang! It's there! You don't understand it? You don't want it? Tough luck, comrade — your children will! (*To* ADA) No peace? You're right, Mrs Simmonds. I'm dirtied up. Listen to me, Dave, and go home before you're dirtied up.

ADA. You've nearly finished that whisky Libby.

DOBSON. Is that all you can say? I've just related a modern tragedy and you're warning me against alcohol. She's a real woman this Ada of yours. A woman dirties you up as well, you know. She and the world—they change you, they bruise you, they dirty you up — between them, you'll see.

DAVE. And you call the idealist soft and flabby do you?

ADA. Let's drop it Dave — I think Libby's had enough.

DOBSON. Oh no, you mean you've had enough. The little

woman senses danger — marvellous instinct for self-preservation. I suppose you two consider you are happily
married for ever and ever and ever. (*Pause.*) I was married
once. God knows how it happened — just after demob. I
used to watch her as the weeks and months went by; I used
to sit and watch fascinated and horrified as — as she
changed. This was before the old man died and we both
went out to work. After supper we'd wash up and she'd
sit by the fire and fall asleep. Just fall asleep — like that.
She might glance at a newspaper or do a bit of knitting,
but nothing else — nothing that might remind me she was
alive. And her face would go red in front of the fire and
she'd droop around and be slovenly. And I just watched
her. She chewed food all the time, you know. Don't
believe me? I watched her! Chewing all the time. Even in
bed, before she went to sleep — an apple or a piece of
gateau — as though terrified she wasn't getting enough
into her for that day. And she became so gross, so undeli-
cate, so unfeeling about everything. All the grace she had
was going, and instead there was flesh growing all around
her. I used to sit and watch it grow. How does one ever
know, for Christ's sake, that a woman carries the seeds of
such disintegration? Then I tried what your brother wants
to do — take a simple girl, a girl from an office, lively, un-
cluttered. Wife number two! Just about the time I in-
herited my five thousand pounds. A real socialist enterprise
and a simple wife. Ironic, really. There was I putting a
vision into practice, and there was she watching me in
case I looked at other women — making me feel lecherous
and guilty. She's the kind that dirties you up. There was I
sharing out my wealth and there was she — always
wanting to possess things, terrified of being on her own.
She marries a man in order to have something to attach to
herself, a possession! The man provides a home — bang!

She's got another possession. *Her* furniture, *her* saucepans, *her* kitchen — bang! bang! bang! And then she has a baby — bang again! All possessions! And this is the way she grows. She grows and she grows and she grows and she takes from a man all the things she once loved him for — so that no one else can have them. Because, you see, the more she grows, ah! the more she needs to protect herself. Clever? Bloody clever! I think I hate women because they have no vision. Remember that, Davey — they haven't really got vision — only a sense of self-preservation, and you will get smaller and smaller and she will grow and grow and you will be able to explain nothing because everything else will be a foreign language to her. You know? Those innocent I-don't-know-what-you're-talking-about eyes?

DAVE. Make an early night Libby, yes?

(DOBSON *rises, suddenly, furious at being told to go to bed. But his own terrible honesty defies him. He shrinks, looks at them for a sort of forgiveness, and then shrugging his shoulders turns and goes, taking maybe something to chew from the table.*)

ADA. Do you realize he was talking about what I might become darling?

DAVE. Are you worried?

ADA. Do we really appear like that to you men?

DAVE. You *are* worried aren't you?

ADA. I suddenly feel unclean.

DAVE. A cynic works that way darling. Perhaps he's right when he says we should use him, sharpen ourself on him. I don't know what to say — the man's certainly been bruised hasn't he? Does that make him more reliable or less — I never know.

ADA. The futile pursuit of an ideal. Suddenly it all makes me sick. Like eating too many good things.

DAVE. Right! Then enough now. We're not going to be dragged into this discussion again. We are not going to go around apologizing for the way we live. Listen to people and we'll go mad. Enough now!

(*Someone is coming from the lane. A torchlight appears. A voice calls. It is* COLONEL DEWHURST.)

COLONEL. Is anyone at home? Hello there. Simmonds.

ADA. It's Dewhurst. At this hour! (*Opens door to him.*) In here Colonel. Come in.

COLONEL. Good evening.

DAVE. Good evening Colonel Dewhurst. Have a seat. Would you like some wine?

COLONEL. This is not a social visit, Simmonds.

DAVE. That sounds very ominous.

ADA. Do have wine Colonel — it's very good.

COLONEL. Please, Mrs Simmonds. You're making it very difficult for me.

DAVE. Difficult?

COLONEL. I've treated you well, Simmonds, haven't I?

DAVE (*not knowing how it's coming*). Ye-es.

COLONEL. That's right, I have. Helped you when you started. Gave you advice.

DAVE. I'm very grateful Colonel, but —

COLONEL. Well, you don't show it!

DAVE. I'm sorry but I don't know what you're talking about.

COLONEL. The lino, the lino! That's what I'm talking about, and you know that's what I'm talking about. Look, Simmonds, you're an intelligent man — you're not the usual sort who works for me, and I didn't expect you to lie. Still, I didn't expect you to steal from me, but you did. Now don't waste time, just tell me and we'll see what we can do: did you or didn't you take two rolls of lino from the shed near the workshop?

DAVE. Those rolls you threw away and said were no use?

262

ADA. Dave —

DAVE. Darling — let *me*. No Colonel, I did not.

COLONEL. But I don't understand why you're lying. In fact I don't understand you at all, Simmonds. What did you come to the country for? It's a different way of life here, y'know. They're a slow people, the country people — slow, but sound. I know where I am with them, and they know their place with me. But with you I could never —

DAVE. Never get the right sort of master-servant relationship?

COLONEL. Yes, if you like. But you didn't like, did you? You spoke to me as if I were a — a —

DAVE. An equal.

COLONEL. I don't like it, Simmonds. I'm not a slave driver, but I believe each person has his place.

DAVE. You're decent like, but it's a favour like?

COLONEL. Are you talking to me about decency, Simmonds?

DAVE. You didn't come all the way up that lane just to find out whether I stole two rolls of lino did you Colonel?

ADA. For God's sake Dave —

DAVE. Now Ada!

COLONEL. Yes I did come all the way up that lane, and I'm damn well furious that I had to. Listen Simmonds, I've got to sack you, because by now all my other men know you took the rolls, and they know I know, and if I don't sack you they'll all think they can get away with pilfering. But thinking you were a decent chap, I thought I'd come here and just tell you what a fool you'd been, and discuss what we could do about it. Now I find you're a petty liar and I'm furious, and I don't care what you do. Good night.

DAVE. But you haven't even any proof — I mean —

COLONEL. You must be insane. And what's outside your back door? (*Silence.*) Well, what is it?

DAVE (*weakly*). You said you didn't want it.

COLONEL. Of course I didn't. Junk! Two and sixpence worth of junk — but that isn't the point.

ADA. What is the point Colonel?

COLONEL. You don't really know the point, do you? We 'ask', Simmonds: in my sort of society we ask. That's all. It's twenty-four hours' notice I'm giving, but there is no need to turn up tomorrow. (*He leaves.*)

ADA. You bring the habits of factory life with you? What got into you?

DAVE. Oh God. What a bloody fool I am.

ADA. But I don't understand. Didn't you *know* the lino was outside and that he might see it?

DAVE. I took a chance that it might be dark —

ADA. Oh my God!

DAVE (*surprised*). I feel so ashamed.

ADA. It was so humiliating — if only you'd admitted it —

DAVE. To be caught for something so petty —

ADA. To be doubly caught for lying as well.

DAVE. Jesus! I feel so ashamed.

(*For some seconds* DAVE *sits, thoroughly crushed.* ADA *is appalled and uncertain what to do.*)

ADA. Well we're not going back to London because of this ridiculous blunder. You're so bloody soft sometimes.

DAVE. Ada I'm sorry.

ADA. You'll have to start your workshop earlier that's all.

DAVE. But we can't afford it.

ADA. Well we'll *have* to afford it. I'm *not* giving up. We'll eat less, we'll buy less, we'll do something but I'm not going away from all this. Thank God the house is still ours anyway. By Christ, Dave — your ideals have got some pretty big leaks in places haven't they?

(DAVE *is deeply hurt by this and* ADA *realizes she has struck deeply. Perhaps this is the first time she has ever hurt* him so deeply. *They wander round the room in silence now, clearing up the table.*)

DAVE. Could you *really* see me leaving?
(*More silence — the battle dies in silence and the wounds heal quietly. The meal is being finally set.*)

ADA. I can help mix cement for the workshop floor you know — I've developed big muscles from drawing water up the well.

DAVE (*looks at her gratefully*). Oh God I feel such a fool.
(*Then after a second* DAVE *lays his hands on* ADA's *shoulders, takes her to a chair, sits her gently on it, places a stool under her feet, takes an olive branch from out of the pot and, first offering it to her, lays it on her lap. Then he looks around and finds a large red towel which he shrouds on her head and shoulders. Then he steps back and kneels in homage. There he remains for a moment till gently he laughs and gradually* ADA *laughs too. And on their laughter —*)

THE CURTAIN FALLS

Scene 2

Late autumn afternoon, 1953. Six years have passed.
    The front wall of the barn has been raised, revealing a furniture-maker's workshop.
    DAVE *is just stepping out of the barn carrying, triumphantly, a chair that he and* SAMMY *have just made.* SAMMY *is* DAVE's *apprentice.* DAVE *is singing (pom-pom) 'Land of Hope and Glory' while* SAMMY *is on his knees applauding and bowing at the spectacle. As* DAVE *majestically lays chair on the 'horse'* SAMMY *speaks. It is fine craftsmanship.*

SAMMY. Looks as though it's sitting down don't it!

265

DAVE. When a chair does that, it works. (*Pause.*) But there's something wrong with this one.

SAMMY. Shall us have it apart?

DAVE. No, no. Leave it a while. Pour us out another cuppa. We'll look at it. (*Walks round chair.*) The legs are too big.

SAMMY. Hell! Have 'em any smaller and you'll be sitting on the floor.

DAVE. True, true. (*Thinks.*) A wrinkle! A little wrinkle! Old Dave's learnt a lot in six years. Give 'em a slight curf with the saw *in between* the joints. Won't need much. Now then, let's have a little clear up shall we? Get the glue on!

SAMMY. When's he coming to see his chair?

DAVE. Who, Selby? Shortly, shortly.

SAMMY. I don't go much on him you know. He run a seed sorting factory. Selby's seeds! Old compost! And they reckon he don't pay his men too well neither.

DAVE. Bit fly eh?

SAMMY. Yearp, fly. And he started as a farm labourer hisself look.

DAVE. Well we've agreed on a good price for the chair anyway.

SAMMY. And you mind you stick to it too. I'll sharpen your chisels. (*Does so.*)

DAVE. The boy say anything to you when you took him to school this morning?

SAMMY. He jabbers a lot don't he?

DAVE. He's like all the Kahns. A funny kid. Comes home with the strangest stories. He's a smasher. Misses his mummy though.

SAMMY. What time train is Ada catchin' from London?

DAVE. Left about twelve this morning I think.

SAMMY. You heard from her? She say how her father was?

DAVE. Not well at all, not well at all poor Harry. This is his second stroke and it seems to have knocked him quite hard. (*He is looking at the chair now.*) I don't think I will. I'll leave the seat as it is. Once you start taking off a piece here and there it makes it worse. It's not all that out of proportion. What say you bor?

SAMMY. Well listen to you then! What say you bor! A proper Norfolk article you're talking like.

DAVE. You taking the mickey out of me? (*Throws a handful of shavings over Sammy's head.*) Are you? (*Another.*) Are you? Are you? Eh?

> (SAMMY *throws back shavings, at which* DAVE *cries* 'War!' *and picks up a stick. A fencing duel takes place till* SAMMY *falls defeated.*)

SAMMY. Hey pack it in ole son, Mister what's-his-name'll be here soon to have a look at this here squatting chair of his.

DAVE Look at this mess you've made. Sweep it up at once. Untidy ole bugger.

> (SAMMY *gathers shavings on his hands and knees with brush and pan. He wants to say something to* DAVE, *and is uncertain how to start.*)

SAMMY. Dave, it'll be a while before Ada come won't it?

DAVE. Yes.

SAMMY. I want a little word with you then.

DAVE. Go on son. I'm listening, but I must get this ready for glueing.

SAMMY. I want to leave soon.

DAVE. That was a very short word. Leave?

SAMMY. I aren't satisfied Dave.

DAVE. Satisfied?

SAMMY. Well I don't seem to be getting anywhere then.

DAVE. But you're learning something boy, you're learnin' to do something with your hands.

SAMMY. But nothing a factory can't do just as well as what we do.

DAVE (*shocked*). Have you ever seen inside a factory? You want to stand by a machine all day? By a planer or a sander or a saw bench?

SAMMY. They change around all the time.

DAVE. Excitement! You change machines! Big difference! All your life Sammy, think of it, all your life.

SAMMY. But you get more money for it.

DAVE. That I do not have an answer to. (*Pause.*) Sammy, remember that chair? Remember what you said about it? It looks as though it's sitting down you said. That's poetry boy, poetry! No not poetry, what am I talking about. Er — it's — it's — O Jesus how do you start explaining this thing. Look Sammy, look at this rack you made for your chisels. Not an ordinary rack, not just bits of wood nailed together, but a special one with dove-tail joints here and a mortise and tenon joint there, and look what you put on the side, remember you wanted to decorate it, so you used my carving tools and you worked out a design. For no reason at all you worked out a design on an ordinary chisel rack. But there was a reason really wasn't there? You enjoyed using those tools and making up that design. I can remember watching you — a whole afternoon you spent on it and you used up three pieces of oak before you were satisfied. Twenty-seven and six you owe me.

SAMMY. Hell, that were only messing around.

DAVE. *Not* messing around. Creating! For the sheer enjoyment of it just creating. And what about the fun we had putting up this workshop?

SAMMY. It's not that I don't enjoy myself Dave.

DAVE. But that's not all cocker. It's not only the fun or the work — it's the place. Look at it, the place where we work. The sun reaches us, we get black in the summer. And any time we're fed up we pack up and go swimming. Don't you realize what that means? There's no one climbing on our backs. Free agents Sammy boy, we enjoy our work, we like ourselves.

SAMMY. You think I don't know these things, hell Dave. But I've seen the boys in the village, I know them, they don't care about things and I see them hang around all their lives, with twopence halfpenny between them an' half a dozen dependents. But I want to get on — don't you think I ought to get on?

DAVE. A bait! A trap! Don't take any notice of that clap-trap for God's sake boy. For every hundred that are lured only one makes it. One, only one. Factories? Offices? When you're in those mate you're there for good. Can't you see that? (*No answer.*) No, you can't can you? Of course you can't. Jesus, I must be mad to imagine I could fight everyone. Sammy, I'm sorry mate — I just —

(*At this moment* ADA *appears. She looks pale and weary.*)

DAVE. Ada! Sweetheart! (*He doesn't know who to talk to first.*)

SAMMY. I'm away home to my tea now Dave. See you tomorrow. How are you Ada? (*Retires quickly.*)

DAVE. Sammy, think again boy, we'll talk some more tomorrow, we'll talk tomorrow, you hear?

ADA. What's been happening?

DAVE. He wants to leave. Work in a factory. Ada, how ill you look. (*Goes to embrace her, she takes his kiss but does not respond.*)

ADA. I met Selby in the village.

DAVE. And?

ADA. He wants to cancel the order for the chair.

DAVE. Cancel it? But it's made.

ADA. The price is too high he says.

DAVE. High? But we agreed — the bastard. That's the third person's done this on me. Blast them, all of them. Twentieth-century, short-sighted, insolent, philistine type bastards! And the world depends upon them, you know

269

that Ada? Oh sweetheart, what an awful welcome.

(*Again he moves towards her but she moves away to sit on a stool.*)

What is it Ada? Why don't you let me touch you all of a sudden, so long and — O my God, it's Harry, idiot I am, I didn't ask, he's not ...

ADA. No, he's not dead.

DAVE. Then how is he?

ADA. He was raving when I got there.

DAVE. Raving? Old Harry?

ADA. The second stroke affected his brain. He was in a padded cell.

DAVE. O God, Ada —

(DAVE *stretches to her but she continues to refuse his comfort.*)

ADA. He didn't recognize me at first. He was lying on his back. You know how large his eyes are. They couldn't focus on anything. He kept shouting in Yiddish, calling for his mother and his sister Cissie. Mummy told me he was talking about Russia. It seems when they first brought him into the ward he threw everything about — that's why a cell. He looked so frightened and mad, as if he were frightened of his own madness.

DAVE. But what brought it on? I mean don't the doctors know?

ADA. A clot of blood. It's reached the brain. And then he recognized me and he looked at me and I said 'Hello Daddy — it's Ada' and he started screaming in Yiddish 'Dir hasst mir, dir hasst mir, dir host mirch alle mul ger hasst!' You hate me and you've always hated me. (*She breaks down uncontrollably.*) Oh darling I haven't stopped crying and I don't understand it, I don't understand it because it's not true, it's never been true.

(DAVE *holds her tightly as she cries, and smothers her with kisses.*)

DAVE. Hush darling, gently, gently. It was a sick man screaming, a sick man, hush — O good God.
(*They stand a while. Then* ADA *pulls away and starts
mechanically unpacking her case.*)

ADA. He smiled and kissed me a lot before I left, it was an
uncanny feeling, but you know Dave (*surprised at the
thought*) I feel like a murderer.

DAVE. *Ada!* You gone mad? A murderer? Stop this nonsense.
You think you were responsible for his illness?

ADA (*calmly*). No, I don't think I was responsible for his illness
and neither did I hate him. But perhaps I didn't tell him I
loved him. Useless bloody things words are. Ronnie and
his bridges! 'Words are bridges' he wrote, 'to get from one
place to another.' Wait till he's older and he learns about
silences — they span worlds.

DAVE. No one made any rules about it. Sometimes you use
bridges. Sometimes you're silent.

ADA. What bridges? Bridges! Do you think I know what
words go to make *me?* Do you think I know why I
behave the way I behave? Everybody says I'm cold and
hard, people want you to cry and gush over them. (*Pause.*)
During the war, when you were overseas, I used to spend
nights at home with Sarah and the family. There was
never a great deal of money coming in and Mummy sometimes got my shopping and did my ironing. Sometimes she
used to sit up late with me while I wrote to you in Ceylon,
and she used to chatter away and then — fall asleep. She'd
sit, in the chair, straight up, and fall asleep. And every
time she did that and I looked at her face it was so sweet, so
indescribably sweet — that I'd cry. There! Each time she
fell asleep I'd cry. But yet I find it difficult to talk to her!
So there! Explain it! Use words and explain that to me.

DAVE. What's going to happen to Sarah, Ada? Do you reckon
we ought to think about returning?

ADA (*turning to him, slowly and deliberately*). Dave, listen to me. My mother is a strong woman. She was born to survive every battle that faces her. She doesn't need me. You say I'm like her? You're right. I'm also strong, I shall survive every battle that faces me too, and this place means survival for me. We — are — staying — put!

(DAVE *takes her hands and kisses them, then her lips. A child's voice calls:* 'Mummy, Ada, Mummy, Ada, Mummy, Ada!')

DAVE. It's the boy. Watch how pleased he'll be, he kept asking when you were coming. I bet you a dollar the first thing he'll want you to do is play your game with him.

ADA. Danny?

DANNY (*off, assuming a gruff voice*). I'm Daniel the lion killer.

ADA. You're who?

DANNY. I've come to slay your lions for you.

ADA. How much do you charge?

DAVE (*taking out his pipe*). Mothers!

DANNY. I charge sixpence a lion.

ADA. The last time I saw you you were so small, I don't know whether I could trust you to slay my lions.

DANNY. I'm as tall as an elephant.

ADA. I can't possibly believe that. Come out and show yourself Daniel the lion killer.

DANNY. I shan't show myself until you play the game with me.

ADA. Oh! And what is the game today Daniel?

DANNY. It is called 'Look I'm alive!'

(DAVE *does a there-I-told-you-so look.*)

ADA. Oh that one. All right. Are you ready?

DANNY. Yes. Now you do it with me.

(*Now* ADA *faces us and goes through the same actions as we must assume* DANNY *does. She starts crouched down, with her face hidden in her arm — as in the womb.*)

ADA. Are you crouched down?

DANNY (*in his own voice*). Yes Mummy.

(DAVE *pulls a face at her so she draws him into the game too.*)

ADA. Do you mind if my friend here plays Mr Life? (DAVE *tries to run away.*) *Dave!*

DANNY. No, hurry up, I'm getting cramp.

(*What happens from now must have the touch of magic and of clowning. The day has gone and now the light fades slowly into evening.*)

DAVE (*bowing first to* ADA, *then to* DANNY). I am — (*pause; to* ADA) what's it?

ADA. You're Mr Life.

DAVE. Oh yes, Mr Life. I am Mr Life. I have spent all day making furniture and now I am going to make a human being. You are clay and I am going to make you into a human being. I am going to breathe the fire of life into you. Hissssss, Hisssssss, Hissssss.

(*As* DAVE *breathes the fire* ADA *unfolds and rises very slowly — this is what* DANNY *is doing unseen — her eyes are closed.*)

DAVE. Now you have life and you can breathe.

(ADA *breathes deeply.*)

DAVE. Now I will give you sight.

(*He snaps his fingers at* DANNY *then at* ADA. ADA *opens her eyes. There is wonder and joy at what is revealed.*)

DAVE. Now I will give you movement.

(DAVE *beckons to* DANNY *then to* ADA. ADA *raises and lowers her arms twice, moving her head from left to right at the same time, full of curiosity and excitement at what she is doing.*)

DAVE. Now I will give you speech. (*He draws something unseen from his mouth and throws it to* DANNY, *then he kisses his finger and places the kiss on* ADA's *lips.*) Tell me, what does it feel like to be a human being?

DANNY (*in his gruff voice*). It's a little strange. But I'm getting used to it. It's very exciting.

273

(ADA *relaxes and becomes herself and involved in the questioning.*)

ADA. Now that you have eyes and tongue to see and talk and limbs to move — move, and tell me what you see.

DANNY (*in his own voice*). Hedges!

ADA. No no Daniel. That's a name, that's not what you see.

DANNY (*in his own voice from now on*). I see thin pieces of wood. Going all over the place. With bumps on them, and thin slips of green like paper, and some funny soft stuff on them.

ADA. *Now* you can use names.

DANNY. They're hedges with leaves and berries.

ADA. Any colours?

DANNY. The hedges are brown, the leaves are green and the berries are red and black.

ADA (*becoming excited*). What else can you see O Daniel?

DANNY. A blue sky with white cloud.

ADA. More?

DANNY. Birds with long necks.

ADA. More?

DANNY. Green fields with brown bumps.

ADA. More?

DANNY. A red brick house and that's where I live.

ADA. Now you are a real human being Daniel who can look and think and talk and you can come out and slay the lions.

(*We hear* DANNY *run right across the back of the stage* (*past barn and hedges*) *crying:* 'I'm coming I'm coming I'm coming!' *and* ADA *crouches down with her arms outstretched to receive him as the night and* —)

THE CURTAIN FALLS[1]

---

[1]The boy could perhaps rush on to the stage as the lights fade. Director's decision.

ACT THREE

Scene 1

It is warm autumn. Three years have passed. 1956. The wall in front of the barn is lowered. No one works there now.

Two women are seated in the garden. CISSIE *and* ESTHER KAHN, *maiden aunts of* ADA. *The first is a trade unionist, the other owns a market stall.* CISSIE *is shelling peas.* ESTHER *is peeling potatoes.*

There is a lovely light in the sky and two deck chairs near the back door.

ESTHER. A guest house they call it.

CISSIE. Esther, stop grumbling — peel!

ESTHER. Three hundred ditches we had to jump over before we even reached the house — and they advertise in newspapers. For peace and quiet and a modest holiday — the Shambles. A very inviting name. Mind you, for a dirty week-end, this place — you know what I mean?

CISSIE (*not* really *minding*). Why must you be so bloody crude Esther?

ESTHER. What's the matter — all these years you been my sister and you don't know me yet?

CISSIE. What time does Dave come back for lunch?

ESTHER. One o'clock.

CISSIE. Ada'll come back from shopping with him, I suppose.

ESTHER. They better be on time else that dinner'll be burnt.

CISSIE. What?

ESTHER. Don't say 'what', say 'ah?' Fine bloody holiday this. Only two mad maiden aunts like us would do this. Do you realize that we haven't stopped working since we've been here? Look at that job we did yesterday. Pulling up weeds. Agricultural workers!

CISSIE. Stop grumbling. You know you're enjoying yourself.

275

ESTHER. You think they make all their other guests work like this? No wonder they get so few. Cissie — I think we should tell them.

CISSIE. What?

ESTHER. Don't say 'what', say 'ah?' We should tell them that people when they go on holiday they don't like digging gardens and feeding chickens.

CISSIE. Don't be daft woman. It's only us. We spoil her. Both her and Ronnie we spoilt.

ESTHER. A guest house they call it. Not even a bleedin' flush lavatory. Just three hundred ditches.

CISSIE. Hush Esther.

ESTHER. What's the matter for Gawd's sake? You frightened someone'll hear me? (*Shouting*) *Cissie, have you stopped peaing yet?*

CISSIE. So help me you're mad.

ESTHER. I'm keeping in training. Though I must say this ain't the most inspiring place for selling underwear. I mean what do their guests do here? The only sights to see are sixty clucking hens waiting to be slaughtered — poor sods — and a two-hundred-year-old barn. A historical monument!

CISSIE. That used to be Dave's workshop.

ESTHER. What did he leave it for?

CISSIE. Ada was telling me that one day about six months ago, he built a beautiful dressing table for someone and he had a lorry come to collect it, and the driver took no care on the bumpy lane so that by the time they reached the main road they'd knocked all the corners off it. A two-hundred-pound job it was, all his own design, ruined! So he found a new workshop in the village.

ESTHER. And he still can't earn money. Poor sod. He works hard that one — and what for? For peanuts that's what for!

CISSIE. Well today may change all that.

ESTHER. You mean the loan?

CISSIE (*nodding*). If he's managed to persuade the bank to loan him money then he can buy machinery and his work'll be easier.

ESTHER. Now *that's* something I don't understand. I can remember him saying when he first moved here that he wanted to make furniture with his own hands. Now he's buying machinery, he'll be like a factory only not big enough to make their turnover. So where's the ideals gone all of a sudden?

CISSIE. Esther, you're a stall-owner, you don't understand these things.

ESTHER. All right, so I'm a coarse stall-owner. I'm a silly cow. So *I'm* a silly cow and *you're* a clever trade union organizer — you explain it to me.

CISSIE. It's all got to do with the work of another socialist furniture-maker, William Morris.

ESTHER. A yiddisha fellow?

CISSIE. He was a famous person. He used to say 'Machines are all right to relieve dull and dreary work, but man must not become a slave to them.'

ESTHER. So?

CISSIE. So Ada says Dave says if he can buy a machine to saw the wood, and another to plane it, that will save him a lot of unnecessary labour and he can still be a craftsman.

ESTHER. I'll tell you something Cissie? Our nieces and nephews are all mad. Look at Ronnie — working in a kitchen, and that silly arse has fallen in love with a waitress.

CISSIE. So what's wrong with a waitress? Beatie Bryant's a very nice girl, very active, bless her.

ESTHER. I know she's a nice girl but she doesn't know what Ronnie's saying half the time.

CISSIE. If it comes to that neither do I. You know where she comes from? About twenty miles from here. Ronnie met her when he came to work in Norwich.

277

(CISSIE *rises and enters kitchen to put peas in pot.* ESTHER *follows.*)

ESTHER. Another wandering Jew. Another one can't settle himself. Hopping about all over the country from one job to another. I'll tell you something Cissie — it's not a joke. Ronnie worries me. He worries me because his father was just the same. You know Harry? Before he fell ill? The way he couldn't stick at one job? The same thing! All over again. It worries me.

CISSIE. Now Esther don't you ever tell him that — you hear me?

ESTHER. Me? I wouldn't say a word! But it worries me. And he wants to spread socialism. Everybody's busy with socialism. 'Aunty Esther' he says 'I've finished making speeches, I'm going to marry a simple girl and hand it all on to her.' So I says to him 'Ronnie' I says 'be careful. Don't hand it on to her *before* you're married.' The meat! (*Turns to oven.*)

(*At this point* ADA *and* DAVE *appear.*)

ADA. What's happened to Aunty Esther?

CISSIE. It's all right darling, she's just gone to look at the meat. She always rushes like that — as if the world was on fire. What's the matter Simmonds? You look all done in.

DAVE. Bank managers. How do you talk to them?

CISSIE. Like I talk to employers when I'm negotiating a strike — as though you're doing them a favour by coming at all.

ESTHER (*coming out of the kitchen*). Fifteen more minutes and we ean eat.

ADA. You're bricks, the pair of you.

ESTHER. You mean we got thick skulls?

CISSIE. Stop grumbling.

ESTHER. All she can say to me is 'Esther stop grumbling.' I'm a happy woman, let me grumble. So tell us, what happened? (*Returns to chair in garden.*)

CISSIE. Wait a minute, let me get my knitting. (*Goes to kitchen.*)

ESTHER. Can't you ever sit still and do nothing?

CISSIE. No I bloody can't. The good lord gave me hands and I like using them.

ESTHER. The good lord gave you an arse but you don't have to be sh ...

CISSIE. *Esther!*

ESTHER. She's so squeamish your aunt.

CISSIE (*returning and sitting on deck chair*). Right, now let's hear what happened — I'm very interested.

ADA. I must go in and lay the table, I can hear from inside.
    (DAVE *moves to the barn and cleans some of his tools.*)

ESTHER. What's the matter with everybody? No one can sit still for five minutes. This one knits, this one must lay the table, that one mucks about with his tools —

CISSIE. He's cleaning his chisels, Esther.

ESTHER. Don't split hairs with me. It's a bleedin' conspiracy to make me feel guilty — well nuts to yers all, I'm sitting still. I'm a lady. A bleedin' civilized lady on holiday. Fan me somebody!

CISSIE. Esther, maybe the kids don't feel like joking.

ESTHER. Dave Simmonds, are you going to tell us what happened at the bank or not?

DAVE. Nothing much. He said I could have an overdraft of two hundred pounds but no loan.

ESTHER. So what you feeling unhappy for? With an overdraft you can lay down deposit on two machines and pay off over three or five years. Who buys anything outright these days anyway.

DAVE. Yeah.

CISSIE. Hey Addie — what kind of school dinners does Danny get?

ESTHER. A real grasshopper mind you've got. Can't you stick to one subject at a time?

CISSIE. Leave off Esther, can't you see the boy doesn't want to talk about it.

(ADA *comes out of the kitchen. She is rubbing her hands and face on a towel very slowly. Although she looks red-eyed from washing, she really has been crying and is covering up with a wash.*)

ADA. They're not bad. A little bit dull but he gets plenty of it.

ESTHER. Have you been crying Ada?

CISSIE. Leave off Esther, I tell you.

ESTHER. For crying out loud what's been happening to you two?

(DAVE *looks up and sees that, in fact,* ADA *has been crying. He lays down his saw, approaches her and takes her in his arms. After a bewildered moment of looking at them and each other —*)

CISSIE *and* ⎫ (*between them*). Ah Ada darling. My pet. Sweet-
ESTHER ⎭ heart. Don't cry love. Ah there poppit, what is it then?

(*Both aunts start fussing the couple but are unable to do anything except commiserate and get in each other's way while moving around trying to get in somewhere. They cannot reach either of the two.* DAVE *and* ADA *stand locked together and rocking, their own misery being the centre of the aunts' faintly comic and frustrated concern.*)

CISSIE (*having tripped over* ESTHER's *feet*). Get back to your deck chair, I'll handle this.

ESTHER. Cissie, carry on knitting and leave off. You always were heavy-handed with people.

CISSIE. That's how it should be. As soon as *you* start handling people you have them in tears.

ESTHER. And you treat every upset as though it was an industrial dispute.

ADA. Listen to those two. Anyone would think we were still fifteen.

DAVE. Feeling better sweetheart?

ADA. How can anyone feel depressed with those two old hens clucking round you.

ESTHER. Here, let me tell you about the time Ronnie made a supper of rice.

CISSIE. That's it, tell them about the time Ronnie made us a supper of rice.

DAVE. Listen to them darling, don't they sound like a music-hall act?

CISSIE. Ronnie invites himself to supper and says he wants to try out a special pork curry —

ESTHER. A very kosher dish he assures us —

CISSIE. We don't even like curry —

ESTHER. Never mind, we agree. What a mess! A whole pound of rice he puts into a saucepan and he starts to boil it — so you know what happens when you boil rice —

CISSIE. It swells!

ESTHER. The whole pound of rice began to swell. And what does he do when it reaches the top of the saucepan? He puts half of it in another saucepan and sets them both to boil. And do you think it was cooked?

CISSIE. Of course it wasn't! And the two saucepans got full again — so he gets two more saucepans and halves them again. For two hours before we got home he was cooking rice —

ESTHER. And by the time we arrived he had five saucepans and two frying pans filled with rice for a supper of three people.

(*Everyone is in a paroxysm of laughter until, as they emerge out of it,* ESTHER *suddenly remembers* —)

ESTHER. Oh yes — there's some mail for you.

DAVE. Thank God — at last!

ESTHER. At last, what?

CISSIE. We thought all you wanted was a loan.

ADA. You have to have people to buy the furniture as well you know.

CISSIE. And there's no people?

ADA. Some, but it's mostly for window sashes.

ESTHER. What's so important with the letter then?

DAVE. The letter is important because three weeks ago I had an inquiry for an originally designed suite of dining-room chairs and table and I sent in an estimate and this should be a reply. If they don't want it, it means I have to carry on doing window sashes.

ESTHER. And what's Ada crying for?

DAVE. She's having a baby.

(*Cries of joy and surprise and 'muzzeltov' and more fussing from the aunts.*)

ESTHER. So what's there to cry about? Are you sure?

ADA. Of course I'm sure you silly bitch.

ESTHER. Right, then if you don't mind I'm going to say something.

DAVE. Esther, I think we're going to mind —

ESTHER. I'm still going to say it.

ADA. Aunts, please, we're really very tired.

ESTHER. For Gawd's sake ! It's not as though we're strangers. We're your aunts. All your life, till we die.

DAVE. What are you going to tell us? We're mad to stay here ? Everyone's told us this. Half our battle here has been against people who for a dozen different reasons have tried to tell us we're mad.

ESTHER. Never mind about madness — but you've changed. You're not the same. Once upon a time we could talk to you. You got troubles? So tell us. What's the matter — you think we're going to laugh?

DAVE. We're tired Esther, leave us alone, yes?

ESTHER. Nice life! Lovely! It's a great pleasure knowing you! Open the letter.

DAVE. I *know* what's in the letter. Dear Mr Simmonds, after having carefully considered your designs and estimate we feel sorry to have to inform you — God! I'm learning to hate people!

ESTHER (*telling a story*). My mother loved her children. You know how I know? The way she used to cook our food. With songs. She used to hum and feed us. Sing and dress us. Coo and scold us. You could tell she loved us from the way she did things for us. You want to be a craftsman? Love us. You want to give us beautiful things? Talk to us. You think Cissie and I fight? You're wrong silly boy. She talks to me. I used to be able to watch everything on television, but she moaned so much I can't even enjoy rubbish any more. She drives me mad with her talk.

DAVE. I talked enough! You bloody Kahns you! You all talk. Sarah, Ronnie, all of you. I talked enough! I wanted to do something. Hands I've got — you see them? I wanted to do something.

ESTHER. Hands is the only thing? I'm a worker too. Haven't I worked? From selling flags at a football match to selling foam cushions in Aylesbury market. From six in the morning till six at night. From pitch to pitch, all hours, all my life! That's not work? It doesn't entitle me to a house? Or a fridge? I shouldn't buy a washing machine? How do you *measure* achievement for Christ's sake? Flower and Dean Street was a prison with iron railings, you remember? And my one ambition was to break away from that prison. 'Buy your flags' I used to yell. 'Rattles at rattling good prices' I used to try to be funny. So I sold rattles and now I've got a house. And if I'd've been pretty I'd've had a husband and children as well and they'd've got pleasure from me. Did money change me? You remember me, tell me, have I changed? I'm still the same Esther Kahn. I got no airs. No airs me. I still say the wrong things and nobody

minds me. Look at me — you don't like me or something?
That's all that matters. Or no, not that, not even like or
dislike — do I harm you? Do I offend you? Is there something about me that offends you?

DAVE (*simply*). You haven't got a vision Esther.

ESTHER. A prophet he is!

DAVE. No! We should turn to *you* for prophecies! With your
twopenny halfpenny flags and your foam cushions? With
your cheap jewels, your market lies and your jerry houses?

ADA. Dave, sweetheart — there's no point — you'll only
upset yourselves — and she doesn't mean —

DAVE. No, no. She can take it. Straight Jane and no nonsense
she says. Let's talk back a little. I know we decided not to
bother to explain but I'm fed up being on the receiving
end. I'll tell them. (*To* ESTHER) Once and for all I'll tell
you — you call me a prophet and laugh do you? Well, I'll
tell you. I *am* a prophet. Me. No one's ever heard of me
and no one wants to buy my furniture but I'm a bleedin'
prophet and don't anyone forget that. As little as you see
me so big I am. Now you look at me. I picked up my
spear and I've stuck it deep. Prophet Dave Simmonds, me.
With a chisel. Dave Simmonds and Jesus Christ. Two
yiddisha boys —

ESTHER. Hatred, Cissie. Look at our nephew-in-law, hatred in
every spit.

DAVE. Well, what have you left me for God's sake? You
want an angel in me? Ten years I spent here trying to
carve out a satisfactory life for my wife and kids and on
every side we've had opposition. From the cynics, the
locals, the family. Everyone was choking with their experience of life and wanted to hand it on. Who came forward
with a word of encouragement? Who said we maybe had
a little guts? Who offered one tiny word of praise?

ESTHER. Praise pretty boy.

DAVE. Yes, praise! It would hurt you, any of you? There isn't enough generosity to spare a little pat on the back? You think we're cranks — recluses? Well, I'll surprise you, look — no long hair, no sandals. Just flesh and blood. Of course we need a little praise. (*Dips in his pocket for coins.*) Or maybe you want me to buy it from you! Like in the market! Here, two half-crowns for a half-minute of praise. I'll buy it! You can't afford to give it away? I'll pay for it! Five bob for a few kind words, saying we're not mad. Here y'are — take it! Take it!

CISSIE. There! You satisfied Esther? Now you've upset him, you happy?

ESTHER (*subdued*). I know, I know. I'm just a silly old cow. You want to build Jerusalem? Build it! Only maybe we wanted to share it with you. Now open the letter.

(DAVE *opens the letter, but before he has had a chance to look at it the* CURTAIN *comes down so that we do not know what it says.*)

Scene 2

Three years later. 1959.

The Simmondses are moving out. SARAH *and* RONNIE *are there helping them. Everyone is that much older.*

SARAH *is sweeping up the kitchen.* ADA *is attending to a third baby, who is in a carry-cot up stage.* DAVE *is just taking a box off stage to where the removal lorry is waiting.* RONNIE *is beside a pile of books that are waiting to be packed away.*

But at this moment they are all listening to the radio.[1]

ANNOUNCER. Captain Davies, Conservative, 20,429. J. R. Dalton, Labour, 10,526. L. Shaftesbury, Liberal, 4,291. Con-

---

[1] Alternatively, the words given here as a radio announcement could be read out by Ronnie from a newspaper, in which case instead of switching off the radio at the end of the announcement Ronnie would crumple up the newspaper.

servative majority 9,903. The Liberal candidate forfeits his deposit. These latest results bring the Conservative majority up to 93 and will ensure the return to power in the House of Commons of the Conservative Party for a third time in succession since the end of the war. Mr Gaitskell went to Transport House this morning to confer with other Labour leaders — he looked very tired —

RONNIE (*switching off*). Well — you've chosen the right time to return anyway. You came in with them and you go out with them — whisht. (*Continues looking through books in silence.*) I'm all washed up. I don't know why the hell you asked me to help with this morbid job.

ADA. Go home then dear boy.

DAVE (*returning with an empty tea chest*). Here's the box to put the books in.

RONNIE. I said I'm all washed up. I'm complaining. (*No response.*) No one listens to me now. Funny that, everybody loo-ves me but nobody listens to me. I can't keep a job and I can't keep a girl so everyone thinks what I say doesn't count. Like they used to say of Dad. Poor old Harry — poor old Ronnie. But you forgive me my trespasses don't you Addie? Look at my sister, she's still beautiful.

DAVE. It was good of you to help us cocker.

RONNIE. *That's* all I ever get away with — gestures. You give someone a hand and they think you're a saint. Saint Ronnie Kahn.

(*All continue with their respective jobs. The removal is in its last stages. DAVE is going round picking up stray tools to place in a tool box. RONNIE sings to himself.*)

RONNIE.

Come O my love and fare ye well,
Come O my love and fare ye well,
You slighted me but I wish you well.
The winter is gone and the leaves turn green,

> The winter is gone and the leaves turn green,
> Your innocent face I wish I never had seen.

You realize you two that having come with explanations you must leave with explanations.

ADA. Is anyone going to care that much Ronnie?

RONNIE. Yes, me! Jesus, one of us has got to make a success of something. You can understand the Labour Party losing the elections again, they change their politics like a suit of clothing or something, but us — well you two, you put it into practice, God knows why you lost.

ADA. Let's forget it Ronnie.

RONNIE (*jumping up*). No, don't let's forget it. You can still change your mind. Let's unpack it all. Pay the removers and try again. There must be something —

DAVE. Don't go on Ronnie, I keep telling you.

RONNIE. But you can't just pack up —

DAVE. I said shut up!

RONNIE.

> The rope is hung and the noose hangs high
> The rope is hung and the noose hangs high
> An innocent man you have all sent to die.

SARAH. What is it, a funeral here?

DAVE. Any chance of a last cup of tea before we go Mum?

SARAH. Tea I can always make.

RONNIE. Tea she can always make.

> There ain't a lady livin' in the land
> What makes tea like my dear old mum —
> No there ain't a lady livin' in the land
> What —

What rhymes with 'mum'?

SARAH. Everything he makes into a joke.

DAVE. Did you ever hear what happened to Beatie Bryant, Ronnie?

RONNIE. No.

DAVE. The girl you wanted to change.

RONNIE. Change! Huh! You know what my father once said to me? 'You can't change people Ronnie' he said, 'you can only give them some love and hope they'll take it.' Well, Beatie Bryant took it but nothing seemed to happen.

DAVE. Three years is a long time to go with a girl.

RONNIE. I don't regret it. Maybe something did happen. After all little Sarah, wasn't it you who was always telling us that you don't know people without something happening?

SARAH. I'm always telling you you can't change the world on your own — only no one listens to me.

RONNIE. We carry bits and pieces of each other, like shrapnel from a war. Ada's like you Sarah, strong! I'm charming, like my father, and weak. O God! Isn't it all terribly, terribly sad. (*Suddenly*) Let's do an Israeli dance before we go — come on, let's dance. (*Starts doing a Zanny Hora on his own.*) The wandering Jews move on — bless 'em. Let there be music, let there be —

ADA. Stop clowning Ronnie, we won't be done in time.

RONNIE. Don't argue! Don't sing! Don't clown!

ADA. You don't have to do anything.

RONNIE. That's right. I don't *have* to do anything — except pack up and go home. We're none of us what you could call 'returning heroes' are we? If only we could squeeze a tiny victory out of it all. God, there must be a small victory somewhere for one of us. Maybe I was a good son eh? Before he died I used to wash Harry and shave him. It took him too long to walk so I used to carry him in my arms, like a cooing baby. Then I'd bounce him on the bed and play with him and he used to laugh, a really full laugh. Funny that, in the last months he couldn't talk but his laughter was full. Mummy even used to try to play cards with him but he couldn't hold them. Sometimes I laid *my* head in *his* arms to make him feel he could still — (*It is too painful to continue.*) No — I don't have to do anything. Only the old worthies are left biding their time, waiting for the new generation. Look at old Mother there, like a patient old tigress — she's still waiting. Nothing surprised you did it Sarah? You still think it'll come, the great millennium?

SARAH. And you don't?

RONNIE. Well, I haven't brought it about — and they (*of* ADA *and* DAVE) haven't brought it about, and the Monty Blatts and Cissie and Esther Kahns haven't brought it about. But then Dad said it would never happen in our lifetime — 'It'll purify itself' he used to say. The difference between capitalism and socialism he used to say was that capitalism contained the seeds of its own destruction but socialism contained the seeds of its own purification. Maybe that's the victory — maybe by coming here you've purified yourselves, like Jesus in the wilderness. Yes? No? (*No response. Places last three books in box, reading titles out like a list of the dead and softly kissing each one.*) *Mother* by Maxim Gorky. *My Son, My Son* by Howard Spring. *Madame Bovary* by Gustave Flaubert. Lovely sound that — Flaubert. Ronnie de Flaubert.

DAVE. Did you ever finish your novel?

RONNIE. No.

DAVE. You've grown older in these last years, haven't you mate?

RONNIE. Yes.

ADA. I don't think there's anything more to pack away.

RONNIE. (*making it up*).

       Pull down the blind, put away the stars,
       The lovers have left their fond house for the town,
       No more leaves will be gathered again
       And the last nightingales have gone.

ADA. Come on darling — put away your books and poems and let's be having you.

RONNIE. *You're* still smiling anyway.

ADA. Well, we shall be back for the summer holidays.

DAVE. Anyone would think it's your experiment that failed, you with your long face.

RONNIE. O my God, how near the knuckle that is.

SARAH. Come and have some tea and stop depressing each other.

RONNIE. And Mother says little. Quietly packs and takes her children home with her.

SARAH. I've been lonely for long enough Ronnie. A few more years and I'll be dead. I'm committing no crimes.

RONNIE. I never know whether to say at this point (*melodramatically*) 'we're all lonely' or not. As soon as I say something, somehow I don't believe it. Don't you find that with things? As soon as you pronounce something it doesn't seem true?

(*A cry of* 'Any more' *comes from off stage.*)

DAVE. The removal men are waiting. Right! Just this last case. Come on Ronnie. The rest of the stuff we'll leave for the holidays.

RONNIE. The radio too?

DAVE. No, bring the radio.

(RONNIE *and* DAVE *pick up packing-case and go off.*)

ADA. Let's make it quick Dave, because Danny and Jake'll be waiting up for us. (*To* SARAH) I wonder how the children'll take to London?

SARAH. Are you sure Aunty Esther met them at the station?

ADA. Yes, we had a telegram.

(RONNIE *and* DAVE *return.*)

RONNIE (*trying to be cheerful*). Righto me hearties. The cheerful side. Let's look at the rainbow. The silver lining. Because

290

remember — in the words of that immortal American prophet — (*Does an Al Jolson act.*)

> When April showers may come your way
> They bring the flowers that bloom in May,
> So when it's raining have no regrets
> Because it isn't raining rain you know it's ...

(*Gives up.*) ... etcetera, etcetera, et bloody cetera!

DAVE. I've found a basement workshop in London and I'll set up shop there.

RONNIE (*sadly*). A basement! The man who started work singing 'Linden Lea' in the open air returns to a basement.

ADA (*after a silence*). The sun is setting Dave. We really must be moving.

DAVE (*picking up again*). Who knows, maybe people will buy furniture in town. They say you can sell them anything in London.

ADA. We've found a house — a roof over our heads.

RONNIE (*jumping on crate*). Oh bloody marvellous!

> We've got sixpence, jolly jolly sixpence
> Di dum dee da to last us all our life
> Pom-pom to lend
> And pom-pom to spend
> And pom-pom to take home to our wives
> *Hallelujah!*

ADA (*finally unnerved*). Ronnie!

DAVE (*after a second*). I can't make you out cock. Not at all I can't make you out.

RONNIE. I'm crying Dave, I'm bloody crying.

(*Everyone is unnerved. Everyone is feeling the reality of leaving. A long pained silence.*)

DAVE. So? We're all crying. But what do you want of us. Miracles?

SARAH. I don't know what's happened to you all. Suddenly

you're talking and then you're shouting and then you're crying. Suddenly you start hitting each other with words.

DAVE. Well, why must hé put us on pedestals.

SARAH. You were the God that fought in Spain, Dave, remember?

DAVE (to RONNIE). Is that it? (Pause.) You can't really forgive me because I didn't speak heroically about Spain, can you?

RONNIE (reflectively). The war that was every man's war.

DAVE. A useless, useless bloody war because Hitler still made it, didn't he, eh? And out went six million Jews in little puffs of smoke. Am I expected to live in the glory of the nineteen thirties all my life?

SARAH. Sick! ... You're all sick or something. We won the last war didn't we? You forgotten that? We put a Labour Party in power and ...

RONNIE (with irony). Oh, yes, that's right! We put a Labour Party in power. Glory! Hurrah! It wasn't such a useless war after all, was it, Mother? But what did the bleeders do, eh? They sang the Red Flag in Parliament and then started building atom bombs. Lunatics! Raving lunatics! And a whole generation of us laid down our arms and retreated into ourselves, a whole generation! But you two. I don't understand what happened to you two. I used to watch you and boast about you. Well, thank God, I thought, it works! But look at us now, now it's all of us.

SARAH. Did you expect the world to suddenly focus on them and say 'Ah, socialism is beautiful,' did you, silly boy? Since when did we preach this sort of poverty?

ADA (turning on SARAH). We were never poor! (Softer to RONNIE, putting an arm round him) You want reassuring, sweetheart? I'll reassure you, shall I? Remember what you said about carrying bits and pieces of each other? Well it's true ...

RONNIE. The justifications!

ADA. Will you shut up and listen to me for Christ's sake? The kind of life we lived couldn't be a whole philosophy, could it?

RONNIE. Did it have to be?

ADA. Exactly! Did it have to be. Any more than your life with Beatie Bryant or Sarah's life with Harry. Whose life was ever a complete statement? But they're going to have to turn to us in the end, they're going to ...

RONNIE. Are you mad? To us?

ADA. Us! Us! Because *we* do the living. We *do* the living.
(*Pause.*)

DAVE. What do you think I am, Ronnie? You think I'm an artist's craftsman? Nothing of that sort. A designer? Not even that. Designers are ten a penny. I don't mind Ronnie — believe me I don't. (*But he does.*) I've reached the point where I can face the fact that I'm not a prophet. Once I had — I don't know — a — a moment of vision, and I yelled at your Aunty Esther that I was a prophet. A prophet! Poor woman, I don't think she understood. All I meant was I was a sort of spokesman. That's all. But it passed. Look, I'm a bright boy. There aren't many flies on me and when I was younger I was even brighter. I was interested and alive to everything, history, anthropology, philosophy, architecture — I had ideas. But not now. Not now Ronnie. I don't know — it's sort of sad this what I'm saying, it's a sad time for both of us — Ada and me — sad, yet — you know — it's not all that sad. We came here, **we** worked hard, we've loved every minute of it and we're still young. Did you expect anything else? You wanted us to grow to be giants, didn't you? The mighty artist craftsman! Well, now the only things that seem to matter to me are the day-to-day problems of my .wife, my kids and my. work. Face it — as an essential member of society I don't really count. I'm not saying I'm useless, but machinery and modern techniques have come about to make me the odd man out. Here I've been, comrade citizen, presenting my offerings and the world's rejected them. I don't count, Ronnie, and if I'm not sad about it you mustn't be either. Maybe Sarah's right, maybe you can't build on your own.

RONNIE. Remember your phrase about people choking with their own experience?

DAVE. I remember a lot of things — come on, let's go.

RONNIE. That was your apology for defeat, was it?

DAVE (wearily). All right, so I'm defeated. Come on, let's go —

RONNIE (desperately). Then where do we look for our new vision?

DAVE (angrily). Don't moan at me about visions. Don't you know they don't work? You child you — visions don't work.

RONNIE (desperately). They do work! And even if they don't work then for God's sake let's try and behave as though they do — or else nothing will work.

DAVE. Then nothing will work.

RONNIE (too hastily). That's cowardice!

DAVE. You call me a coward? You? I know your kind, you go around the world crooning about brotherhood and yet you can't even see a sordid love affair through to the end. I know your bloody kind.

ADA. Dave! This is so silly —

DAVE. Well, I've tried haven't I? Everybody wants explanations and I've tried. Do you think I want to go?

RONNIE. It wasn't sordid, you know Dave. I know I didn't see it through to the end but it wasn't sordid. Beatie Bryant could have been a poem — I gave her words — maybe she became one. But you're right. There isn't anything I've seen through to the end — maybe that's

why you two were so important to me. Isn't that curious?
I say all the right things, I think all the right things, but
somewhere, some bloody where I fail as a human being.
Like my father — just like poor old Harry. O Christ!
Look at me.

(RONNIE *sinks to his knees in utter despair.*
They stand and watch him a while.
ADA *moves to him, but* DAVE *holds her back.*
SARAH *is about to move to him but* DAVE *stops her with*
'Sarah!'
RONNIE *is to receive no more comfort. No one can help him*
now but himself.
Slowly, very slowly, he unfolds and they all watch him.
Slowly, very slowly, he rises to his feet. He knows what is
wanted of him but still cannot do more than stand in a sort of
daze, looking from one to another — then —)

DAVE (*to* ADA). Darling, did you post those letters off?

ADA (*she understands that they must indicate that they are going on*).
Yes, Dave, and the estimates went off too.

DAVE. Where did you put the drawings?

ADA (*indicating brief-case*). It's all right, they're here. All those
you've decided to keep I've rolled up into one pile. The
rejects I burned last night.

DAVE. Now don't forget, first thing tomorrow morning I
must get in touch with the electricians and tell them to
start wiring the place up. Then there's that appointment
with Mrs What's-her-name for her bloody awful wardrobe.

(ADA *goes over to pick up the carry-cot.*)

ADA. When we've finished unpacking tonight we'll make a
list of all the things we must do — just before we go to
bed. (*She and* DAVE *pick up cot.*) Come on Simmonds
number three, we'll soon be back again for your holidays,
you can still grow up here, yes you can, or won't *you* care?

DAVE. Ronnie — lock up and stick the key in your pocket, there's a good lad. Sarah, you take your daughter's bags, God knows what she's got in them.

(DAVE *picks up his brief-case and he and* ADA *go off with the carry-cot, still talking.*)

ADA. Are you sure you turned the calor gas off properly?

DAVE. Positive. Now look darling — you mustn't let me forget to phone those electricians — Hey! Did we pack my drawing boards away?

ADA. Yes, yes, Simmonds. In those first boxes, don't you remember?

DAVE. Funny, I don't remember...

ADA (*to* SARAH *and* RONNIE). Come on, you two, the men are waiting.

(*They have gone off by now.* RONNIE *has locked the door and* SARAH *is waiting for him. He takes one of the baskets from her and puts an arm on her shoulder.*)

RONNIE. Well Sarah — your children are coming home now.

SARAH. You finished crying, you fool you?

RONNIE. Cry? We must be bloody mad to cry, Mother.

(SARAH *goes off leaving* RONNIE *to linger and glance once more around. Suddenly his eye catches a stone, which he picks up and throws high into the air. He watches, and waits till it falls. Then he cups his hands to his mouth and yells to the sky with bitterness and some venom —*)

RONNIE. We — must — be — bloody — mad — to cry!

(*The stage is empty.*
Soon we hear the sound of the lorry revving up and moving off.
A last silence.
Then —)

A LAST SLOW CURTAIN

HOOLYIT HOOLYIT

1. Hool-yit hool-yit baiz-a vin-ten Yetzt iss ei - er
2. Brent a licht-el er-getzt toon-kle Lesht mit tzor-en

tseit   Long vet dor - en   noch de-er vin-ter
aus   Rize die sho-ben   fon d - ie lut-ten

Zu - mer i - is no-och vi - ite   Long vet dor-en
Fen-ster ri-ist a - rau-aus   Rize die sho-ben

noch de-er vin-ter   Zu-mer i - is no-och vite.
fon d-ie lut-ten   Fen-ster ri-ist a - raus.

COME OH MY LOVE

Old American Folk Song

297

Chips with Everything

CHARACTERS

Conscripts

ARCHIE CANNIBAL 239
WINGATE (Chas) 252
THOMPSON (Pip) 276
SEAFORD (Wilfe) 247
ANDREW MCCLORE 284
RICHARDSON (Ginger) 272
COHEN (Dodger) 277
SMITH (Dickey) 266
WASHINGTON (Smiler) 279

Officers

CORPORAL HILL
WING COMMANDER
SQUADRON LEADER
PILOT OFFICER
P.T. INSTRUCTOR, FLT SGT

GUARD
NIGHT CORPORAL
FIRST CORPORAL
SECOND CORPORAL
AIRMAN

The song 'The Cutty Wren', which appears on page 327, is reprinted from *If I had a Song,* a collection of children's songs published by the Workers' Music Association, 136A Westbourne Terrace, London W 2.

ACT ONE

SCENE ONE

An R.A.F. hut.

> [*Nine new conscripts enter. They are subdued, uncertain, mumbling.* CORPORAL HILL *appears at door, stocky, Northern, collarless man. He waits till they notice him, which they gradually do till mumbling ceases, utterly – they rise to attention. After a long pause*]

HILL: That's better. In future, whenever an N.C.O. comes into the hut, no matter who he is, the first person to see him will call out 'N.C.O.! N.C.O.!' like that. And whatever you're doing, even if you're stark rollock naked, you'll all spring to attention as fast as the wind from a duck's behind, and by Christ that's fast. Is that understood? [*No reply.*] Well, is it? [*A few murmurs.*] When I ask a question I expect an answer. [*Emphatically*] Is that understood!

ALL [*shouting*]: Yes, Corporal!

HILL: Anyone been in the Air Cadets? Any of the cadets? Anyone twenty-one or more then? Nineteen? [*Two boys,* ANDREW *and* DICKEY, *raise their hands. To one*] Month you were born?

ANDREW: July, Corporal.

DICKEY: May, Corporal.

HILL [*to Dickey*]: You're senior man. [*To Andrew*] You're assistant. Shift your kit to top of hut. Not now – later.

> [HILL *scrutinizes the rest. He lays his hand on the two smallest – Dodger and Ginger.*]

These small boys, these two, they're my boys. They'll do the jobs I ask them when I ask them; not much, my fires each day, perhaps my bunk – my boys. But they won't do my polishing – I do that myself. No one is to start on them, no one is to bully them, if they do, then they answer to me. [*Pause.*] You can sit now.

> [*Reads out list of names, each recruit rises and sits as called. Boys sit on their beds, waiting;* HILL *paces up and down, waiting his time. Then*]

Right, you're in the R.A.F. now, you're not at home. This hut, this

303

place here, this is going to be your home for the next eight scorching weeks. This billet here, you see it? This? It's in a state now, no one's been in it for the last four days so it's in a state now. [*Pause.*] But usually it's like a scorching palace! [*Pause.*] That's the way I want it to be cos that's the way it's always been. Now you've got to get to know me. My name is Corporal Hill. I'm not a very happy man, I don't know why. I never smile and I never joke – you'll soon see that. Perhaps it's my nature, perhaps it's the way I've been brought up – I don't know. The R.A.F. brought me up. You're going to go through hell while you're here, through scorching hell. Some of you will take it and some of you will break down. I'm warning you – some of you shall end up crying. And when that happens I don't want to see anyone laughing at him. Leave him alone, don't touch him.

But I'll play fair. You do me proud and I'll play fair. The last lot we 'ad 'ere 'ad a good time, a right time, a right good scorching time. We 'ad bags o' fun, bags o' it. But I will tear and mercilessly scratch the scorching daylights out of anyone who smarts the alec with me – and we've got some 'ere. I can see them, you can tell them. I count three already, you can tell them, by their faces, who know it all, the boys who think they're GOOD. [*Whispered*] It'll be unmerciful and scorching murder for them – all. Now, you see this wireless here, this thing with knobs and a pretty light that goes on and off? Well that's ours, our wireless for this hut, and for this hut only because this hut has always been the best hut. No other hut has a wireless. I want to keep that. I like music and I want to keep that wireless. Some people, when they get up in the morning, first thing all they want to do is smoke, or drink tea – not me, I've got to have music, the noise of instruments.

Everyone's got a fad, that's mine, music, and I want to be spoilt, you see to it that I'm spoilt. Right, if there's anyone here who wants to leave my hut and go into another because he doesn't like this 'un, then do it now, please. Go on, pick up your kit and move. I'll let 'im. [*No movement.*] You can go to the Naafi now. But be back by ten thirty, cos that's bleedin' lights out. [*Moves to door, pauses.*] Anyone object to swearing? [*No reply. Exit.*]

[*Stunned. A boy rushes in from another hut.*]

BOY: What's your'n say?

SMILER [*imitating*]: My name is Corporal Hill, I'm not a happy man.

BOY [*imitating a Scotsman*]: My name is Corporal Bridle – and I'm a bastard!

SCENE TWO

The Naafi.
[*One boy strumming a guitar*]

WILFE:
    Dear mother come and fetch me
    Dear mother take me home
    I'm drunk and unhappy
    And my virginity's gone.

    My feet are sore and I'm weary
    The sergeant looks like dad
    Oh, a two bob bit would buy me a nip
    And a Naafi girl in my bed.
    Now Eskimo Nell has gone back to the land
    Where they know how to – Eight weeks!
    EIGHT STUPID WEEKS, MOTHER!

CHAS: I've left two girls at home, two of them, and I've declared passionate love to them both – both. Poor girls, promised I'd marry them when it was all over. They'll miss me.

WILFE: Wouldn't be so bad if my mother could hear me, but she's as deaf as a bat.

PIP: Bats are blind.

WILFE: Oh dear me, bats are blind, deary, deary me fellows.

PIP: Look old son, you're going to have me for eight painful weeks in the same hut, so spend the next five minutes taking the mickey out of my accent, get it off your chest and then put your working-class halo away because no one's going to care – O.K.?

CHAS: Where are you from then?

PIP: My father is a banker, we idolize each other. I was born in a large country house and I'm scorching rich.

CHAS: You're going to do officer training then?

PIP: No! My father was also a general!

WILFE: Oh my father was a general
And I'm a general's son
But I got wise to the old man's lies
And kicked him up his you know, you
know, you know, you know what I mean.
Now Eskimo Nell has gone back to the land –
EIGHT STUPID WEEKS, MOTHER!

SMILER: Give over, Wilfe, give over.

GINGER: Well roll on Christmas, roll on I say.

DODGER: So what then? You'll be back after four days, and then four more weeks of this –

GINGER: But I'll be married.

DODGER: You'll be what?

GINGER: I'm getting married two weeks from tomorrow –

CHAS: Bleedin' daft to get married. I got two girls back home, one's blonde and one's dark – it's the Jekyll and Hyde in me. Married? Bleedin' daft!

PIP: You mean you can actually think of better things to do than produce babies?

CHAS: You shut your classical mouth you, go away, 'oppit! 'Oppit or I'll lay you down. I haven't liked you from the start.

PIP: Oh sit down, there's a good boy, I wouldn't dream of fighting you.

SMILER: You don't mind being a snob, do you?

PIP: One day, when I was driving to my father's office, the car broke down. I could have got a taxi I suppose, but I didn't. I walked. The office was in the City, so I had to walk through the East End, strange – I don't know why I should have been surprised. I'd seen photographs of this Mecca before – I even used to glance at the *Daily Mirror* now and then, so God knows why I should have been surprised. Strange. I went into a café and drank a cup of tea from a thick, white, cracked cup and I ate a piece of tasteless currant cake. On the walls I remember they had photographs of boxers, autographed, and they were curling at the edges from the heat. Every so often a woman used to come to the table and wipe it with a rag that left dark streaks behind which dried up into weird patterns. Then a man came and sat next to me – WHY should I have been surprised? I'd seen his face before, a hundred times on the front pages of papers reporting a strike. A market man, a porter, or a docker. No, he was too old to be a docker. His eyes kept watering, and each time they did that he'd take out a neatly folded handkerchief, unfold it and, with one corner, he'd wipe away the moisture, and then he'd neatly fold it up again and replace it in his pocket. Four times he did that, and each time he did it he looked at me and smiled. I could see grains of dirt in the lines of his face, and he wore an old waistcoat with pearl buttons. He wasn't untidy, the cloth even seemed a good cloth, and though his hair was thick with oil it was clean. I can even remember the colour of the walls, a pastel pink on the top half and turquoise blue on the bottom, peeling. Peeling in fifteen different places; actually, I counted them. But what I couldn't understand was why I should have been so surprised. It wasn't as though I had been cradled in my childhood. And then I saw the menu, stained with tea and beautifully written by a foreign hand, and on top it said – God I hated that old man – it said 'Chips with everything'. Chips with every damn thing. You breed babies and you eat chips with everything.

[*Enter* HILL.]

HILL: I said ten thirty lights out, didn't I? Ten thirty I said. I want to see you move to that hut like wind from a duck's behind –

WILFE: And O Jesus mother, that's fast mother, that's eight weeks and that's fast!

HILL: That's fast, that's fast, into the hut and move that fast. Into the hut, into the hut, in, in, into the hut. [*Looks at watch. Pause.*] Out! I'll give you . . .

SCENE THREE

Parade Ground: morning.

HILL: Out! I'll give you sixty seconds or you'll be on a charge, one, two, three, four – come on out of that hut, twenty-five, twenty-six, twenty-seven, twenty-eight. AT THE DOUBLE! Now get into a line and stop that talking, get into a line. A straight line you heaving nig-nogs, a straight line.

This is the square. We call it a square-bashing square. I want to see you bash that square. Right, now the first thing you've got to know, you've got to know how to come to attention, how to stand at ease and easy, how to make a right turn and how to step off.

Now to come to attention you move smartly, very smartly, to this position: heels together. STOP THAT! When I was born I was very fortunate, I was born with eyes in the back of my neck and don't be cheeky. Legs apart and wait till I give the command SHUN. When I give the command SHUN, you will move sharply, very sharply, to this position. Heels together and in a line, feet turned out to an angle of thirty degrees, knees braced, body erect and with the weight balanced evenly between the balls of the feet and the heels.

Shoulders down and back level and square to the front.

Arms hanging straight from the shoulders.

Elbows close to the sides.

Wrists straight.

Hands closed – not clenched.

Back of the fingers close to the thighs.

Thumbs straight and to the front, close to the forefinger and just behind the seam of the trousers. Head up, chin in, eyes open, steady and looking just above their own height. Come on now, heels together, body erect and evenly balanced between the balls of the feet and the heels – you didn't know you had balls on your feet did you – well you have, use them.

Stand up straight there – keep your mouth shut and your eyes

308

open and to the front. Right, well, you are now standing – somewhat vaguely – in the position of attention.

To stand at ease you keep the right foot still and carry the left foot to the left so that the feet are about – do it with me – so that the feet are about twelve inches apart. At the same time force the arms behind the back, keeping them straight, and place the back of the right hand in the palm of the left, thumbs crossed, fingers and hands straight and pointing towards the ground. At the same time transfer the weight of the body slightly to the left so as to be evenly balanced. Keep your arms straight and don't bend at the waist. [*Inspects them.*] Right hand inside your left, *your* left not his. Try to make your elbows meet.

When you hear me give the command SQUAD, I want you to jump to that position, smarten up, as if you were going somewhere. We'll try it – stand easy, relax, just relax, but keep your hands behind your back, don't slouch, don't move your feet and don't talk – just relax, let your head look down, RELAX! IF YOU DON'T RELAX I'LL PUT YOU ON A CHARGE!

Squad, squad – SHUN! As you were, I want you to do it together. Squad – SHUN! As you were. Squad – SHUN! STAND AT EASE!

To make a Right Turn: keeping both knees straight, turn through ninety degrees to the right swivelling on the heel of the right foot and the toe of the left raising the toe of the right and the heel of the left in doing so. Keeping the weight of the body on the right foot, on completion of this movement the right foot is flat on the ground, the left leg to the rear and the heel raised – both knees braced back and the body in the position of attention. Bring the left foot into the right, good and hard, and for the time being I want that left knee good and high, slam your foot in good and hard and keep still.

Squad, squad – SHUN.

Turning to the right – RIGHT TURN.

All right you creepy-crawly nig-nogs, moon men that's what you are, moon men. I want it done together. As you were.

Squad, turning to the right – RIGHT TURN.

Now, to Step Off. When I say by the front – quick march, I don't want your pretty left foot forward anyways, like this, no, it's got to be scorching smart, like a flash of greased lightning. ONE!

Like this [*Petrified stance of a man about to step off.*] ONE! Like that, and I want that left hand up as high as you can get it and your right level with your breast pocket.

Now, on the word – MARCH – I want you only to take a step forward, *not* to march. I want you only to take a step forward, just pretend, got that? Some dimwitted piece of merchandise is sure to carry on. Now then, watch it. SQUAD – by the front – quick MARCH!

[*Sure enough two boys march off and collide with those standing still, and one in the front marches off out of sight.*]

Stop that laughing. I'll charge the next man I see smile.

[*Stands, watching the other one disappear.*]

All right, Horace, come back home. [*Airman returns, sheepishly.*] You nit, you nit, you creepy-crawly nit. Don't you hear, don't you listen, can't you follow simple orders, CAN'T YOU? Shut up! Don't answer back! A young man like you, first thing in the morning, don't be rude, don't be rude. No one's being rude to you.

Stop that laughing. I'll charge the next man I see smile. [*To Smiler*] You, I said wipe off that smile. I said wipe it off.

SMILER: I'm not smiling, Corporal, it's natural, I was born with it.

HILL: Right then, don't ever let me see that face frown or I'll haul you over the highest wall we've got. [*Approaching one of the two marching ones*] You. If you'd been paying attention you might 'ave done it correctly, eh? But you weren't, you were watching the little aeroplanes, weren't you? You want to fly? Do you want to reach the thundering heavens, my little lad, at an earlier age than you imagined, with Technicolor wings? KEEP YOUR EYES ON ME. [*To all*] You better know from the start, you can have it the hard way or you can have it the easy way, I don't mind which way it is. Perhaps you like it the hard way, suits me. Just let me know. At ease everyone. Now, we'll try and make it easier for you. We'll count our way along. We'll count together, and then maybe we'll all act together. I want everything to be done together. We're going to be the happiest family in Christendom and we're going to move together, as one, as one solitary man. So, when I say 'attention' you'll slam your feet down hard and cry 'one'. Like this. And when I say 'right turn' you'll move and bang your foot down and cry 'one-pause-two'. Like this. Is that clear? Is that beyond the intellectual comprehensibilities of any of you? Good! SQUAD – wait for it – atten-SHUN!

SQUAD: ONE!

HILL: As you were, at ease. Did I say slam? Didn't I say slam? Don't worry about the noise, it's a large square, no one will mind. Squad – atten-SHUN.

SQUAD: ONE!

HILL: As you were. Let's hear that 'one'. Let's have some energy from you. I want GOD to hear you crying 'ONE, ONE, ONE – pause TWO!' Squad – atten-SHUN!

SQUAD: ONE!

HILL: Right TURN!

SQUAD: ONE – pause – TWO!

HILL: By the left – quick – MARCH!

[*The boys march off round the stage, sound of marching and the chanting of* 'One, One, One – pause – Two! One, One, One – pause – Two!']

SCENE FOUR

Sound of marching feet. Marching stops. The lecture hall.
    [*Boys enter and sit on seats. Enter the* WING COMMANDER, *boys rise.*]

WING COMMANDER: Sit down, please. I'm your Wing Commander. You think we are at peace. Not true. We are never at peace. The human being is in a constant state of war and we must be prepared, each against the other. History has taught us this and we must learn. The reasons why and wherefore are not our concern. We are simply the men who must be prepared. You, why do you look at me like that?

PIP: I'm paying attention, sir.

WING COMMANDER: There's insolence in those eyes, lad – I recognize insolence in a man; take that glint out of your eyes, your posh

311

tones don't fool me. We are simply the men who must be prepared. Already the aggressors have a force far superior to ours. Our efforts must be intensified. We need a fighting force and it is for this reason you are being trained here, according to the best traditions of the R.A.F. We want you to be proud of your part, unashamed of the uniform you wear. But you must not grumble too much if you find that government facilities for you, personally, are not up to standard. We haven't the money to spare. A Meteor, fully armed, is more important than a library. The C.O. of this camp is called Group Captain Watson. His task is to check any tendency in his officers to practical jokes, to discountenance any disposition in his officers to gamble or to indulge in extravagant expenditure; to endeavour, by example and timely intervention, to promote a good understanding and prevent disputes. Group Captain Watson is a busy man, you will rarely see him. You, why are you smiling?

SMILER: I'm not, sir, it's natural, I was born like it.

WING COMMANDER: Because I want this taken seriously, you know, from all of you. Any questions?

WILFE: Sir, if the aggressors are better off than us, what are they waiting for?

WING COMMANDER: What's your name?

WILFE: 247 Seaford, sir.

WING COMMANDER: Any other questions?

[*Exit. Enter* SQUADRON LEADER. *The boys rise.*]

SQUADRON LEADER: Sit down, please. I'm your squadron leader. My task is not only to ensure respect for authority, but also to foster the feelings of self-respect and personal honour which are essential to efficiency. It is also my task to bring to notice those who, from incapacity or apathy, are deficient in knowledge of their duties, or who do not afford an officer that support which he has a right to expect or who conduct themselves in a manner injurious to the efficiency or credit of the R.A.F. You are here to learn discipline. Discipline is necessary if we are to train you to the maximum state of efficiency, discipline and obedience. You will obey your instructors because they are well trained, you will obey them because they can train you efficiently, you will obey them because it's necessary

312

for you to be trained efficiently. That is what you are here to learn: obedience and discipline. Any questions? Thank you.

[*Exit. Enter* PILOT OFFICER. *The boys rise.*]

PILOT OFFICER: Sit down please. I'm your pilot officer. You'll find that I'm amenable and that I do not stick rigidly to authority. All I shall require is cleanliness. It's not that I want rigid men, I want clean men. It so happens, however, that you cannot have clean men without rigid men, and cleanliness requires smartness and cere- mony. Ceremony means your webbing must be blancoed, and smartness means that your brass – all of it – must shine like silver paper, and your huts must be spick and span without a trace of dust, because dust carries germs, and germs are unclean. I want a man clean from toe nail to hair root. I want him so clean that he looks unreal. In fact I don't want real men, real men are dirty and nasty, they pick their noses – and scratch their skin. I want unreal, super- real men. Those men win wars, the others die of disease before they reach the battlefields. Any questions? You, what are you smiling at?

SMILER: I'm not, sir, it's natural. I was born like that.

PILOT OFFICER: In between the lines of that grin are formed battal- ions of microbes. Get rid of it.

SMILER: I can't, sir.

PILOT OFFICER: Then never let me hear of you going sick.

[*Exit. Enter* P.T. INSTRUCTOR, FLIGHT SERGEANT.]

P.T.I.: As you were. I'm in charge of physical training on this camp. It's my duty to see that every minute muscle in your body is awake. Awake and ringing. Do you hear that? That's poetry! I want your body awake and ringing. I want you so light on your feet that the smoke from a cigarette could blow you away, and yet so strong that you stand firm before hurricanes. I hate thin men and detest fat ones. I want you like Greek gods. You heard of the Greeks? You ignorant troupe of anaemics, you were brought up on tinned beans and television sets, weren't you? You haven't had any exer- cise since you played knock-a-down-ginger, have you? Greek gods, you hear me? Till the sweat pours out of you like Niagara Falls. Did you hear that poetry? Sweat like Niagara Falls! I don't want your stupid questions!

[*Exit.*]

PIP: You have babies, you eat chips and you take orders.
CHAS: Well, look at you then, I don't see you doing different.
  [*They march off. Sound of marching feet.*]

SCENE FIVE

Sound of marching feet and the men counting. The hut. Billet inspection.
  [ANDREW, *the hut orderly, tidying up. Enter the* PILOT OFFICER]

ANDREW [*saluting*]: Good morning, sir.
PILOT OFFICER: Haven't you been told the proper way to address an
  officer?
ANDREW: Sorry sir, no sir, not yet sir.
  [PILOT OFFICER *walks around.* ANDREW *follows awkwardly.*]
PILOT OFFICER: There's dust under that bed.
ANDREW: Is there, sir?
PILOT OFFICER: I said so.
ANDREW: Yes, you did, sir.
PILOT OFFICER: Then why ask me again?
ANDREW: Again, sir?
PILOT OFFICER: Didn't you?
ANDREW: Didn't I what, sir?
PILOT OFFICER: Ask me to repeat what I'd already said. Are you
  playing me up, Airman? Are you taking the mickey out of me?
  I can charge you, man. I can see your game and I can charge you.
ANDREW: Yes, you can, sir.
PILOT OFFICER: Don't tell me what I already know.
ANDREW: Oh, I wouldn't, sir – you know what you already know.
  I know that, sir.
PILOT OFFICER: I think you're a fool, Airman. God knows why the
  Air Ministry sends us fools. They never select, select is the answer,
  select and pick those out from the others.
ANDREW: What others, sir?
PILOT OFFICER: Don't question me!

314

ANDREW: But I was only thinking of –

PILOT OFFICER: You aren't paid to think, Airman, don't you know that? You aren't paid to think. [*Long pause.*] No, it's no good trying that line. [*Sits.*] Why pretend? I don't really frighten you, do I? I don't really frighten you, but you obey my orders, nevertheless. It's a funny thing. We have always ruled, but I suspect we've never frightened you. I know that as soon as I turn my back you'll merely give me a V sign and make a joke of me to the others, won't you? And they'll laugh. Especially Thompson. He knows you're not frightened, that's why he's in the ranks. But I'll break him. Slumming, that's all he's doing, slumming. What's your name?

ANDREW: Andrew McClore, sir.

PILOT OFFICER: I don't suppose Thompson's really slumming. There *is* something about you boys, confidence, I suppose, or cockiness, something trustworthy anyway. I can remember enjoying the Naafi more than I do the Officers' Mess. What was your job?

ANDREW: Electrician, sir.

PILOT OFFICER: My father was an electrician. He used to play the piano. He really played beautifully. Tragic – my God – it was tragic.

ANDREW: Had an accident, sir?

PILOT OFFICER: That would be your idea of tragedy, wouldn't it? My father never had that sort of accident; he couldn't, he owned the factory he worked for. It's the other things that happen to people like him. The intangible accidents. No, his fingers remained subtle till he died, and he touched the keys with love whenever he could, but no one heard him. That was the tragedy, Andrew. No one heard him except – four uncaring children and a stupid wife who saw no sense in it. God, Andrew, how I envied that man. I could have bought so much love with that talent. People don't give love away that easily, only if we have magic in our hands or in our words or in our brush then they pay attention, then they love us. You can forget your own troubles in an artist's love, Andrew; you can melt away from what you were and grow into a new man. Haven't you ever wanted to be a new man? [*Places hand on McClore's knee.*]

ANDREW: Don't do that, please, sir.

315

PILOT OFFICER [*change*]: Don't ever rely on this conversation, don't ever trust me to be your friend. I shall not merely frighten you, there are other ways – and you will need all your pity for yourself. I warn you not to be fooled by good nature, we slum for our own convenience.

[*Enter a* FLIGHT SERGEANT.]

FLIGHT SERGEANT: When is – I beg your pardon, sir.

PILOT OFFICER: You can take over now, Flight. [*Exit.*]

FLIGHT SERGEANT: When is this place going to be straight?

ANDREW: Pardon, Sergeant?

FLIGHT SERGEANT: *Flight* Sergeant!

ANDREW: Sorry, FLIGHT Sergeant.

FLIGHT SERGEANT: When is this place going to be straight, I asked?

ANDREW: I've just straightened it, Serg – or Flight – or Flight Sergeant.

FLIGHT SERGEANT: You what? If I come in here tomorrow and I can't eat my dinner off that floor I'll have you all outside on fatigues till midnight. Have you got that?

ANDREW: Yes, Flight Sergeant.

FLIGHT SERGEANT: Well, keep it. Tight! Tight! Tight, tight –

['Tight, tight, tight', *mixes to sound of marching feet, men counting.*]

SCENE SIX

The billet at night. The boys are tired. Beds are being made, brasses, shoes, webbing attended to.

ANDREW: And then he says:'I shall not merely frighten you, there are other ways, and you will need all your pity for yourself.' Man, I tell you it was him was frightened. A tall meek thing he is, trying to impress me.

HILL: It's not him you want to be frightened of, it's royalty. Royalty! I hate royalty more than anything else in the world. Parasites! What do they do, eh? I'm not in this outfit for them, no bloody fear, it's the people back 'ome I'm here for, like you lot. Royalty –

PIP: Good old Corporal Hill, they've made you chase red herrings, haven't they?

ANDREW: And he had something to say about you too, Pip Thompson. He said you were slumming, laddie, slumming; he said: 'Thompson knows you're not frightened, that's why he's in the ranks – but he's slumming.'

PIP: So he thinks you're not frightened? He's right – you're not, are you? But there *are* other ways – he's right about that too.

DODGER: You know, I've been looking at this hut, sizing it up. Make a good warehouse.

GINGER: A good what?

DODGER: Warehouse. It's my mania. My family owns a pram shop, see, and our one big problem is storage. Prams take up room, you know. Always on the look-out for storage space. Every place I look at I work out the cubic feet, and I say it will make a good warehouse or it won't. Can't help myself. One of the best warehouses I ever see was the Vatican in Rome. What you laughing at? You take a carpenter – what does he do when he enters – what does he do when he enters a room, eh? Ever thought about that? He feels how the door swings open, looks straight across to the window to see if the frame is sitting straight and then sits in the chair to see if it's made good – then he can settle down to enjoy the evening. With me it's pregnant women. Every time I see pregnant women I get all maternal. You can have your women's breasts all you want and her legs. *Me*, only one spot interests me – one big belly and we've made a sale. Can't help it – warehouses and pregnant women.

DICKEY: Hey, Cannibal my dear associate, what are you so engrossed in?

CANNIBAL: It's a book about ideal marriage, now leave me be.

DICKEY: Why you dirty-minded adolescent you – put it away.

DODGER: Here, let's have a read.

[*He and some others crowd round to read on.*]

PIP: 252 WINGATE! – give me a hand with this bed, will you, please.

CHAS: Why I bloody help you I don't know, not at all I don't.

PIP: Because you like me, that's why.

CHAS: *Like* you? Like *you*? You're the lousiest rotten snob I know.

PIP: And you like snobs.

CHAS: Boy, I hate you so much it hurts. You can't even make a bed properly.

PIP: It was always made for me.

CHAS: There you go. See what I mean. Boasting of your bleedin' wealth and comfort. Well, I don't want to know about your stinking comforts, don't tell me, I don't want to hear.

PIP: Oh, yes you do. You love to hear me talk about my home. We have a beautiful home, Charles, twenty-four rooms, and they're all large and thick with carpets.

CHAS: Modern?

PIP: No, built in the time of George III.

CHAS: I don't want to know.

PIP: They started to build it in 1776 when George Washington was made commander-in-chief of the American colonists and the great-grandfathers of the Yanks were issuing the Declaration of Independence. A jubilant period, Charles – exciting. Did you know that while my great-great-grandfather was trading with the East India Company in the land of the strange chocolate people, bringing home the oriental spoils, the American grandfathers were still struggling to control a vast land at a time when there was no communication? But they didn't struggle long. Each time my great-grandfather came home he heard more bad news about those traitorous Americans. Returning from India in 1830, with a cargo of indigo, he heard, twenty-three years after everyone else, that the steamboat had been invented. Terrible news. Returning in 1835 with a cargo of teak they told him about the strange iron horse that ran on wheels. Terrible, terrible, news. Returning in 1840 with a cargo of coriander he was so enraged that he refused to believe it possible to send messages through the air, and so he died without ever believing in the magic of the telegraph. What do you think of that, Charles boy? Still, my favourite relative was his father, a beautiful boy, the kind of boy that every aunt wanted to mother and every cousin wanted to marry. The only thing was he was incredibly stupid, much more than you, Charles, and strangely enough he was called Charles also. My family talk about him to this very day. You see, the fact was that very few people ever realized he was so stupid because he was such a handsome boy and very

318

rarely spoke. And because of his silence everyone thought he was very wise, and this was so effective that he increased our family fortune by double. [*Nearly everyone is listening to him by now.*] You want to know how? Well, it was like this. Shortly after the shock of losing America, the English were disturbed by another event – another shock that rocked the whole of Europe and set my family and all their friends shaking. One day, the French kings and princes found themselves bankrupt – the royalty and the clergy never used to pay any taxes, you see they left that on the shoulders of the middle class and the commoners, and yet they still managed to become bankrupt. So what did they do? They called a meeting of all the representatives of all the classes to see what could be done – there hadn't been such a meeting for over a century, what a party! What a mistake! because, for the first time in a long while, the commoners not only found a means of voicing their discontent over the paying of taxes, but they suddenly looked at themselves and realized that there were more of them than they ever imagined – and they weren't fools. Now, they voiced themselves well, and so loudly that they won a victory, and not simply over the tax problem, but over a dozen and one other injustices as well. Big excitement, jubilation, victory! In fact, they found themselves so victorious and so powerful that they were able to cut off the heads of poor Louis XVI and Marie Antoinette and start what we all know as the French Revolution.

CHAS: What about Charlie, the silly one?

PIP: Patience, my handsome boy, don't hurry me. Now, my family had a lot of interests in France and its royalty, so they decided to send this beautiful boy out to see what was happening to their estates and fortunes. And do you think he did? Poor soul, he couldn't understand what the hell was happening. The royalty of all Europe was trembling because of what the French did to Louis and Marie, and he just thought he was being sent on a holiday. To this day we none of us know how he escaped with his life – but, not only did he escape with his life, he also came back with somebody else's life. A French princess! And would you believe it, she was also a simpleton, a sort of prototype deb with a dimple on her left cheek. Her family had given her all their jewels, thinking that no

319

one would touch her, since she was so helpless, and indeed no one did. No one, that is, except our Charles. He met her on his way to Paris in a Franciscan monastery and asked her to teach him French. There were her relatives being beheaded one by one and there was she, chanting out the past tense of the verb 'to be'. You can guess the rest, within four weeks he was back in England with a lovely bride and four hundred thousand pounds'-worth of jewellery. They built a new wing to the house and had seven children. The rooms glitter with her chandeliers, Charlie boy – and – well, just look at the way your mouth is gaping – you'll get lockjaw.

HILL: Don't you tell stories, eh? Don't you just. I bet you made that one up as you went along.

PIP: That's right, Corporal, the French Revolution was a myth.

CHAS: Tell us more, Pip, tell us more stories.

PIP: They're not stories, Charlie boy, they're history.

CHAS: Well, tell us more then.

PIP: What's the use?

CHAS: I'm asking you, that's what's the use. *I'm* asking *you*.

[PIP *picks up his webbing to blanco. The others withdraw and pick up what they were doing.* CHARLIE *is left annoyed and frustrated.* HILL *takes a seat next to the fire and plays a mouth-organ. In between sounds he talks.*]

HILL: I was pleased with you lads today. You're coming on. When you did those last about turns I felt proud. You might even be better than the last lot we had. Know that? And by Christ that last lot were good. But there's one of you needs to buck up his ideas, I shan't mention names.

SMILER: I try, Corporal.

HILL: Well, you want to try harder, my son. Look at you.

SMILER: I look at myself every day, Corporal.

HILL: That stupid smile of yours, if only you didn't smile so much. Can't you have an operation or something? I'll go bleedin' mad looking at that for another five weeks.

DODGER: Oh, my gawd, listen to this! Listen what it says here. 'Between two hundred and three hundred million spermatozoa are released at one time of which only one succeeds in fertilizing the female ovum.' Jesus! All them prams!

320

GINGER: Give us a good tune, Corp, go on.

HILL: You're my treasure, aren't you, eh, Ginger lad? Don't know what I'd do without you. What shall I play for you, you name it, I'll play it.

GINGER: Play us the 'Rose of Tralee'.

HILL: You want the 'Rose of Tralee', my beauty? You shall have it then.

> [CORPORAL HILL *plays, the boys rest, work, write letters, and* *listen.*]

GINGER: When's the Christmas Eve party?

DODGER: Tomorrow a week, isn't it?

HILL: Uh-huh.

> [*Continue sound of mouth-organ – change to*]

SCENE SEVEN

The Naafi. Christmas Eve Party.
> [*The rock-'n-'roll group play vigorously. The boys jiving, drinking,* *and singing. Officers are present.*]

WING COMMANDER: Look at them. Conscripts! They bring nothing and they take nothing. Look at them. Their wild dancing and their silly words – I could order them at this moment to stand up and be shot and they'd do it.

SQUADRON LEADER: You're drinking too much, Sid.

WING COMMANDER: Civilians! How I hate civilians. They don't know – what do they know? How to make money, how to chase girls and kill old women. No order, no purpose. Conscripts! They bring their muddled lives and they poison us, Jack; they poison me with their indifference, and all we do is guard their fat bellies. I'd sacrifice a million of them for the grace of a Javelin Fighter, you know that?

SQUADRON LEADER: Don't let them see you scowl. Smile, man, smile. It's a Christmas Eve party. We're guests here.

SMILER [*to Wilfe*]: Go and offer the Wing Commander a drink, then, go on.

WILFE: Leave off, will you, man? All evening you have been pestering me. What do I want to go giving officers drinks for?

SMILER: Go up to him and say 'with the compliments of our hut, sir', go on.

WILFE: I'll pour a bottle on you soon if you don't leave off.

SMILER: Your fly button's undone.

WILFE: Where? Smiler, I'll bash you – you tantalize me any more this evening and I'll bash that grin right down to your arse, so help me, I will.

SMILER: Listen to him. Wilfe the warrior. Do you talk like this at home? Does your mummy let you?

WILFE: Now why do you talk to me like that? Why do you go on and on and on? Do I start on you like that? Take this away, will you boys, take him away and drown him.

SMILER: Go after one of them Naafi girls, go on, Wilfe. Go and find out if they're willing.

CANNIBAL: Naafi girls! Camp bloody whores, that's all they are.

DICKEY: Well, he's woken up. Cannibal has spoken, come on, me ole cocker, say more.

CANNIBAL: Who's for more drinks?

DICKEY: Good old Cannibal! He uttered a syllable of many dimensions. The circumlocircle of his mouth has moved. Direct yourself to the bar, old son, and purchase for us some brown liquid. We shall make merry with your generosity.

CANNIBAL: I don't know where he gets the words from. He lies in his bed next to me and he talks and he talks and he sounds like an adding-machine.

DICKEY: You're under-educated, my old son – you're devoid of knowledgeable grey matter. You should've gone to a technical school like me; we sat in study there and ate up books for our diluted pleasure. We developed voluble minds in that technical college and we came away equipped with data. Data! That's the ticket – the sum total of everything. Direct your attention to the bar I say, and deliver us of that inebriating liquid, my hearty.

CANNIBAL: Ask him what he means. Go on, someone! I don't know. He lies on his bed next to me and he talks and he mumbles and

322

talks and he mumbles. One night he woke up and he shouted: 'Kiss me, Mother, kiss your dying son.'

DICKEY: You lie in your teeth, O dumb one. Buy the drinks.

CANNIBAL: And another night he crept up to me and he was crying. 'Let me in your bed,' he moaned, 'let me get near you, you're big and warm.'

DICKEY: You're lying, Cannibal. Don't let me hear more of your lies.

CANNIBAL: Shall I tell them how you pray at nights?

[DICKEY *throws his beer over Cannibal and they fight.*]

WING COMMANDER: Separate those men! Hold them! Stop that, you two, you hear me, an order, stop that! [*They are separated.*] Undisciplined hooligans! I won't have fighting in my camp. Is this the only way you can behave with drink in you? Is it? Show your upbringing in your own home where it grew but not here, you hear me? Not here! This is Christmas Eve. A party, a celebration for the birth of our Lord, a time of joy and good will. Show me good will then. I will not, will not, will not tolerate your slum methods here. This is a clean force, a clean blue force. Go to your huts, stay there, stay there for the rest of the evening and don't wander beyond ten feet of your door. Disobey that order and I shall let out the hell of my temper so hard that you'll do jankers the rest of your National Service.

[DICKEY *and* CANNIBAL *leave. On the way*, DICKEY *trips over, and* CANNIBAL *helps him to his feet.*]

WING COMMANDER: They don't even fight seriously – a few loud words, and then they kiss each other's wounds. God give us automation soon.

SQUADRON LEADER: You suffer too much, Sid.

WING COMMANDER: Nonsense! And forget your theories about my unhappy childhood. Mine is a healthy and natural hatred.

SQUADRON LEADER: I haven't time to hate – it takes me all my time to organize them.

WING COMMANDER: Look at them. What are they? The good old working class of England. Am I supposed to bless them all the time for being the salt of the earth?

SQUADRON LEADER: They provide your food, they make your clothes, dig coal, mend roads for you.

WING COMMANDER: Given half the chance you think they would? For me? Look at them, touching the heights of ecstasy.

PIP: They're talking about us – the officers.

CHAS: What are they saying?

PIP: They're saying we're despicable, mean, and useless. That fight disturbed the Wing Commander – we upset him.

ANDREW: Don't say ' we ' and imagine that makes you one of us, Pip.

PIP: Don't start on me, Andy, there's a good man.

ANDREW: Don't do us any favours.

PIP: Don't start on me, Andy, there's a good man. I don't have to drop my aitches in order to prove friendship, do I?

ANDREW: No. No, you don't. Only I've known a lot of people like you, Pip. They come drinking in the pub and talk to us as though we were the salt of the earth, and then, one day, for no reason any of us can see, they go off, drop us as though that was another game they was tired of. I'd give a pension to know why we attract you.

WING COMMANDER: What do you know about that one, Jack, the one with the smart-alec eyes and the posh tones?

SQUADRON LEADER: Thompson? Remember General Thompson, Tobruk, a banker now?

WING COMMANDER: So that's the son. Thompson! Come here, Airman.

PIP: Sir?

WING COMMANDER: Enjoying yourself?

PIP: Thank you, sir.

WING COMMANDER: Gay crowd, eh?

PIP: I imagined you would dislike conscripts, sir.

WING COMMANDER: I haven't met you before, Thompson; your father impressed me but you don't.

PIP: Is that all, sir?

WING COMMANDER: I can have you, boy. I can really have you – remember that.

CHAS: What'd he want, Pip, what'd he say?

PIP: He wouldn't dare. Yes, he would. He's going to test you all. The old fool is really going to play the old game. I wonder what method he'll choose.

324

WILFE: What d'you mean, old game, what old game?

PIP: How he hates you; he's going to make an announcement. Listen how patronizing he'll be. Whatever happens, do as I tell you – don't question me, just do as I tell you.

ANDREW: If you have a war with that man, Pip, don't use me as fodder, I'm warning you.

PIP: Help, Andy, I'm helping, or do you want to be made fools of?

WING COMMANDER: Silence everybody, your attention please, gentlemen – Thank you. As you all know we hoped, when we organized this gay gathering for you, that we'd have a spot in the evening when everyone would get up and do a turn himself. A dirty recitation, or a pop song. I'm sure that there's a wealth of native talent among you, and now is the chance for you to display it in all its glory, while the rest of us sit back and watch and listen. My officers are always complaining of the dull crowds we get in this camp, but I've always said no, it's not true, they're not dull, just a little inhibited – you – er know what inhibited means, of course? So now's the time to prove them wrong and me right. You won't let me down, will you, lads? Who's to be first? Eh? Who'll start?

PIP: Very subtle, eh, Andy?

WILFE: Will someone tell me what's going on here? What's so sinister about a talent show?

WING COMMANDER: The first, now.

PIP: Burns, Andrew –

ANDREW: Burns?

PIP: Your bloody saint, the poet –

ANDREW: I know he's a poet but –

PIP: Recite him, man, go on, get up there and recite.

ANDREW: Recite what? I –

PIP: In your best Scottish accent now.

ANDREW: Hell, man [once there] I – er – Burns. A poem.
[Recites it all, at first hesitantly, amid jeers, then with growing confidence, amid silence.]

> This ae nighte, this ae nighte,
> *Every nighte and alle,*

325

Fire and fleet and candle-lighte,
And Christe receive thy saule.

When thou from hence away art past,
Every nighte and alle,
To Whinny-muir thou com'st at last;
And Christe receive thy saule.

If ever thou gavest hosen and shoon,
Every nighte and alle,
Sit thee down and put them on;
And Christe receive thy saule.

If hosen and shoon thou ne'er gav'st nane
Every nighte and alle,
The whinnes sall prick thee to the bare bane;
And Christe receive thy saule.

From Whinny-muir when thou art past,
Every nighte and alle,
To Purgatory fire thou com'st at last;
And Christe receive thy saule.

If ever thou gavest meat or drink,
Every nighte and alle,
The fire sall never make thee shrink;
And Christe receive thy saule.

If meat and drink you ne'er gav'st nane,
Every nighte and alle,
The fire will burn thee to the bare bane
And Christe receive thy saule.

This ae nighte, this ae nighte,
Every nighte and alle,
Fire and fleet and candle-lighte,
And Christe receive thy saule.

[*Ovation.*]

WING COMMANDER: Come now, something more cheerful than that. How about a song – something from Elvis Presley.

[*Band and boys begin pop song.*]

PIP: Not that, not now.

WING COMMANDER: Lovely, yes, that's it, let's see you enjoying yourselves.

PIP: Don't join in, boys – believe me and don't join in.

WILFE: What *is* this – what's going on here?

WING COMMANDER: Look at them – that's them in their element.

PIP: Can't you see what's happening, what he's thinking?

WING COMMANDER: The beer is high, they're having a good time.

PIP: Look at that smug smile.

WING COMMANDER: Aren't they living it up, just, eh? Aren't they in their glory?

PIP: He could lead you into a swamp and you'd go.

WING COMMANDER: Bravo! Bravo! That's the spirit! Make merry – it's a festive occasion and I want to see you laughing. I want my men laughing.

[*Loud pop song. Pip moves to guitarist and whispers in his ear. Boy protests, finally agrees to sing* 'The Cutty Wren', *an old peasant revolt song. Boys join in gradually, menacing the officers*]

ALL:

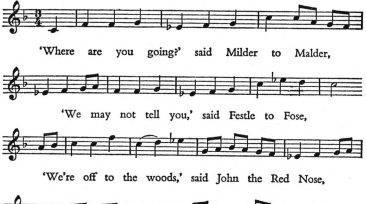

'Where are you going?' said Milder to Malder,

'We may not tell you,' said Festle to Fose,

'We're off to the woods,' said John the Red Nose,

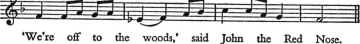

'We're off to the woods,' said John the Red Nose.

'What will you do there?' said Milder to Malder.
'We may not tell you,' said Festle to Fose.

327

'We'll shoot the cutty wren,' said John the Red Nose,
'We'll shoot the cutty wren,' said John the Red Nose.

'How will you shoot him?' said Milder to Malder.
'We may not tell you,' said Festle to Fose.
'We've guns and we've cannons,' said John the Red Nose,
'We've guns and we've cannons,' said John the Red Nose.

'How will you cut her up?' said Milder to Malder.
'We may not tell you,' said Festle to Fose.
'Big hatchets and cleavers,' said John the Red Nose,
'Big hatchets and cleavers,' said John the Red Nose.

'How will you cook her?' said Milder to Malder.
'We may not tell you,' said Festle to Fose.
'Bloody great brass cauldrons,' said John the Red Nose,
'Bloody great brass cauldrons,' said John the Red Nose.

'Who'll get the spare ribs?' said Milder to Malder.
'We may not tell you,' said Festle to Fose.
'Give them all to the poor,' said John the Red Nose,
'Give them all to the poor,' said John the Red Nose.

WING COMMANDER: Quite the little leader, aren't you, Thompson? Come over here, I want a word with you in private. Stand to attention, do your button up, raise your chin – at ease. Why are you fighting me, Thompson? We come from the same side, don't we? I don't understand your reasons, boy – and what's more you're insolent. I have every intention of writing to your father.

PIP: Please do.

WING COMMANDER: Oh, come now. Listen, lad, perhaps you've got a fight on with your father or something, well that's all right by me, we all fight our fathers, and when we fight them we also fight what they stand for. Am I right? Of course I'm right. I understand you, boy, and you mustn't think I'm unsympathetic. But it's not often we get your mettle among conscripts – we need you. Let your time here be a truce, eh? Answer me, boy, my guns are lowered and I'm waiting for an answer.

PIP: Lowered, sir?

WING COMMANDER: You know very well what I mean.

[WING COMMANDER *and* OFFICERS *leave*.]

HILL: Well, a right mess you made of that interview. If there's any

328

repercussions in our Flight, if we get victimized cos of you, boy, I'll see you –

PIP: Don't worry, Corp, there won't be any repercussions.

CHAS: Well, what in hell's name happened – what was it all about?

SMILER: This party's lost its flavour – let's go back to the hut, eh? I've got a pack of cards – let's go back and play cards.

CHAS [*of Pip*]. Talk to him is like talking to a brick wall. PIP!

SCENE EIGHT

The Naafi.

PIP: You've got enemies, Charles boy. Learn to know them.
     [*The others have gone.*]

CHAS: Enemies? I know about enemies. People you like is enemies.

PIP: What do *you* mean when you say that, Charles?

CHAS: Oh, nothing as clever as you could mean, I'm sure.

PIP: Come on, dear boy, we're not fighting all the time, are we? You mustn't take too much notice of the way I talk.

CHAS: You talk sometimes, Pip, and I don't think you know that you hurt people.

PIP: Do I? I don't mean to.

CHAS: And sometimes there's something about your voice, the way you talk – that – well, it makes me want to tell you things.

PIP: You were telling me about enemies you like.

CHAS: You're embarrassed.

PIP: You were telling me –

CHAS: Now why should I embarrass you?

PIP: – enemies you like.

CHAS: No, about people you liked who were enemies. There's a difference. I'm surprised you didn't see the difference.

PIP: Go on.

CHAS: Go on what?

PIP: What do you mean?

CHAS: Mean?

329

PIP: What you just said.

CHAS: Well, I said it. That's what it means.

PIP: Oh, I see.

CHAS: I do embarrass you, don't I?

PIP: A bit. Are you an only child, Charles?

CHAS: I got six brothers. You?

PIP: Four brothers.

CHAS: What I meant was people say things meaning to help but it works out all wrong.

PIP: You could have meant a number of things, I suppose.

CHAS: Words do mean a number of things.

PIP: Yes, Charles.

CHAS: Well, they do.

PIP: Mm. I'm not sure why we started this.

CHAS: Well, you said we got enemies, and I was saying –

PIP: Oh, yes.

CHAS: There, now you've lost interest. Just as we were getting into conversation you go all bored.

PIP: Don't nag at me, Charles.

CHAS: Charlie.

PIP: Oh, I can't call you Charlie – it's a stupid name.

CHAS: Now why did you have to say that? Making a rudeness about my name. Why couldn't you leave it alone. I want to be called Charlie. Why couldn't you just call me Charlie? No, you had to criticize.

PIP: All right, Charlie then! Charlie! If you don't mind being called Charlie you won't ever mind anything much.

CHAS: You're such a prig – I don't know how you can be such a barefaced prig and not mind.

PIP: I'm not a prig, Charles, that's so suburban – a snob perhaps but nothing as common as prig, please. Tell you what, I'm a liar.

CHAS: A liar?

PIP: Yes – I haven't got four brothers – I'm an only son.

CHAS: So am I.

PIP: You? Yes – I might've guessed. Poor old Charlie. Terrible, isn't it? Do you always try to hide it?

CHAS: Yes.

PIP: Not possible though, is it?

CHAS: No. Funny that – how we both lied. What you gonna do when they let us out of camp?

PIP: When is it?

CHAS: Next Friday.

PIP: Oh, go into the town, the pictures perhaps.

CHAS: Can I come?

PIP: Yes, I suppose so.

CHAS: Suppose so! You'd grudge your grandmother a coffin.

PIP: But I've just said you could come.

CHAS: Yes, dead keen you sounded.

PIP: Well, what do you want?

CHAS: Don't you know?

PIP: Oh, go to hell!

CHAS: I'm sorry, I take it back, don't shout. I'll come – thanks. [*Pause.*] If I was more educated you think it'd be easier, wouldn't it, between us?

PIP: What do you mean 'us'?

CHAS: Let me finish –

PIP: For God's sake don't start wedding me to you –

CHAS: Just let me –

PIP: And don't whine –

CHAS: You won't let me –

PIP: You are what you are – don't whine.

CHAS: Let me bloody finish what I was going to say, will you! You don't listen. You don't bloody listen.

PIP: I'm sorry –

CHAS: Yes, I know.

PIP: I'm listening.

CHAS: Oh, go to hell – you –

PIP: I'm sorry, I take it back, don't shout, I'm listening.

CHAS: I didn't say *I* thought it'd be easier if I was more educated – I said *you'd* think it'd be easier, I thought *you'd* think it. And I was just going to say I disagreed – then you jumped.

PIP: Yes, well, I thought – yes, well, you're right Charles, quite right. It's no good wanting to go to university –

CHAS: Facts, that's all it is.

PIP: Like me and work – manual labour. The number of intellectuals and artists who are fascinated by manual labour. Not me though, Charles. I haven't the slightest desire to use my brawn, prove myself a man, dirty my nails.

CHAS: And facts don't mean much to me either.

PIP: It's dull, repetitive, degrading.

CHAS: Intelligence counts, not facts. Stick your education, your university. Who cares why Rome was built.

PIP: Van Gogh with the miners; Hemingway, hunting.

CHAS: Even if I knew all about that it wouldn't make it any easier.

PIP: God, how I despise this yearning to be one of the toilers.

CHAS: I knew someone who used to wear a bowler cos he thought it made him look educated.

PIP: The dignity of labour!

CHAS: But it wouldn't make it any easier –

PIP: The beauty of movement!

CHAS: Not between us –

[*They smile.*]

SCENE NINE

The hut.

SMILER: What shall it be – poker, pontoon?

WILFE: I'm for bed.

SMILER: 'I'm for bed', little boy is tired.

WILFE: You can go on man – nothing seems to affect you.

CANNIBAL: What happened? They kick you out too?

SMILER: We got sick – you game for poker?

DICKEY: The squalor overcame you, eh? Ah, well, welcome back to the delinquents.

[*Enter* HILL.]

HILL: Well, I've got a right bunch, haven't I, a real good crowd, that's a fact.

GINGER: Come off it, Corp – you know we're O.K. on the square.

DODGER: That's all that counts, isn't it, Corp?

HILL: My boys – even them, my own little boys let me down.

SMILER: It's poker, Corp, you playing?

HILL: I shan't say anything now because you're away home in two days – but when you come back it's rifle drill and bayonet practice – and that's tough, and if you slack – I'm warning you – no more easy life, it'll be back to normal for you all.

DODGER: Play us a tune, Corp.

HILL: You don't deserve no tunes – a kick up the arse you deserve, the lot, where it hurts, waken you up.

[CHARLES, SMILER, PIP, and DICKEY *sit down to play. The others lie in their beds, and* HILL *plays the mouth-organ.*]

GINGER: There's a bloody great moon outside. Dodge, you seen it? With a whopping great halo.

DODGER: Nippy, too. Who wants some chocolate? My uncle has a sweet shop. [*Produces dozens of bars.*]

DODGER: Ginge, what trade you going to apply for?

GINGER: Driver – I'm going to get something out of this mob – it's going to cost them something keeping me from civvy street. Driving! I've always wanted to drive – since I don't know how long. A six BHP engine, behind the wheel controlling it–nyaaaaaaarr. I dream about it. I dream I'm always in a car and I'm driving it, but I got no licence. I always know I've never driven a car, but somehow it comes easy to me and I've never got a ruddy licence. I'm always being chased by cops – and I keep dreaming it, the same dream. I got no licence, but I'm driving a car and the police are after me. What'll I dream about when I can drive a car, I wonder.

DODGER: You won't. Stands to reason you won't need to; when you got the real thing you don't pretend. How about some tea? Ginger, my cock, make some tea on the stove and we'll eat up these biscuits also.

CANNIBAL: Dreams is real you know, they may be pretending in your sleep, but they're real. I dreamt my girl was a prostitute once and when I see her next day she looked like one and I give her up.

DODGER: What's wrong with prostitutes? We need them, let's keep them I say. Nationalize them. Stuck in clubs like poor bleedin' ferrets.

WILFE: Don't it make you sick, eh? Don't it make you sick just – these eight weeks, these two years, the factory – all of it? Don't it make you just bleedin' sick? I SAID SICK, MOTHER, SICK! Poor dear, she can't hear a word.

[*Pause. Mouth-organ. Warm hut.*]

CANNIBAL: I'm going to get in that Radar-Plotting lark. All them buttons, them screens and knobs. You have to learn about the stars and space for that.

DICKEY: That's astronomy, my fine fellow. The code of the heavens. Radar! Radar is the mystic digits of sound-waves; you have to have an enlightened degree of knowledge for that. Cannibal, my son, you're not arrogant enough, not standard enough for that. But I could – oh yes, I could rise to the heights of radar. I've put in for that.

SMILER: I think I'll go into Ops. Bring the planes in. Operations calling D17, are you receiving me, are you receiving me – over! D17 calling flight-control, I'm receiving you – left jet gone, I said gone, think I'll have to make a forced landing, stand by for emergency. Nyaaaaaaah passssssssss, brrrrrrrrrr – we'll all learn a trade and then 'oppit – nyaaaaaaaaaaaaa. . . .

[*Pause.*]

ANDREW: I like us. All of us, here now. I like us all being together here. In a way you know I don't mind it, anything. Old Corp and his mouth-organ – all of us, just as we are, I like us.

[*Pause. Mouth-organ. Warm hut.*]

GINGER: We've run out of coke you know – water won't ever boil.

PIP: Then we'll pinch some.

DICKEY: What?

PIP: That's all right with you isn't it, Corp? You don't mind a little raiding expedition?

HILL: You think you'll get in the coke yard? You won't, you know, mate; there's a wire netting and a patrol on that.

PIP: We'll work out a plan.

CHAS: Oh, knock it off, Pip, we're all in bed soon.

PIP: Think we can't outwit them?

DODGER: You won't outwit them, mate, they've got it all tied up neat, not them, me old *lobus*.

PIP: If you can't outwit them for a lump of coke, then they deserve to have you in here for a couple of years.

HILL: I know what you are, Thompson – you're an agent provocative.

WILFE: I'm game, how do we do it?

GINGER: We could snip the wire and crawl through.

PIP: No. We want to raid and leave no sign.

ANDREW: What do we put it in?

DICKEY: Buckets.

DODGER: Too noisy.

PIP: Buckets with sacking at the bottom. How high is the netting?

HILL: About six feet. You'll need a ladder.

WILFE: Take it from the fire hut near by.

CANNIBAL: What if there's a fire?

WILFE: Let it burn.

PIP: No, no risks. Efficient, precise, but humane. They happen to be the only qualities for absolute power. That's what we want – absolute success but without a price. Coke in ten minutes, with no one caught and no one but us the wiser. Trust me?

SCENE TEN

A large square of wire netting.
   [*A* GUARD *walks round it. Boys are in the shadows.*]

PIP: Now watch him – he walks round slowly – we can make three moves for each round except the last one and that requires speed. I want the first three stages started and finished between the time he disappears round the first corner and before he turns the third. If he changes his course or hurries his step or does anything that means one of us is caught, then we all, all of us make an appearance. He can't cop the lot. Right? [*All exeunt.*]
   [GINGER *dashes to wire, and places chair – dashes to other side of stage.* PIP *runs to chair, jumps up and over.* DODGER *runs to take chair away and joins Ginger. The* GUARD *appears and carries on*

335

round. DODGER *runs back, places chair.* WILFE *runs to chair with another, jumps on it, and drops chair into Pip's hands, runs off.* DODGER *runs on, and withdraws chair. The* GUARD *appears, and continues.* DODGER *runs on with chair again.* ANDREW *runs with buckets to chair, jumps up and passes them to Pip.* GINGER *runs to take chair away.* GUARD *appears, and continues. In like process, two buckets are returned 'full' of coke. In the last stage,* PIP *jumps back over netting, leaving chair.* GINGER *and* DODGER *appear with two stools.* DICKEY *dashes on to top of two stools, leans over wire and reaches down for chair, which he throws to Andrew.* DODGER *and* GINGER *run off with two stools.* GUARD *appears, and continues. This scene can be, and has to be, silent, precise, breathtaking, and finally very funny.*]

SCENE ELEVEN

The hut again.
[*Mouth-organ.* DODGER *pouring out tea, drinking, eating. Silence.*]

DICKEY: Yes. Yes – very satisfactory. Very pleasing. I wouldn't've thought we could do it.

CHAS: No more you wouldn't have done it without Pip.

DICKEY: Do I detect in young Charles the ineffable signs of hero worship?

CHAS: You'll detect black and blue marks, that's what you'll detect.

DICKEY: I think we've got a love affair in our midst.

CHAS: Just because I respect a man for his nerve? You gone daft?

DICKEY: No, I think my mental balance is equilibralized, it's you I fear for my Charlie boy. First you start off baiting young Thompson here and now you can't take your eyes off him.

PIP: Don't act the goat, Dickey.

DICKEY: I'm correct in my observations though aren't I, Lord Thompson?

PIP: No observation you make is correct, Dickey, you just remember other people's.

DICKEY: But you have a marvellous mind, don't you?

CHAS: He has.

DICKEY: Now there's a question. Would we have pinched the coke without Pip's mind?

HILL: You always need leaders.

PIP: Always!

HILL: Well, don't you always need leaders?

PIP: Always, always!

HILL: Yes, always, always!

PIP: Always, always, always! Your great-great-grandfather said there'll always be horses, your great-grandfather said there'll always be slaves, your grandfather said there'll always be poverty and your father said there'll always be wars. Each time you say 'always' the world takes two steps backwards and stops bothering. And so it should, my God, so it should –

WILFE: Easy, Airman, easy.

GINGER: Hey, Dodge – come and look outside now. Have you ever seen a halo as big as that! – look at it.

DODGER: Means frost.

ANDREW: This ae nighte, this ae nighte,
             Every nighte and alle,
          Fire and fleet and candle-lighte,
             And Christe receive thy saule.

SLOW CURTAIN

ACT TWO

SCENE ONE

The hut, dark early morning.
 [*Enter night* GUARD.]

GUARD: Hands off your cocks and pull up your socks, it's wake to the sun and a glorious day. [*Pulls off blankets of one near by.*] Rise, rise, rise and shine – Christmas is over. CHRISTMAS IS OVER. [*Exit.*]
 [*There have been moans and movements. Return to silence. Enter* HILL. *Pause.*]
HILL: CHRISTMAS IS OVER, he said.
 [*Moans and movements.*]
 It's over, done, finished. You're 'ome. You're 'ome again and it's rifles today. Rifles and a stricter routine. You've been slacking. I've warned you and told you and today is judgement day, especially for you, Smiler – today is especially judgement day for you. You too, Airmen Wilfe Seaford, and Archie Cannibal, you shan't be passed. I intend making you the smartest squad in the glorious history of flying – and I will. But you – A/C2 Thompson – you're too good for me, too smart. The Wing Commander and all the officers in charge of this camp have got their guns on you and they're aiming to throw the book at you – the whole, heavy scorching book, so you beware and guard your mouth. I've heard, I know – so guard your mouth. CHRISTMAS IS OVER. [*Exits.*]
WILFE: Christmas is over and don't we know it. Rouse yourself, Smiler, or you'll get us all in the cart.
SMILER: Leave off.
WILFE: Rouse yourself, I say – I aren't suffering cos of you. Get up or I'll turn you under your bed.
 [*No reply.* WILFE *does so.* SMILER *rises from under the rubble and angrily fights with Wilfe till separated by others.*]
ANDREW: Cut it out or I'll lay you both.

338

DICKEY: It's the basic animal rising to undiluted heights in them. A nasty morning, my boys, a nasty morning, nasty tempers, and a nasty undiluted life.

CANNIBAL: And you can shut your undiluted mouth for a start, too. I'm not stomaching you the rest of the time.

DICKEY: What side of the bed did you rise from?

CANNIBAL: I'm fit for you, so don't worry.

[*Enter* HILL *with rifles.*]

HILL: Come and get them. Don't grab them, don't drop them, and don't lose them. We start with them first thing after breakfast and I intend to train you so hard that you'll not be happy unless they're in bed with you.

[*Exit. Immediately, half the boys start playing cowboys and Indians, dropping behind beds and crawling on the floor, firing them at each other, 'BANG. BANG.' Enter* HILL.]

HILL: The next man to pull that trigger, his feet won't touch the ground.

[SMILER *clicks one unintentionally.*]

You – I've wanted to pounce on you, Smiler.

SMILER: It slipped, Corp – an accident.

HILL: You say accident, I say luck. I'm charging you, Smiler, just a little charge, a few days' jankers to start with – that's all.

PIP: Why don't you charge us all, Corporal?

HILL: YOU SHUT UP. You, I've warned. All of you, I've warned. The joke's over, the laughing's done. Now get ready. [*Exit.*]

DODGER: We used to have a master who'd crack a joke, and then look at his watch to see we didn't laugh too long.

HILL: All right, get fell in, the lot of you.

SCENE TWO

The parade ground.
[*The men in threes.*]

HILL: The first thing is – not to be afraid of it. It won't hurt you and if you handle it correctly you can't hurt it. [*Only one boy laughs.*] I know you think they're nice, boys. With one of them in your hand you feel different, don't you, you feel a man, a conquering bloody hero? You want to run home and show your girl, don't you? Well, they're not toys – you can kill a man wi' one o' them. Kill 'im! Your napkins are still wet – you don't really understand that word 'kill', do you? Well, you can be killed. There! Does that bring it home to you? A bullet can whip through your flesh and knock breath out of *you*. Imagine yourself dying, knowing you're dying, you can feel the hole in your body, you can feel yourself going dizzy, you can feel the hot blood, and you can't breathe. You want to breathe but you can't, the body you've relied on all these years doesn't do what you want it to do, and you can't understand it. You're surprised, you're helpless, like those dreams where you're falling – only dying isn't a dream because you know, you know, you know that you're looking at everything for the last time and you can't do a bloody thing about it, that's dying. And that's a rifle. So don't let me catch anybody aiming it at anybody – loaded or not. Now, you hold it here, just below the barrel, pushing it out slightly to the right and forward, with the butt tucked well in at the side of your feet – so – well in firm, straight, at ease – and at the command to 'shun' I want that rifle brought smartly in at the precisely same moment. So. Atten-shun! Together, and your hand holding firmly on to that rifle. I don't want that rifle dropped – drop that rifle and I want to see you follow it to the ground. Right. Squad – atten-shun!

SQUAD: One!

[SMILER *drops gun.*]

HILL: Leave it! Smiler, you nasty squirming imbecile! Can't you hear me? Can't you hear anything? Don't anything go through your thick skull? Look at you. Slob! Your buttons, your blanco, your shoes – look at them. They're dull. You're dull! You're like putty. What keeps you together, man? You're like an old Jew – you know what happens to Jews? They go to gas chambers. Now pick it up. Squad – atten-shun!

SQUAD: One!

HILL: Now to slope and shoulder arms, you make three movements. Watch me, follow me and you won't make a mess of it. I'll do it slowly and I'll exaggerate the movements. Shoulder ARMS! One pause, two pause, three. Slope ARMS! One pause, two pause, three. Again [*Repeats.*] Now – you do it. Squad! Shoulder ARMS!

SQUAD: One pause, two pause, three.

HILL: Slope ARMS!

SQUAD: One pause, two pause, three.

    [*Repeats order.*]

HILL: You're no good, Smiler, you're no good. Shoulder ARMS! Smiler, one pace forward march. The rest, about turn. By the left, quick march.

    [*The squad march off, all except* SMILER. *The wall of the guardroom drops into place as scene changes to*]

SCENE THREE

The guardroom.

    [SMILER *at the slope. Enter* HILL *and two other corporals.*]

FIRST CORPORAL: This him?

HILL: That's him.

SECOND CORPORAL: What's your name, lad?

SMILER: Smiler.

SECOND CORPORAL: I said your name, lad.

SMILER: 279 A/C2 Washington, Corporal.

FIRST CORPORAL: Washington, is it? You mustn't lie then, ha-ha! If you mustn't lie, then tell us, is your mother pretty? Is she? Answer me, lad. Do you know it's dumb insolence not to answer an N.C.O.? We'll make that six day's jankers, I think. Answer me, lad.

SMILER: Yes. She was.

FIRST CORPORAL: Have you ever seen her undressed? Eh? Have you, lad? Have you seen her naked?

SECOND CORPORAL: Wipe that smile off your face, lad.

SMILER: I'm not smiling, Corporal, it's natural, I was born like it.

FIRST CORPORAL: Arguing with an N.C.O. We'll make that nine days' jankers.

HILL: All right Smiler, order arms, slope arms, order arms, slope arms, slope arms, slope arms.

[*The two corporals walk round him.*]

FIRST CORPORAL: You're a slob, Smiler.

SECOND CORPORAL: A nasty piece of work.

FIRST CORPORAL: You're no good, lad.

SECOND CORPORAL: No good at all. You're an insult.

FIRST CORPORAL: Your mother wasted her labour.

SECOND CORPORAL: Your father made a mistake.

FIRST CORPORAL: You're a mistake, Smiler.

SECOND CORPORAL: A stupid mistake.

FIRST CORPORAL: The Queen doesn't like mistakes in her Air Force.

SECOND CORPORAL: She wants good men, Smiler, men she can trust.

FIRST CORPORAL: Stand still, boy. Don't move. Silent, boy. Still and silent, boy.

HILL: That'll do for a taster, Smiler. That'll do for the first lesson. Tomorrow we'll have some more. We'll break you, Smiler, we'll break you, because that's our job. Remember that, just remember now – remember – About TURN! By the left – quick march, eft – ite, eft – ite. Remember, Smiler, remember.

[*Exit.*]

SCENE FOUR

WING COMMANDER'S *office.*

[*With him at a table are* SQUADRON LEADER *and* PILOT OFFICER.]

WING COMMANDER: Just remember who we're dealing with – remember that. I don't want a legal foot put wrong – I just want him broken in.

PILOT OFFICER: Not broken in, sir, but loved – he's only lost temporarily, for a short, natural time, that's all.

WING COMMANDER: Bloody little fool – sowing seeds of discontent to semi-educated louts; what do they understand of what he tells them?

SQUADRON LEADER: Gently, Sid, anger'll only make it easier for him to be stubborn.

PILOT OFFICER: Leave it to me, sir. I think I know how to do it, I think I know the boy very well.

WING COMMANDER: I know the boy, by Christ I know him, I've known them all and I've broken them all.

[HILL *marches Pip into the room and goes.*]

PIP: You called me to see you, sir.

WING COMMANDER: Take your hat off, blast you, Thompson, take it off, lad, in front of an officer.

SQUADRON LEADER: Please sit down, won't you, Thompson, sit down and be at ease for a little while; we'd simply like a chat with you.

WING COMMANDER: Your square bashing is coming to an end. We're concerned about you. We have to find you something to do. It has to be decided now.

SQUADRON LEADER: I think, Wing Commander, if you'll excuse me, it would be more correct to say that Personnel must decide that in London, but we can recommend from here, isn't that the case? We are on the spot, so we can recommend.

PILOT OFFICER: We see, Thompson, that you've put down administration orderly as your first and only choice. A very strange choice.

WING COMMANDER: A damn fool choice, boy, your brains, your carriage and background, damn perversity!

SQUADRON LEADER: You know what administration orderly implies, don't you, son?

WING COMMANDER: Anything and everything – waste, absolute waste.

SQUADRON LEADER: Anything from dishwashing to salvage, from spud-bashing to coal-heaving.

[*Pause.*]

PILOT OFFICER: Listen Pip, excuse me, sir?

WING COMMANDER: Yes, yes, carry on.

PILOT OFFICER: Let's drop the pretence. We're the same age and class, let's drop this formal nonsense. The Air Force is no place to carry on a family war, Pip. This is not a public school, it's a place where old boys grow into young men, believe me. Don't force me to start listing all your virtues and attributes. We're not flatterers, but don't let's be falsely modest either – that's understood between us, I'm sure. God, when I think of what I did to try and get out of coming into this outfit – two years wasted I thought. But waste is what you yourself do with time – come on man, if people like us aren't officers, then imagine the bastards they'll get. This is a silly game, Pip – why look, you're even sulking. Admin orderly! Can you see yourself washing dishes?

PIP: It might be a pretence to avoid responsibility.

PILOT OFFICER: You, Pip? Come now! It may be that you want to prove something to yourself. I don't know, why don't you tell us?

PIP: Your tactics are obvious, please don't insult my intelligence. I do not feel obliged to explain my reasons to you.

WING COMMANDER: You'll do what you're told.

PILOT OFFICER: It's not a question of obligation, no one's forcing –

PIP: I have no wish to –

PILOT OFFICER: But there's no one forcing you –

PIP: I said I have no wish to –

PILOT OFFICER: But-no-one-is-forcing-you –

PIP: I have no wish to explain anything to you I say.

[Pause.]

WING COMMANDER: Corporal Hill!

[Enter HILL.]

HILL: Sir?

WING COMMANDER: The men in your squad are slobs. Their standard is low and I'm not satisfied. No man passes out of my camp unless he's perfect – you know that. Pull them together, Corporal Hill, fatigues, Corporal Hill. They're a wretched bunch, wretched, not good enough.

HILL: Yes, sir [Exit from room.]

All right, fall in, the lot of you.

[Boys enter.]

You're slobs, all of you. Your standard is low and I'm not satisfied. No man passes out of my hut unless he's perfect, I've told you that before. You're a wretched bunch – a miserable, wretched bunch, and since you're not good enough, it's fatigues for you all. Squad will double mark time.

[*They do so for one minute. Exeunt at the double. The Inquisition resumes.*]

WING COMMANDER: Carry on, P.O.

PILOT OFFICER: Right, Thompson, I have some questions to ask you. I don't want clever answers. You wish to be an administration orderly?

PIP: That is correct, sir.

PILOT OFFICER: Doesn't it occur to you that that very act, considering who you are, is a little – revealing? It's a rather ostentatious choice, isn't it?

PIP: It could be viewed like that.

PILOT OFFICER: You enjoy mixing with men from another class. Why is this? Do you find them stimulating, a new experience, a novelty, do you enjoy your slumming?

PIP: It's not *I* who slum, sir.

PILOT OFFICER: I suppose you feel guilty in some way for your comfortable and easy upbringing; you feel you must do a sort of penance for it.

PIP: A rather outdated cause to be a martyr for, don't you think, sir?

PILOT OFFICER: Possibly, Thompson, possibly. You enjoy their company, though, don't you?

PIP: I enjoy most people's company.

PILOT OFFICER: Not ours, though.

PIP: Certain standards are necessary, sir.

PILOT OFFICER: A very offensive reply, Thompson – it's almost a hysterical reply – a little too desperately spoken, I would say. But look, we haven't stiffened, we aren't offended, no one is going to charge you or strike you. In fact we haven't really taken any notice. We listen to you, we let other people listen to you but we show no offence. Rather – we applaud you, flatter you for your courage and idealism but – it goes right through us. We listen but we do not hear, we befriend but do not touch you, we applaud but we do not act. To tolerate is to ignore, Thompson. You will not really become an administration orderly, will you?

PIP: What I have written, stays.

PILOT OFFICER: You will not be a foolish, stiff, Empire-thumping officer – no one believes in those any more. You will be more subtle and you will learn how to deal with all the Pip Thompsons who follow you. I even think you would like that.

PIP: What I have written stays. You may recommend as you please.

PILOT OFFICER: Yes, we shall put you up for officer training.

[OFFICERS *exeunt. Scene changes to*]

SCENE FIVE

The Square. A dummy is hanging. It is bayonet practice for the squad.

HILL: Even officers must go through this. Everyone, but everyone must know how to stick a man with a bayonet. The occasion may not arise to use the scorching thing but no man passes through this outfit till he's had practice. It's a horrible thing, this. A nasty weapon and a nasty way to kill a man. But it is you or him. A nasty choice, but you must choose. We had a bloke called Hamlet with us once and he had awful trouble in deciding. He got stuck! I don't want that to be your fate. So! Again, hold the butt and drop the muzzle – so. Lean forward, crouch, and let me see the horriblest leer your face can make. Then, when I call 'attack' I want to see you rush towards that old straw dummy, pause, lunge, and twist your knife with all the hate you can. And one last thing – the scream. I want to hear you shout your lungs out, cos it helps. A hoard of screaming men put terror in the enemy and courage in themselves. It helps. Get fell in, two ranks. Front rank will assume the on-guard position – ON GUARD! Run, scream, lunge.

[HILL *demonstrates it himself. One by one, the men rush forward at the dummy, until it comes to* PIP. *He stands still.*]

I said attack. Thompson, you, that's you. Are you gone daft? I've given you an order – run, scream, you. Are you refusing to obey? A/C Thompson I have ordered you to use your bayonet. You scorching, trouble-making, long-haired, posh-tongued, lump of aristocracy – I'll high jump you, court martial you. I'll see you rot

346

in every dungeon in the force. Oh, thank your lucky stars this ain't the war, my lad; I'd take the greatest pleasure in shooting you. You still refuse? Right – you men, form up a line behind this man; I'll need you all for witnesses. A/C2 Thompson, I am about to issue you with a legitimate order according to Her Majesty's rules and regulations, Section Ten paragraph five, and I must warn you that failing to carry out this order will result in you being charged under Section ten paragraph sixteen of the same book. Now, when I say attack, I want to see you lower your gun in the attack position and race forward to lunge that dummy which now faces you. Is that order understood?

PIP: Yes, Corporal.

HILL: Good. I am now about to give the command. Wait for it and think carefully – this is only practice and no one can be hurt. Within ten seconds it will all be over, that's advice. Attack.

[*Silence. No movement.*]

Squad – slope ARMS! A/C2 Thompson – I'm charging you with failure to obey a legitimate order issued by an N.C.O. in command under Her Majesty's Air Force, and may God help you, lad.

[*All march off except* THOMPSON.]

SCENE SIX

[*Enter* ANDREW.]

ANDREW: Idiot.

PIP: You?

ANDREW: Who the hell is going to be impressed?

PIP: You, Andrew?

ANDREW: Yes, Andrew! I'm asking you – who the hell do you think is going to be impressed? Not me. The boys? Not them either. I've been watching you, Pip – I'm not impressed and neither are they.

PIP: You don't really think I'm interested in the public spectacle, Andy, you can't? No, no I can see you don't. Go off now. Leave me with it – I've got problems.

347

ANDREW: No one's asking you to make gestures on our behalf.

PIP: Go off now.

ANDREW: Don't go making heroic gestures and then expect gratitude.

PIP: Don't lean on me, Andy – I've got problems.

ANDREW: I don't think I can bear your martyrdom – that's what it is; I don't think I can bear your look of suffering.

PIP: I'm not suffering.

ANDREW: I don't know why but your always-acting-right drives me round the bend.

PIP: I'm not a martyr.

ANDREW: It's your confident cockiness – I can't stand your confident cockiness. How do you know you're right? How can you act all the time as though you know all right from wrong, for God's sake.

PIP: Don't be a bastard Jock.

ANDREW: I'm trying to help you, idiot. The boys will hate any heroic gesture you make.

PIP: Andy, you're a good, well-meaning, intelligent, person. I will die of good, well-meaning, and intelligent people who have never made a decision in their life. Now go off and leave me and stop crippling me with your own guilt. If you're ineffectual in this world that's your look-out – just stay calm and no one will know, but stop tampering with my decisions. Let *them* do the sabotaging, they don't need help from you as well. Now get the hell out – they wouldn't want you to see the way they work.

[*Exit* ANDREW.]

SCENE SEVEN

PILOT OFFICER: It goes right through us, Thompson. Nothing you can do will change that. We listen but we do not hear, we befriend but do not touch you, we applaud but do not act – to tolerate is to ignore. What did you expect, praise from the boys? Devotion from your mates? Your mates are morons, Thompson, morons. At the slightest hint from us they will disown you. Or perhaps you wanted a court martial? Too expensive, boy. Jankers? That's for the yobs. You, we shall make an officer, as we promised. I have studied politics as well, you know, and let me just remind you of a tactic the best of revolutionaries have employed. That is to penetrate the enemy and spread rebellion there. You can't fight us from the outside. Relent boy, at least we understand long sentences.

PIP: You won't impress me with cynicism, you know.

PILOT OFFICER: Not cynicism – just honesty. I might say we are being unusually honest – most of the time it is unnecessary to admit all this, and you of all people should have known it.

PIP: I WILL NOT BE AN OFFICER.

PILOT OFFICER: Ah. A touch of anger, what do you reveal now, Thompson? We know, you and I, don't we? Comradeship? Not that, not because of the affinity of one human being to another, not that. Guilt? Shame because of your fellow beings' suffering? You don't feel that either. Not guilt. An inferiority complex, a feeling of modesty? My God. Not that either. There's nothing humble about you, is there? Thompson, you wanted to do more than simply share the joy of imparting knowledge to your friends; no, not modesty. Not that. What then? What if not those things, my lad? You and I? Shall I say it? Shall I? Power. Power, isn't it? Among your own people there were too many who were powerful, the competition was too great, but here, among lesser men – here among the yobs, among the good-natured yobs, you could be king. KING. Supreme and all powerful, eh? Well? Not true? Deny it – deny it, then. We know – you and I – we know, Thompson.

PIP: Oh, God –

PILOT OFFICER: God? God? Why do you call upon God? Are you his son? Better still, then. You are found out even more, illusions of grandeur, Thompson. We know that also, that's what we know, that's what we have, the picture you have of yourself, and now that we know that, you're really finished, destroyed. You're destroyed, Thompson. No man survives whose motive is discovered, no man. Messiah to the masses! Corporal Hill! [*Exit.*]

HILL [*off stage*]. Sir?

SCENE EIGHT

[*Enter* HILL.]

HILL: I have instructions to repeat the order, Thompson. The powers have decided to give you another chance. I don't know why, but they know what they're doing, I suppose. When I give the order 'attack' I want you to lean forward, run, thrust, and twist that blade in the dummy. Have you understood?

PIP: Yes, Corporal.

HILL: Run, thrust and twist that blade – good. ATTACK.

[PIP *pauses for a long while, then with a terrifying scream he rushes at the dummy, sticking it three times, with three screams.*]

SCENE NINE

The hut.

[CHARLES *and* PIP.]

CHAS: What they say, Pip? What they want you for, what did they say? Hell, look at your face, did they beat you? Did they make you use the bayonet? They did, didn't they? I can tell it from your face. You're crying – are you crying? Want a cigarette? Here, have a cigarette. The others have all gone to the Naafi, it's New Year's Eve, gone for a big booze-up. Bloody fools – all they do is drink. I think I'll give it up, me. Well, what did they say, man – talk to me? You know why I didn't go to the Naafi – I – I was waiting for you. It seemed fishy them calling you in the evening, so I waited to see. Pip? I'm telling you I waited for you. I wanted to tell you something, I want to ask you a favour; I've been meaning all these last days to ask you this favour. You see – you know me, don't you, you know the sort of bloke . . . I'm – I'm, I'm not dumb, I'm not a fool, I'm not a real fool, not a bloody moron and I thought, well,

I thought maybe you could, could teach me – something, anything. Eh? Well, not anything but something proper, real.

PIP: Ask someone else – books, read books.

CHAS: Not books! I can't read books, but I can listen to you. Maybe we'll get posted to the same place, and then every evening, or every other evening, or once a week, even, you could talk to me a bit, for half an hour say. Remember how you talked that night about your grandfathers, about all those inventions and things. Well, I liked that, I listened to that, I could listen all night to that. Only I want to know about something else, I want to know about – I don't even know how to put it, about – you know, you know the word, about business and raw materials and people working and selling things – you know, there's a word for it –

PIP: Economics.

CHAS: Enocomics – that's it.

PIP: Economics not enocomics.

CHAS: EE-mon-omics.

PIP: No, Ee –

CHAS: Ee

PIP: Con

CHAS: Con

PIP: Om

CHAS: Om

PIP: Ics.

CHAS: Ics.

PIP: Economics.

CHAS: Economics. There, about that, could you? I'd listen, you could draw diagrams and graphs; I wasn't bad at maths.

PIP: Someone else, Charles, not me, someone else.

CHAS: There you go. You're a hypocrite – a hypocrite you are. You take people to the edge. Don't you know what I'm asking you, don't you know what I'm really asking you?

PIP: Ask someone else.

CHAS: But I want to be with you – I want to. Ah, you give me a pain in the neck, you do, you're a coward. You lead and then you run away. I could grow with you, don't you understand that? We could do things together. You've got to be with someone, there's got to be someone you can trust, everyone finds someone and I found you – I've never asked anyone before, Jesus, never –

PIP: Ask someone else.

CHAS: Someone else. Someone else. It's always someone else, you half-bake you, you lousy word-user you. Your bleedin' stuffed grandfathers kept us stupid all this time, and now you come along with your pretty words and tell us to fend for ourselves. You clever useless leftover you. Oh, you're cocky, aren't you – Ask someone else. The truth is – you're scared, aren't you? You call us mate, but you're a scared old schoolboy. The pilot officer was right, you're slumming. You're a bleedin' slummer –

PIP: And he also said 'we will listen to you but we will not hear you, we will befriend you but not touch you, we will tolerate and ig-nore you'.

CHAS: Well, what did that mean?

PIP: We'll do anything they want just because they know how to smile at us.

CHAS: You mean *I'll* do what they want, not you boy. You're one of them – you're just playing games with 'em, and us mugs is in the middle – I've cottoned on now. [*Long pause.*] I'll do what *you* want, Pip.

PIP: Swop masters? You're a fool, Charles, the kind of fool my parents fed on, you're a fool, a fool –

[*Fade in the sound of marching feet and the Corporals repeating the insults they heaped upon Smiler and change to*]

SCENE TEN

A roadway.

[SMILER *has run away from camp. He is desperate, haggard and tired. Mix:* 'You're a fool, Charles' *to* 'You're a slob, Smiler' 'A nasty piece of work' 'You're no good, lad', *etc., rising to crescendo –*]

SMILER: LEAVE ME ALONE! Damn your mouths and hell on your

stripes – leave me alone. Mad they are, they're mad they are, they're raving lunatics they are. CUT IT! STUFF IT! Shoot your load on someone else, take it out on someone else, why do you want to pick on me, you lunatics, you bloody apes, you're nothing more than bloody apes, so damn your mouths and hell on your stripes! Ahhhhh – they'd kill me if they had the chance. They think they own you, think that anyone who's dressed in blue is theirs to muck about, degrade. YOU BLOODY APES, YOU WON'T DEGRADE ME! Oh my legs – I'm going home. I'll get a lift and scarper home. I'll go to France, I'll get away. I'LL GET AWAY FROM YOU, YOU APES! They think they own you – Oh my back. I don't give tuppence what you say, you don't mean anything to me, your bloody orders nor your stripes nor your jankers nor your wars. Stick your jankers on the wall, stuff yourselves, go away and stuff yourselves, stuff your rotten stupid selves – Ohh – Ohhh. Look at the sky, look at the moon, Jesus look at that moon and the frost in the air. I'll wait. I'll get a lift in a second or two, it's quiet now, their noise is gone. I'll stand and wait and look at that moon. What are you made of, tell me? I don't know what you're made of, you go on and on. What grouses you? What makes you scream? You're blood and wind like all of us, what grouses you? You poor duff bastards, where are your mothers? Where were you born – I don't know what grouses you, your voices sound like dying hens – I don't know. That bloody lovely moon is cold, I can't stay here. I'll freeze to death. That's a laugh, now that'd fool them. Listen! A bike, a motor-bike, a roaring bloody motor-bike.[*Starts thumbing.*]London, London, London, London, LONDON! [*The roar comes and dies.*] You stupid ghet, I want a lift, can't you see I want a lift, an airman wants a lift back home. Home, you bastard, take me ho'ooooome. [*Long pause.*] Now they'll catch me, now they'll come, not much point in going on – Smiler boy, they'll surely come, they're bound to miss you back at camp – eyes like hawks they've got – God! Who cares. 'Stop your silly smiling, Airman' – 'It's not a smile, Corp, it's natural, honest, Corp. I'm born that way. Honest Corp, it's not a smile. . . .'

[*Enters hut.*]

353

SCENE ELEVEN

The hut.
[CHARLES *and* PIP *as we left them.* SMILER *is now with them.*]

SMILER: The bastards won't believe it's natural. Look at me, me!
[*A very broken* SMILER *stands there.* SMILER *turns to* PIP *for help. Pip approaches him and takes him gently in his arms. They sway a moment.*]
SMILER: Wash my feet for me.
[SMILER *collapses.* PIP *lays him on the ground. He is about to remove his shoes –*]
CHAS: Leave him. I'll do it.
[CHARLES *doesn't know what to do to begin with. Surveys* SMILER. *Then – picks him up and lays him on his bed, looks at him; thinks; takes off his shoes and socks.*]
CHAS: His feet are bleeding.
[*Takes a towel and pours water from pot on it; washes Smiler's feet; a long unconscious moan from* SMILER; *clock strikes midnight; sound of boys singing 'Auld Land Syne'.* CORPORAL HILL's *voice, loud.*]
HILL [*off stage*]: You pass out with the band tomorrow – rifles, buttons, belts, shining, and I want you as one man, you hear me? You'll have the band and it'll be marvellous; only you Smiler, you won't be in it, you'll stay behind a little longer, my lad – HAPPY NEW YEAR.
[*Silence. One by one the rest of the men come in, returning from the Naafi. They make no sound, but their movements are wild and drunk. No sound at all – like a TV with sound turned off, till they see Smiler.*]
DODGER: Look at his feet. The rotten bastards, look at his feet.
ANDREW: What'd he do?
CHAS: Tried to hop it.
ANDREW: Couldn't make it?
CHAS: Walked for miles and then came back.
CANNIBAL: They had it in for him, you've got no chance when they got it in for you.

GINGER: He's staying behind, you know? I reckon they'll make him do another two weeks of this.

DICKEY: Give me the chance, just give me one chance and I'd have them. Five minutes in civvy street and I'd have them chasing their own tails.

WILFE: Ah, you wouldn't, man – you talk like this now but you wouldn't, and you know why? Cos you'd be just as helpless there, you'd be just as much wind and nothing there, man. 'Just gimme the boss,' you'd say, 'just gimme him for one hour in uniform and I'd teach him what a man is.' That's all you'd say, civvy street, the forces – it's the same, don't give me that.

GINGER: What about Smiler's stuff?

CANNIBAL: I'll do it.

CHAS: No, you won't, I'm doing it.

CANNIBAL: All right, all right, then. Blimey, what's gotten into you? Jumping at me like that – I don't much want to do my own buggers, let alone his. Takes all the guts out of you, don't it. Look at him, lying there like a bloody corpse. His feet are cold.

DODGER: He's like a baby. Sweet as a sleeping baby. Have you ever watched a baby sleep? It always looks as though it's waiting for something to happen, a grown-up seems to be hiding away but a nipper seems to trust you, anyone. He's done it, ain'tee, eh? He's really had it –

CHAS: For Christ's sake, give over – you talk like he was dead or something. Come on. help cover him.

[*As many as possible manoeuvre Smiler so that his jacket and trousers come off, with the least disturbance. This action is done lovingly and with a sort of ritual.* DODGER *takes a comb to Smiler's hair and* CHARLES *gently wipes a towel over his face. Then they tuck him in bed and stand looking at him. Unknown to them the* PILOT OFFICER *has been watching them.*]

PILOT OFFICER: Beautiful. Tender and beautiful. But I'm sorry, gentlemen, this man is needed in the guardroom.

[*Enter* HILL.]

HILL: Squad – shun!

[*The men slowly come to attention, except* CHARLES, *who, after a*

355

pause, moves to his bed and sits on it. One by one the other boys, except PIP, *also sit on their beds in defiance.*]

PILOT OFFICER: Corporal – take that smiling airman to the guard-room.

CHAS: YOU'LL LEAVE HIM BE!

PILOT OFFICER: And take that man, too.

GINGER: You won't, Corporal Hill, will you?

PILOT OFFICER: And that man, take the lot of them, I'll see them all in the guardroom.

PIP: You won't touch any of them, Corporal Hill, you won't touch a single one of them.

PILOT OFFICER: Do you hear me, Corporal, this whole hut is under arrest.

PIP: I suggest, sir, that you don't touch one of them. [PIP *and the* PILOT OFFICER *smile at each other, knowingly, and* PIP *now begins to change his uniform, from an airman's to an officer's.*] We won't let him, will we Charles – because you're right. Smiler has been badly treated and you are right to protect him. It's a good virtue that, loyalty. You are to be commended, Charles, all of you; it was a brave thing to do, protect a friend. We lack this virtue all too often, don't you agree, sir? These are good men, sometimes we are a little hasty in judging them – don't you agree, sir, a little too hasty? These are the salt of the earth, the men who make the country, really. Don't worry, Charles, nor you, Ginger, nor you, Andrew – none of you, don't worry, you shan't be harmed – it was a good act. We like you for it, we're proud of you, happy with you – you do agree, don't you, sir? These are men we need and these are the men we must keep. We are not hard men, Charles – don't think ill of us, the stories you read, the tales you hear. We are good, honest, hard-working like yourselves and understanding; above all we are understanding, aren't we, sir? There, that's a good fit, I think. [*The* PILOT OFFICER *hands a list over to Pip.* PIP *reads out the list.*]

PIP: 239 A/C2 Cannibal – [CANNIBAL *rises to attention*] adminis-tration orderly, posted to Hull. [*Stands at ease. Same procedure for others.*]

252 A/C2 Wingate – administration orderly, posted to Oxford.

247 A/C2 Seaford – administration orderly, Cyprus.

284 A/C2 McClore – typing pool, Malta.

272 A/C2 Richardson – administration orderly, Aden.

277 A/C2 Cohen – administration orderly, Halton.

266 A/C2 Smith – administration orderly, Lincoln.

279 A/C2 Washington – put back three weeks to flight 212 – decision of employ will be made at a later date.

Squad – Squad, SHUN.

[*Sudden loud sound of brass band playing the R.A.F. March Past.*]

SCENE TWELVE

Music of March Past. The Parade Ground. Passout Parade. The men march into position. A flagpole is moved in.

HILL: Squad atten-shun! Shoulder arms! Right turn! By the left quick march! Lift your heads, raise them, raise them high, raise them bravely, my boys. Eft-ite, eft-ite, eft-ite, eft. Slope that rifle, stiffen that arm – I want to see them all pointing one way, together – unity, unity. Slam those feet, slam, slam, you're men of the Queen, her own darlings. SLAM, SLAM! SLAM! Let her be proud. Lovely, that's lovely, that's poetry. No one'll be shot today, my boys. Forget the sweat, forget the cold, together in time. I want you to look beautiful, I want you to move as one man, as one ship, as one solid gliding ship. Proud! Proud! Parade, by centre, quick march, saluting to the front.

[*Men salute to audience, return back to face* WING COMMANDER. *Music stops.* WING COMMANDER *on a rostrum. Officers around him.*]

WING COMMANDER [*a long, broad, embracing smile*]: I am satisfied. Good. Good men. One of the best bunch I've had through my gates. Smart, alert, keen. Two years of service in Her Majesty's Air Force lie ahead of you, I am confident of the service you will give, you have turned out well, as we expected, nothing else would have done, just as we expected. God speed you.

[GINGER *comes to attention. Lays rifle on ground. Steps forward to flagpole and takes ropes in his hands.*]

357

HILL: Parade about turn.

[*Men now facing audience again.*]

SQUADRON LEADER: Parade, for colour hoisting. PRESENT ARMS!

[*Ginger very very slowly hoists the R.A.F. colours. Let it be a tall pole. 'The Queen' is played, and there is a*]

SLOW CURTAIN